D0031164

THE SOUTHWEST HISTORICAL SERIES

EDITED BY

LEROY R. HAFEN

XI

Encampment of Gold Miners at Pike's Peak

From a contemporary wood-engraving of 1859

OVERLAND ROUTES
to the Gold Fields, 1859
from contemporary diaries

Arkansas River Route
Platte River Route
Leavenworth and Pike's Peak Express Route
Smoky Hill Trail, etc.

Edited by

LEROY R. HAFEN, PH.D., LITT.D.
Historian of the State Historical Society of Colorado
Author of The Overland Mail, Colorado, Fort Laramie, etc.

THE ARTHUR H. CLARK COMPANY
Glendale, California, U.S.A.
1942

TO

CHAUNCEY THOMAS

Western Writer and Stimulating Critic

CONTENTS

ILLUSTRATIONS

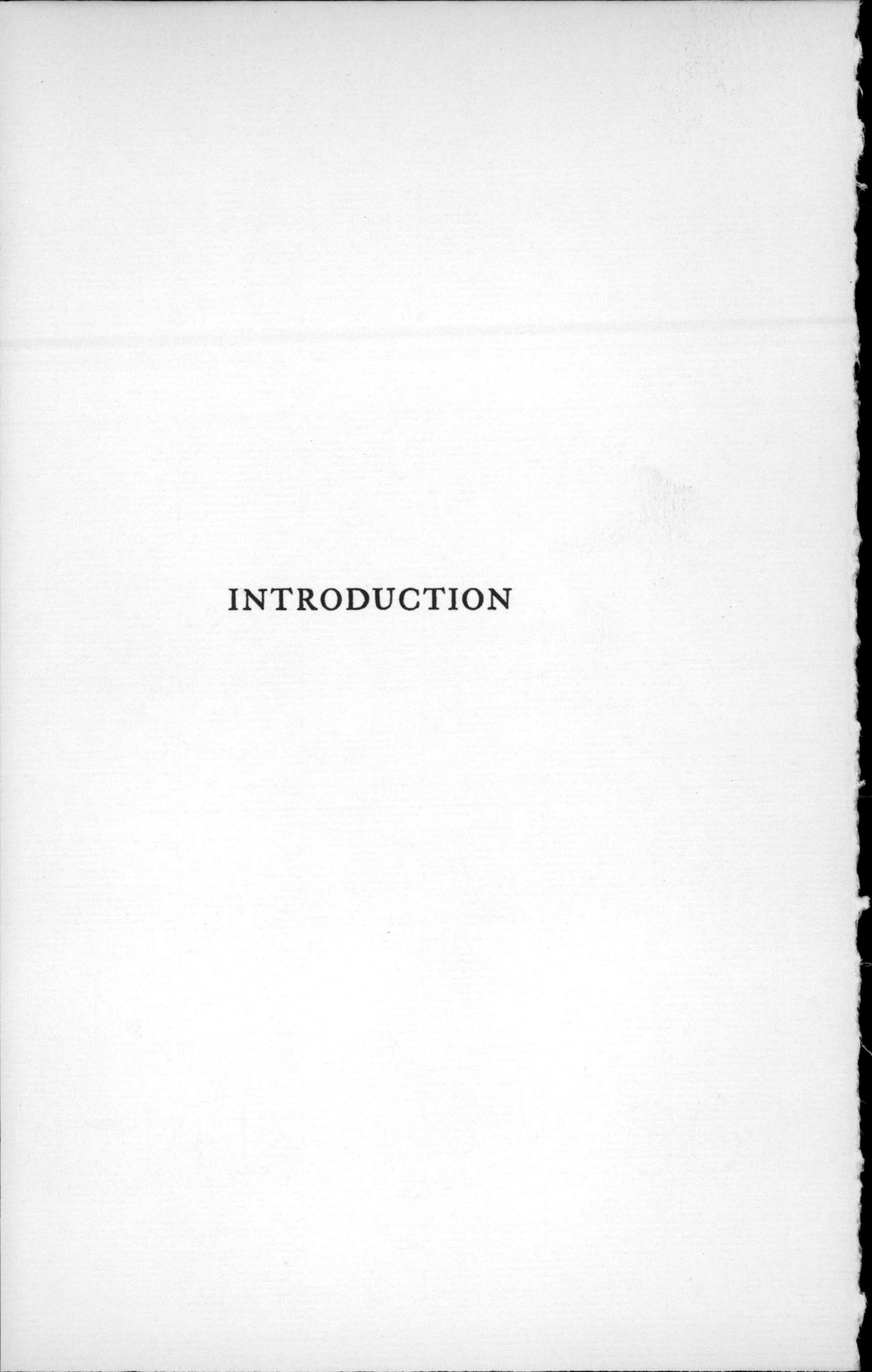

INTRODUCTION

INTRODUCTION

Many good contemporary records of the Pike's Peak gold rush of 1859 are extant. In volume IX of this *Southwest Historical Series* the guidebooks issued for gold-seekers and emigrants were presented and discussed. Volume X was devoted to contemporary letters and newspaper reports. We now endeavor to round out the picture by publishing diaries of trips to the mines.

Long ago it was recognized that diaries are among the most valuable sources for historical data. Such records not only give eye-witness accounts of events and developments, but they present as well the attitude, color and flavor of the times.

The California gold rush of 1849 produced numerous diaries. Scores of these have been unearthed and published. As a result we have a great storehouse of information on that historic trek. The gold rush of a decade later to the Pike's Peak region, though participated in by as many people as went overland to California in 1849, has produced fewer diaries by far than did the earlier gold rush. The novelty of a western trip had probably worn off somewhat by 1859 and the distance to the front range of the Rockies was considerably less than that to the Pacific coast. These factors may in part account for the keeping of fewer journals. Of course more diaries of the Pike's Peak gold rush will undoubtedly come to light from time to time, as this stampede in western history is given more attention.

The Pike's Peak gold rush journals of 1859 that have been chosen for publication here, cover the principal routes to the mining country. Competent and observing diarists have been found for most of the trails. Two of the men were experienced journalists – E.H.N. Patterson and A.D. Richardson. Charles C. Post was a practicing attorney before he turned prospector; he later became Attorney-general of Colorado. Edwin R. Pease was a school teacher. Of A.M. Gass's background we are ignorant, but his diary is good. E. D. Boyd, civil engineer, and R. F. Burton, English traveler and author, were competent observers.

Inasmuch as the routes of the various diarists are shown on the map at the end of this volume, we shall not offer written descriptions of the roads taken.

THE ARKANSAS ROUTE

THE ARKANSAS ROUTE
Diary of Charles C. Post
Editor's Introduction

When Charles C. Post decided to go to the Pike's Peak gold country in the spring of 1859, he was practicing law at Decatur, Illinois. He had come to this Illinois city in 1851 and here began the study of law in the office of his brother, Captain John P. Post. Upon admission to the bar in 1854, he remained with his brother, and for the five succeeding years they practiced law together.

Charles C. Post was born on a farm in Saline, Washtenaw county, Michigan, on november 29, 1831.[1] His parents Jeremiah and Lucy (Winter) Post, were natives of Vermont and Connecticut, respectively, and had migrated to Michigan in 1829. On the Michigan farm and in the country school young Charles grew up. At the age of twenty he went to Decatur, Illinois, and began his legal career. On may 16, 1856, he was married to Miss Angelina Kaufman.

The story of his trip to the mines of western Kansas is told in the diary that follows. After arriving at Denver he went to Gilpin county and engaged in gulch

[1] This is the date given in Mr. Post's biography which appears in the *Encyclopedia of Biography of Colorado* (Chicago, 1901), 316. His biographical sketch in the Baskin *History of Clear Creek and Boulder Valleys, Colorado* (Chicago, 1880), 530, gives the year of birth as 1832. Relatives in Denver state that the earlier date is correct.

mining. He was elected to the convention which met in Denver in august, 1859, to form a constitutional government. He was elected a member of the legislature of the Provisional Government of Jefferson Territory. He was one of the three judges appointed in 1860 to constitute the judiciary of Jefferson Territory. But the Territorial government was not recognized by Congress and did not go into full operation.

Mr. Post lived in Central City for twelve years and there built a reputation as a versatile attorney. In 1868 he was elected district attorney for the Second Judicial District of Colorado. He moved to the thriving mining city of Georgetown in 1872, where he engaged largely in mining litigation. He served several terms as county attorney. Until 1892 he was a Democrat; then he joined the Populists. In 1900 he was elected Attorney-general of Colorado on a fusion ticket of the Populists, Silver Republicans and Democrats. He served one term in this office, 1901-1903. Following a protracted illness, Mr. Post died in Denver on november 22, 1906.

The diary reproduced here is in possession of Charles C. Post's daughter, Mrs. Ada W. Dickerson, by whose kind permission it is now published for the first time.[2]

[2] At the end of the copy of the diary used is the following note, written at Decatur, Illinois, september 2, 1859, by J. P. Post (brother of Charles) and addressed to their father and mother; "The foregoing Journal of Charles was copied by his wife in considerable less space than the original. Angie (the wife) has done it faithfully and I suppose you all will take pleasure in reading it as we have." This copying may account for some slight errors in spelling and construction that appear in the diary used here. Some changes in punctuation, the spelling out of figures, and a few other minor changes have been made by the editor, in conformity with the typography of this *Series.*

The diary of A. E. Raymond, a manuscript in possession of the State Historical Society of Colorado, covers the same route from Kansas City to Denver as does Post's diary. Raymond left Kansas City april 16, more than three weeks ahead of Post, and arrived in Denver on june 3, 1859. The two diaries are valuable for checking against each other. Another good journal for the same route is that of Dr. George M. Willing, who reached Denver june 13, 1859. This diary was edited by Dr. R. P. Bieber and was published in the *Mississippi Valley Historical Review,* XIV, 360-378.

The editor considers it unnecessary and inadvisable to annotate in detail this Charles C. Post diary of a trip along the Arkansas route to the Pike's Peak gold region. Most of the route is along the Santa Fe Trail, well known and adequately described in other works. The descriptions of the route written in 1858 by Luke Tierney, William B. Parsons, and Augustus Voorhees were published in volume IX of this *Southwest Historical Series.* Various letters reproduced in volume X give data on the road up the Arkansas. See also Appendix D at the end of this volume.

DIARY

MAY 3rd. [1859]. Started for Pike's Peak, Wooden Bloc, northwest corner of old square, in flames, by the light of which the omnibus found no difficulty in finding the depot.[3] Train started at three o'clock, a.m., to Springfield, and arrived at last named place at five o'clock in morning during a heavy rain. Had an excuse for breakfast at the junction, which together with the rascally baggage boys and the rain vexed me somewhat, took cars on to St. Louis, Alton & Chicago R.R. and arrived at station on Bloody Island opposite St. Louis at one and one-half o'clock p.m., ferried Mississippi and found brother Lemm at landing waiting for us. After greeting I recollected that I had an overcoat when I left Springfield, must have left it on cars. Lemm and I recrossed and found it safely locked in depot baggage room. Took bus for Everett House, found Dr. Baldwin and Charley Cutter ready for dinner, when dispatched took bus for upper ferry and arrived in camp at four o'clock. Found Dr. Rease and brother and son, G. W. Free. Mr. Reude and C. B. Spooner encamped in a beautiful grove with all the luxuries surrounding (except orange grove) necessary for a pleasant camp (frog pond included). Our cook, "The Doctor" (synonymous terms) showed an exhibition of his culinary skill and the way the pork and beans, bread and potatoes disappeared was proof positive that we

[3] This, apparently, was in Decatur, Illinois, as it was from this point that Post set out for the gold fields. See the preceding biographical sketch.

Charles C. Post
From a photograph, about 1900

had not reckoned without our host when we chose Dr. for our cook. We pitched our tent expecting a heavy rain and I never enjoyed a better night's sleeping in my life, excepting the doctor thought my blanket better than his and kicked his off and cabbaged mine. In consequence I awoke once, "a thing greatly to be regretted."

MAY 4th. The Dr. for breakfast done some ham and potatoes brown, which with warmed over beans and delicious bread and tea we satisfied ourselves and again remarked the great skill of our cook whose great patience was greatly tried in washing all the dirty dishes in camp, but he came out of the greasy ordeal unsoiled, an index of his cleanliness as a dish washer. Went again to St. Louis to procure provisions etc., for our trip across the "Plains," which being done I started in search of Richard Whitley, who as I thought had not yet arrived from Centralia, whither he had gone on the twenty-seventh ult. Walked about three miles and back (to Illinois or Frog Town), took ferry and bus for upper ferry and found the boys had struck tents and loaded ferry boat. We then had a nice time getting stock aboard the Minnehaha for Kansas City, but got them aboard about nine o'clock at night and went to bunk almost exhausted. But went to sleep and woke not till broad day.

THURSDAY, MAY 5th, 1859. After breakfast called on D. C. Woods, atty., to arrange affairs of White House and of Wm. K. York, after which went out for corn and hay for stock. Had to go three miles, pay nine cents for seventy pounds in cob. Took bus, arrived at boat just in time; got corn aboard, no hay. We are now steering up Missouri river, or as Lemm calls it, Big

Muddy. Four o'clock p.m. The river looks as though one could walk on it, so muddy and thick.

FRIDAY, MAY 6th. Still plowing the big muddy, passed towns of St. Charles, Augusta, Washington, Herman, Portland, St. Anburt [Aubert] and arrived at Jefferson City at eight o'clock, p.m. All the above towns excepting Herman and Jefferson City are insignificant in every point except for old fogyish looking and dilapidated buildings and scarce in that line.[4] Jefferson, the capital of Missouri, is a disgrace to any state as a capital. There is nothing there excepting the old capitol to call attention and it only as a focus around which centers the "Hon's." whose wisdom or rather lack of it concocts laws to govern the great state of Missouri. Went uptown with Dick Cutter and Dr. Baldwin, made purchase of pipes and back to the boat. Cars from St. Louis arrived at forty minutes past nine o'clock, large number of passengers came aboard here and away we went again.

SATURDAY, MAY 7th. Made slow progress, boat heavily ladened, a mean set of stewards and waiters, insolent and insulting. This day and night passed Rockport [Rocheport], Boonville, Arrow Rock, Glasgow and Cambridge. All better towns than on lower Missouri river. At Glasgow a man going to Pike's Peak, in attempting to jump off "Minnehaha" to wharf boat, fell in the river. He struggled bravely with the sand and water for life. Boards, ropes, etc. were thrown to him, but he seemed destined to find a watery grave. When the first mate, Thomas Hawthorn, stripped off his coat and hat and nobly plunged in to save the unfortunate man, and just as he reached him the poor fellow caught hold of a rope thrown to him and both were pulled

[4] All the towns named are still on the modern map.

aboard. He was almost gone. What a noble act in the mate, thus to peril his own life to save that of an entire stranger who had merely stepped aboard of the boat to procure passage for a party of which he was a member to Leavenworth, enroute for Pike's Peak. When the boat was in act of leaving, he fell in and it is a fact that not one in a hundred persons who get into the Missouri river with clothes on get out alive, in consequence of the great amount of sand mixed with the water and the swift current. More noble and more justly could a biographer write in indelible lines the record of the generous and noble Thomas Hawthorn, first mate of the "Minnehaha," in rushing into almost certain death to save the life of a fellow, than the murderous life of a Bonaparte, Alexander or Caesar, but it will be passed as naught and the mate will be forgotten.

SUNDAY, MAY 8th. Arrived at the beautiful town of Waverly, in Lafayette county. Boat had one hundred ton freight to discharge, went ashore for hay to feed oxen, met an old friend, J. J. Gordon, who resides in Waverly. Had a good time, got some hay, and the morning being very fair – took a stroll over the town. The prairie back of Waverly looks just like old Macon, only a little more rolling. Went aboard of boat, made Lexington at six p.m. It is the most considerable town on Missouri river below Kansas City. The bluffs for ten miles on Lexington, or south, side of river present only one grand coal bed, it being dug out commencing in a strata about seven feet thick which crops out about ten feet above high water mark. They drift in, I don't know how far, and haul it out to river bank on small wooden railroads with trucks, nothing could be more convenient. Coal even better than Danville.

MONDAY, MAY 9th. At nine o'clock arrived at Kansas City and got freight landed all safe and sound. Cattle looking rather gaunt, not having had anything but corn since we went aboard the boat. Went to work to load freight in one wagon, which being done, we drove to grove east of McGees Addition and encamped to wait for flour which could not get aboard of our boat, but had to ship by the "J. D. Ferry" which will be up to-morrow. This is a beautiful city, situated on a number of hills or bluffs, has about nine thousand souls, is only three years old, does a heavy business for New Mexico and all southwest country. It is a point that suits me much, and had I not determined on Pike's Peak, I'd have Ann Laura and little Charley[5] here shortly and locate.

TUESDAY, MAY 10th, 1859. Camp No. 1. Dr. woke me just in time for breakfast, a beautiful morning. After breakfast we unpacked our wagons in order to make a final packing for the plains. Went to levee, found the "J. D. Ferry" not yet arrived; waited until four p.m. and no Ferry. Went back to camp, ate supper, took a long stroll with brother, learned after dark that the Ferry had arrived at levee so we can load in morning and in evening get on to the prairie where our stock can get more grass.

WEDNESDAY, MAY 11th. 1859. Camp No. 2. Went to town, got our flour, had to pay the small sum of three dollars and fifty cents for storage. After getting back to camp and loading we hitched on and started at half past two o'clock for a cattle range. Arrived at Westport, four miles from Kansas City, at four o'clock. Westport is a fine little town and at this place or Kansas

[5] His young children.

City we could get complete outfits as cheap and cheaper than in St. Louis, counting in the freight up the Missouri river. Good oxen can be had here for from fifty dollars to seventy-five dollars per yoke. Left Westport at half past four, went three and one-half miles and found this a very good camp ground. Grass has been fed off rather short, all the better for our stock, it being the first they have had. We pitched our tents on a slope and after supper went to bed, all of us very tired.

THURSDAY, MAY 12th. Still in Camp No. 2. Last night it commenced to rain and still continues to pour, but we kept perfectly dry in our tents. I borrowed a mule of a Missouri company and rode to Westport to get a lock chain for our wagon. Got back at dark and am now writing on my knee by candle light.

FRIDAY, MAY 13th. Camp No. 3. Started at half past twelve, roads very heavy. Made eight miles into K.T. [Kansas Territory] over the finest rolling prairie I ever saw; splendid farms fenced with stone wall, the material being taken from the hills on the farms. We overtook today a curiosity in the shape of a wind wagon. It is a four wheeled vehicle, about nine feet across schooner rigged a very large sail. The whole weighs three thousand pounds. It plowed right through the mud, but cast anchor in a deep ravine where the wind failed to fill the sail and she stopped, the old captain has got out or applied for a patent, he says when he gets it perfected he will bet ten thousand dollars he can get to the Rocky mountains in six days; he is another Maddock.[6] We encamped near a beautiful boiling spring which abound in this country. Our oxen came very near bursting from eating the grass which is from eight to ten inches high.

[6] For an account of this wind wagon, see the preceding volume in this *Series*, page 297.

I begin to like camp life first rate. This is a great country, about the best I ever saw, saving there is but little timber. But they have good substitutes in plenty, coal rock, gravel and lime. The prairie is a little too rolling for good plow land.

SATURDAY, MAY 14th. Camp No. 4. It rained again last night and all the morning until half past eleven o'clock a.m. We then got our cattle to our wagons and after lunch made only four and one-half miles and camped again. The roads which by the way, are generally good and are traveled more than any roads I know of in Illinois, are very muddy. We passed the first timber, which is a poor excuse for such, today at what is called Indian creek. Our camp is in sight of the town of Olathe, the county seat of Johnson county.

SUNDAY, MAY 15th. Camp No. 5. We could not get any wood where we camped last night and consequently had to move, we made fifteen and one-half miles today. Our camp is one and one-half miles west of Bull creek, which is quite a stream and good timber, what there is of it. The belt is very narrow, not exceeding twenty rods. Our camp is right in front of a fine stone house and once natural lawn. We got plenty of good buttermilk and we launched into it accordingly. Cattle are all thriving. The character of the world, timber scarce, lots of lime and building rock, gravel and splendid water.

MONDAY, MAY 16th. Camp No. 6. This day made twelve miles, character of country same as yesterday, not quite so rolling perhaps. Rained some, encamped on a place drained by the forks of the old and new road, it having been changed by fencing. Nothing of interest today. Last night it rained a perfect hurricane, but we kept our tents right side up by holding the poles down, there was no thunder but a continual blaze of lightning.

TUESDAY, MAY 17th. Camp No. 7. Rained pretty much all forenoon, afternoon fine. Traveled all day, made about thirteen miles. I, in pulling on my boots, burst the backs of both of them (if I had old Monroe here I would pull his old grey wool all out). It is a shame to be imposed upon so, I paid six dollars for them. Encamped in a comfortable place, wood and spring water handy. We are now in Douglas county, Lawrence, county seat. Character of country same as yesterday.

WEDNESDAY, MAY 18th. Camp No. 8. Rained this morning, got late start. Encamped near house of a Frenchman, a very intelligent man. I thought he was an Englishman. Made today about eight miles. We have up to this day met and passed sixteen Santa Fe trains, averaging about twenty wagons, each making eight miles, when mule teams and twelve when oxen. So the trade must be an immense one, they carry average five hundred pounds per load, I do not count those loading in Kansas, number about six trains. [The ambiguity in the preceding two sentences may be due to errors in copying the original diary.] Character of this country today a little less rolling than before.

THURSDAY, MAY 19th. Camp No. 9. Got early start, traveled about fourteen miles and encamped about six miles west of Creek No. 110,[7] in sight of town of Burlingame. Plenty of wood, water and grass. Six of our oxen ran off in the night but we found them early enough to start at seven o'clock, which is too early. This day I traded off one yoke of steers for a good horse. Country beautiful, settlements getting scarce.

[7] A branch of Marais des Cygnes river.

FRIDAY, MAY 20th. Camp No. 10. Today we passed Burlingame, a town situated on Switzer creek. It is the next best town on the road from Westport, being second to Olathe. Dragoon creek [8] and Soldier creek, the last takes its name from the fact of General Kearny's losing one day of seventy-four men and next day forty-six men, here in 1846 when on his way to Mexico.[9] We encamped about three miles east of Chicken creek and for first time set guard. I was on first watch, from dark till twelve o'clock; Lemm on second watch. Country still the same.

SATURDAY, MAY 21st [1859]. Camp No. 11. Got early start. Passed Chicken, Log Claim, Elm creeks and Osage river and encamped about eight miles east of Bluff creek, having made about eighteen miles, being the biggest day's drive yet made and Bluff creek is the first creek that empties into the Neosho river. I noticed as soon as we got on to the high ground west of the Osage that the soil was different from what we had yet seen, being composed of soil lime and flint conglomerate rock, the whole face of the country being more or less covered with fine flint and lime pebbles, some as sharp as glass. The high ground is worthless for anything but grazing purposes and the fine rock it contains.

SUNDAY, MAY 22nd. Camp No. 12. Although it is sunday a majority of the company voted to go to Council Grove,[10] where we are encamped on bluff east about

---

[8] The crossing of Dragoon creek was about six miles west of Burlingame, according to W. B. Parsons (See volume IX of this *Series*, page 172).

[9] General Stephen W. Kearny's Army of the West on its march to Santa Fe during the Mexican War.

[10] This well-known camping place, on the Neosho river, was named for the council with Osage Indians held here in august, 1825. Here, in the westernmost grove of abundant hardwood timber, the traveler usually laid in a supply of extra axle trees, ox bows, etc.

one mile, with a large number of trains in sight bound for the land of gold. We came eighteen miles this morning and arrived at our camp ten minutes before twelve o'clock. We dinnered, unloaded our wagons, dried fruit and beans, cloth etc., which from the much rain had got damp but not injured. The company are all in good health. Lemm has a cold but it doesn't prevent him from taking his pork and beans, bread etc., as usual. At Rock creek I took rifle and horse and followed creek down about four miles expecting to kill a deer, but saw none and no other game except two wolves, large gray ones; didn't get a shot at them. Got into camp, went to town, which consists of a large three story stone Mission House under charge of Methodist Episcopal church South, three large stores, black-smith shop and seven residences. This is the county seat of Mains [Morris] county, one hundred and thirty-one miles west of Kansas City, situated on the Neosho river. Here is the Kansas tribe Indian reservation. They are very numerous here, numbering in all about one thousand. Some of them are becoming a very little civilized, but most of them are mean, lazy devils. This is the last point where supplies can be had and there is everything here that a man wants if he has got money enough to buy it with. Flour is worth six dollars per one hundred pounds, bacon sixteen cents and so on. We went to bed tonight and were lulled to sleep by the howls of wolves and yells of Indians, which is the only use or good or hurt they can be put to or do.

MONDAY, MAY 23rd. Camp No. 13. The cattle being hitched we went through the Neosho, which is barely fordable, and traveled sixteen miles to Diamond Spring.[11] One encampment the country is worthless ex-

[11] For a note on Diamond Spring, see volume IX, 174.

cept the bottom lands (it strongly resembles some parts of Minnesota) until we reached Elm creek, eight miles west of Council Grove, which creek is the last of the Neosho waters we will pass. The country after we passed Elm creek commenced improving and at Diamond Springs is as beautiful as any in K.T. I stayed at Council Grove until half past two o'clock to write letters and galloped sixteen miles to our camp. The spring here is the largest I ever saw, it yields a stream not less than half the size of the Sangamon river when at low water. The wind blew big guns all day and still is blowing; we had hard work in pitching our tents.

TUESDAY, MAY 24th. Camp No. 14. This day we traveled about twenty-one miles. The country is very fair farming land with plenty of water. We stopped for dinner about one mile from what is known as the last [Lost] spring and drank slew water and cold coffee. This spring lays about one-half mile off of the main road. We were not a little vexed when Lemm found the spring so near after dinner and we vented our wrath by drinking immense quantities of the last water. After noon C. N. Cutter and myself went hunting antelope, which were said to abound here. We went about four miles north of the road, where I saw the first antelope I ever saw. It was a male with tall curling horns and looked very much like a deer only larger bodied, shorter and not so nimbly and symmetrically made. They are considerably heavier than our common deer. It was so far off that I could not shoot it, so I gave it chase and gained on it till it crossed a ravine and it was a short time out of sight. We then saw it and gave fresh chase, but could not come up with it. We saw a great many when returning to the road but could not get a shot at them, they were so shy. I rode over twenty miles and was more tired than any night since I have been out. I must go to bed as it is my watch after midnight.

WEDNESDAY, MAY 25th. Camp No. 15. I called up the company at four o'clock, breakfast ready. It then commenced raining and we had to go into Spoon's tent to eat it as we had not struck ours. A real norther set in and continued three hours. Our oxen broke for a ravine. We got hitched up at nine o'clock and drove to Cottonwood river [12] by noon. Here is the only chance for wood until we get to Little Arkansas river, seventy miles. We accordingly laid in a good supply as it was raining and so we could not burn buffalo chips. We passed Cottonwood and encamped eight miles west, having made about fifteen miles. We passed as fine country as we have yet seen and encamped in the Great buffalo range and expecting to see them tomorrow.

THURSDAY, MAY 26th. Camp No. 16. We were blessed last night and this morning with more rain from the north, high winds. It slackened about two o'clock and we started. It was so cold we had on our gum and overcoats and then we suffered considerably from the cold. I drove until eleven o'clock on horseback, Lemm and Dick riding in the wagon. Lemm then relieved me, and Reude and me started afoot for Remming [Running] Turkey creek [13] and reached it about noon, two and one-half miles in advance of the company. There is no timber here until about ten miles down. We saw buffalo for first time, a large herd, four or five miles off

[12] A branch of Neosho river. The crossing was at the present town of Durham, Marion county. A. E. Raymond reached here on april 29, 1859, and recorded in his diary (manuscript in the library of the State Historical Society of Colorado): "Here is a U.S. mail station. There is but one house here."

[13] A little west of present Canton, McPherson county.

south in afternoon. We met a large train going back, having heard bad news from Pike's Peak, but it is a fact that not one we have yet met have struck a shovel in the ground for gold, but have taken others' say so for it. This evening we saw any quantity of buffalo and one gang coming nigher than was prudent for them. I straddled my horse with revolver and U.S. yogher and gave chase and came up in one hundred yards of them about two and one-half miles from camp and dismounted and fired my yogher which wounded the buffalo, scared the horse, which ran for camp and left me to come back afoot with the glory of shooting the first buffalo. It is now nine o'clock and I will retire.

FRIDAY, MAY 27th. Camp No. 16. We were aroused at day break by the cry "Buffalo! Buffalo!!" from our guard and got up to keep them from stampeding our oxen. The whole of the vast plains seemed alive southward. We fired our guns and turned them from us. We again gave chase and got a fine large bull. We took the tongue and about forty pounds of steak and let him lay to enrich the already fertile plains. The buffalo are next to the camels, the ugliest beasts alive. They run just like a fat hog and not any faster than a common steer. I can ride up to them now. Started and all along the road we met teams returning, but we did not during the whole day find a man who had been any farther than Bent's Fort and the Arkansas, but returned doubtless on the say so of persons who like themselves had never been there or were hired liars. I met three men with whom I was acquainted, H. P. Miller of Mouline, James Davidson of Christian and one Dotz of Bloomington. They said the reason they returned was because they had only two months provisions. We traveled about eighteen miles today; passed big Turkey creek,[14] which is a running stream only after a shower. Here is a ranch and mail station, but no post office. They charged us ten cents per bucket for riley well water. The country is very level, not enough however to make the prairie soft. The soil is first rate. We encamped on the Big Muddy, three miles from the little Arkansas river. The Big Muddy is a high water stream, some deep gulches where water stands the year round. The grass is the poorest here of any since we left Camp No. 2, being mostly buffalo grass which is said to be very nutritious. This is my guard night so I will retire, first stating that our buffalo steak was better than any beef steak I ever ate.

SATURDAY, MAY 28th [1859], Camp No. 17. The oxen being hitched, we moved for Little Arkansas and before we got one-half mile Lemm hailed us to wait until he brought in some more steak out of another buffalo which one of our party killed, which being loaded we got down to the river, a little stream except during rains. Its bed is some thirty feet lower than the prairie, which in most places comes down to the bank, with a very few cottonwood trees here and there.[15] This is the first timber on the road since we left Cottonwood river. The soil on the creek is mixed with considerable sand. I saw some rock at a distance and examined some which is in the piers to a bridge across the stream. It is a kind of lime granite, very heavy. The bridge was built last season by Gains & Wheeler, the owners of it and the ranch, twenty-five cent toll and ten gallons of water or

[14] A branch of Little Arkansas. There are several forks of Turkey creek; the crossings were a little below McPherson.

[15] Little Arkansas flows southeastward and enters the Arkansas at present Wichita.

twenty-five cents for ten gallons, and cross at ferry. We crossed at ferry and got our kegs filled at a spring above one-fourth mile. Cutter and myself stopped one mile west of river, stopped to let our horses graze. We heard and saw a large number of prairie dogs. They are about twice as large as our fox squirrels, very light yellow color, live in holes like gophers. We reached Chaves creek, nine miles, at noon. Roads since we left the river are a little sandy with clay and mole mixture packed as hard and are as smooth as white ash dressed flooring. We passed Oral creek which has a little timber on it and is a running creek. Came here to Little Cow creek [16] which has ash, clm, and walnut timber and some undergrowth. No running water, but very good, clear, still water. The grass is very short, kept so by the great number of buffalo which were in sight in innumerable herds at sunset. There is a prospect of rain tonight. The whole camp are asleep except Dick Whitley and a Cumberland county, Illinois boy (whose company have joined ours for the trip) who are on watch tonight.

SUNDAY, MAY 29th. Camp No. 18. We had no rain this day until about three p.m. and as the grass was very short on Little Cow creek we concluded to move to Big Cow creek two miles and camp for the day. The prairie between the two creeks is mostly high and rolling and looks like rich soil. We arrived at Big Cow creek at ten a.m. and encamped up the stream from ford about two miles. This creek is very much as the Little Arkansas was, with a deep lake as it is called on west side running its whole length and full of water some twenty-five or thirty feet above bed of stream; plenty of fish (blue cat) in both lake and stream, lake about twenty rods from stream. There are some two hundred teams encamped

[16] Near present Lyons.

along this creek, some going to and some turning back from the Peak. We made the acquaintance of Dr. Beach, who keeps a ranch on east side of creek. He is a young man who together with his father and four hired men are trading with the Indians, the Kiowahs, and slaughtering buffalo, the meat of which they prepare by salting, smoking and drying and hauling to Kansas City, where they find a ready sale of it at twenty-five cents per pound. They are making a fortune. The doctor is a very intelligent and courteous gentleman and a graduate of Cleveland Medical college. He was very kind and gave us much very valuable information. We busied ourselves in reading, writing, mending and washing, etc. It rained part of the p.m. and still looks like more rain.

MONDAY, MAY 30th. Camp No. 19. It rained some last night and Dr. B. had three attacks of his old complaint during the night, all severe and he is quite unwell today. I feel very sleepy and tired. We traveled all the a.m. over as fine prairie as I ever saw, road number one. I killed four prairie dogs, which abound here at midday. We encamped near a large and high sand hill which I climbed and had a fine view of the country. Twas very hot and mosquitoes very bad. We reached the big bend of the Arkansas river [17] eighteen miles from last camp at three o'clock p.m. The stream here is about twenty rods wide and is about ankle deep on an average. The water is thick with sand but is cool and tastes well. We passed on up the river two and one-half miles to camp, where we found lots of grass, wood, water and mosquitoes. We all went to river to bathe and found one place deep enough and I never felt better than at pres-

[17] The road reached the Arkansas some ten miles east of present Great Bend.

ent except for the mosquitoes. We have got a large number of buffalo chip fires and our oxen tied, so we can go to sleep without any anxiety except from the Indians, which were said to be encamped here two thousand in number, but we have seen no sign of them yet.

TUESDAY, MAY 31st. Camp No. 19. This day we passed Allison's ranch [18] (or fort), Walnut creek, and encamped about two miles from river. No water except slew water, which is so thick we could almost pick it up with our fingers. Dick Whitley got on to my horse at noon and about three o'clock hailed the wagons with the news that he had killed a big buffalo bull. He was very much excited and tired himself out. We halted and concluded to encamp and save as much meat as we wanted. We done so and are feasting on fresh buffalo again. We saw more buffalo today than we have seen before.

WEDNESDAY, JUNE 1st. Camp No. 20. This has been a glorious, pretty day, with roads as good as one could wish for. Prairie fine, some sand mixed with soil. Got an early start, saw lots of buffalo. I gave chase to one lot and shot one, he stopped, but went on again and laid down about one mile from road. We went out and cut a little more buffalo steak and tongue. We passed Pawnee rock which is a curiosity; it is an angle of a bluff with a detached or two detached rocks about the size of the old court house in Decatur set on a small base about ten

[18] David Kellogg, upon reaching this point on october 1, 1858, recorded in his diary: "Bill Allison, a one-armed plainsman, has a stockade here and trades with the Indians." "Across the Plains in 1858, Diary of Daniel (David) Kellogg," in *The Trail* (Denver, Colorado), v, number 7, page 7. A. E. Raymond reports in his diary that Allison's Ranch was "built of Poles inclosed with Sod. The roof is nearly flat one story high. The Stone Walls and Sods inclose about an Acre of Land. This affords a strong protection against Indians. Here is a Mail Station, Store, Tavern, Corn & Hay etc." – Raymond's diary, *op. cit.*, may 5, 1859. See also volume IX of this *Series*, page 175.

feet across. This rock seems to have been burnt or the sun has hardened and blackened the outside, which being penetrated we found nothing but soft sand stone.[19] We went on after dinner to Ash creek and camped at night on west bank of Pawnee Fork [20] of Arkansas river. Grass short. Three Indian tepees about two miles down creek, which makes Dick Whitley and Cutter very uneasy.

THURSDAY, JUNE 2nd. Camp No. 21. Morning broke upon us with great splendor and we got an early start and in two hours came to the forks of the Santa Fe road, one taking across the high uplands (without any water save in pools and slews and very short grass) due west sixty miles to the river and the other keeping to left along the banks of the river or in close proximity thereto, with plenty of good water, grass, buffalo chips and wood, seventy-five miles. We halted for lunch near the mouth of a high water creek called Coon creek and encamped on bank of river. Grass fine and cattle in clover. We here met a Pike's Peaker who had gone to the mines in september last. He gave us encouraging news, says from one to three dollars can or could be made there in winter and spring. He lives in K.T. and will return if things are favorable in the latter part of season. We all took a bath in the river, which is here from one to four feet deep.

FRIDAY, JUNE 3rd [1859]. Camp No. 22. Beautiful weather, got early start, traveled twenty miles over fine roads on bottom lands, soil quite sandy, produces very

19 Pawnee Rock was a notable landmark on the Santa Fe Trail. A. E. Raymond records in his diary: "We passed Pawnee Rocks which is visible ten miles in advance of the emigrant which presents a bold and majestic front."

20 Pawnee Fork enters the Arkansas at present Larned, Kansas. The prospecting parties of 1858 encountered large bands of Indians here. See volume IX, 99.

good grass. Sage weed, numerous flowers and lots of prairie dogs, pig weeds, red root, parsley and quite such productions as grow in Illinois. A long old road, no timber on or along Cottonwood. We had a fine camping ground, were visited by two Arapahoe Indians, camped close to us. It is my watch till midnight.

SATURDAY, JUNE 4th. Camp No. 23. It turned quite cold in night and we were compelled to resort to overcoats, etc. Got early start, oxen traveled briskly, we made some twenty-two miles and camped near river again. Had company of our two Indian friends, but we gave them to understand we could spare them and they "Puchacheed." Character of country still the same.

SUNDAY, JUNE 5th. Camp No. 24. We concluded to travel until noon as we did not have large enough range for our cattle; quite cool, pleasant driving. Our road led up on the high land in consequence of the bluffs running down to river, which is rarely the case on the north side of river, but on south side the sand hills for a a great portion of the way lead into river. I was riding ahead of train and found a beautiful pool in a basin some thirty feet lower than the top of bluff with an outlet to the river. I have not yet seen anywhere an account of this pool, so I named it Crescent Pool; it is about seventy-five miles from Pawnee Fork. I carved my name and address in the rocks, also the name of the pool; it is a beautiful spot. We encamped at eleven o'clock for day and night at old fort Atkinson, nothing of it remains except a bridge with four sides showing the outline of walls which were of sod.[21]

MONDAY, JUNE 6th. Camp No. 25. Got early start, weather fine and at two and one-half o'clock p.m. came

[21] For data on this fort, see volume IX of the *Series,* page 177.

to the crossing of the river of the Santa Fe road. We here had to go again on to bluff and I think that I never traveled over so desolate and uninteresting eight miles of road in my life. Saw nothing but small dried up buffalo grass. Once in a while a wolf, and a dreary waste as far as the eye could reach to the north. We did not reach our encampment on river until dark. Traveled twenty-six miles, all of us very tired.

TUESDAY, JUNE 7th. Camp No. 26. Did not start until eight o'clock, drove about fifteen miles before and after dinner and broke down. Dr. Baldwin's old wagon proved of no account, the right hind wheel smashed in going down a small hill, so we had to encamp for day and night and went to work unloading wagons, which being done we cast about to find some timber for false spokes, but could find none, so we used a part of top pieces of wagon box, spare ox bows etc. Got wheel very well fixed, loaded up and drove half mile to camp, finding wagon was not able to carry load. We were offered the chance by our Cumberland county boys, Charles McMillin and brothers, to put the most of our load on their wagon and hitched two yoke of our oxen in with theirs. We accepted their very kind offer and were glad to go to bed well satisfied. Weather, grass, buffalo chips and water fine.

WEDNESDAY, JUNE 8th. Camp No. 27. After changing our heavy load in McMillin wagon we started. Roads good all day, bluffs run down to river on this side at only one point, easy grade. The old oxen done fine, load just right for them. I drove all day; rode most of the way; good grass, buffalo chips, willow brush and river water improving. Evening cloudy, no rains, camped near river, caught some Blue Cat fish.

THURSDAY, JUNE 9th. Camp No. 28. Fine cool morning, got early start, roads good, rather sharp for cattle's feet in some places. Some of the cattle show signs of tender feet. We passed some very high sand banks on our right and one high beautiful mound. Good grass, willow brush and river water all day; camped on river bank, nothing of unusual interest. Country same as on previous days, made twenty miles.

FRIDAY, JUNE 10th. Camp No. 29. We had a beautiful fine shower this morning, which done us all (including wagons and stock) good; fine day for traveling. Bluffs run down to river at one place quite a steep grade, both up and down, plenty of buffalo chips, grass and river water. Roads tolerably good, made twenty miles and camped at a fine spring and creek. Reudc, Dubois, and Rose found a lame cow which they drove into camp. My watch, we have a full moon which gives us almost as much light as the sun in day time. Had a very pleasant watch. Chas. Mc. watched with me; he is a wholesouled and honest gentleman.

SATURDAY, JUNE 11th. Camp No. 30. Started at seven o'clock, traveled ten miles and camped on river for day and night to let our oxen rest. Roads good, no wood; water and grass plenty, day beautiful but warm, bottom land first rate, easy to be irrigated. Camped on river, had a good time all afternoon.

SUNDAY, JUNE 12th. Camp No. 31. Started early, came to and passed Big Timber,[22] which consists of about two or three hundred cottonwood trees, very large but low and scrubby. We were very much refreshed in their shade, it being quite a luxury, not having enjoyed

[22] This was the lower end of the Big Timber, just above the mouth of Sand creek and a little east of present Lamar, Colorado. The timber area

shade for one hundred and seventy-five miles. We made twenty-five miles, camped at dark on river, which is now very high. No buffalo chips, nothing but willow brush, mosquitoes very troublesome, grass good, very pleasant all day. We were all very tired and weary. A Bareau company camped near, the first for one hundred and fifty miles; we out traveled most all other teams.

MONDAY, JUNE 13th. Camp No. 32. This was another day of disaster, although the morning was cool and fair roads and cattle in good plite and everything promising a good day's journey towards the Peak, the place where our hope is centered, yet we only traveled six miles when Dr. Rose's wagon gave out. The box in one behind hub broke and caught the skein and twisted the spindle almost off and no timber on this side of river for a new axle. Some swam the river for timber while Dr. and myself took out the tongue and cut it off and spliced the axle, making an entirely new arm and took the out side band off of our hub for a new box, put in a new cottonwood tongue and got it all done by six o'clock at night; retired very much fatigued.

TUESDAY, JUNE 14th. Camp No. 33. This morning started early, had rather a bad road all day. Quite warm in middle of day. Made only fifteen miles, camped on river five miles below Bent's Fort. It is now blowing big guns, no rain. I watched after-part of night. Timber has been quite plentiful all day, grass poor, river water. We this day heard very flattering accounts of the mining prospect.

WEDNESDAY, JUNE 15th [1859]. Camp No. 34.

extended up the river some twenty miles and was a favorite resort for Arapahoes and Cheyennes. For a detailed map of the route from the eastern border of Colorado to present Pueblo, see G. B. Grinnell, *Bent's Old Fort and its Builders*.

Teams all right, Dr.'s wagon ditto, got early start. Cutter and self went forward to Bent's Fort. It is a very good fort built of stone laid in clay mortar, one hundred and fifty feet by two hundred, on a high rocky bluff on very bank of river; can be approached only from one way.[23] Two white, two Mexicans and a family of Arapahoes are now sole tenants. It has been built four years by Bill Bent and brother, first governor of New Mexico, who some twenty-five years ago came to this country, married an Arapahoe squaw by whom he has one son and two daughters.[24] Bent has accumulated an immense fortune and this spring has sold his fort to government for ten thousand dollars. He lives in Westport, Missouri. His children are well educated. His wife died some eight years ago. The fort will soon be encamped by soldiers.[25] Camped on river; wood, water and grass plenty; made some fifteen or sixteen miles, roads flinty and hilly.

THURSDAY, JUNE 16th. Camp No. 34. Morning fair, but warm and hot in middle of day, night quite cold. This morning while riding with Dr. Rose, I discovered and caught the first view of the Spanish Peaks,[26] straight ahead of teams, our course then being a little west of southwest. They looked like a dark blue cloud and might have been mistaken for such but that a dark cloud

---

[23] For a description of this post, Bent's New Fort, see volume IX, 101, 178.

[24] William Bent married a Cheyenne woman. His brother, Charles, the first American governor of New Mexico, married a Spanish woman, a sister of Mrs. Kit Carson.

[25] After conversion into a military post it was named Fort Wise for Governor Henry A. Wise of Virginia. At the outbreak of the Civil war, and following the secession of Virginia, the name was changed to Fort Lyon, honoring General Nathaniel Lyon, who lost his life in the engagement at Wilson's creek, Missouri, august 10, 1861. On account of floods, Fort Lyon was later moved to its present location near Las Animas, Colorado.

[26] These peaks, known to the Spaniards and Indians as the Huajatolla

was behind them and for their out-line. We this day traveled over high rolling roads very flinty and hard. Oxen flinched considerably and will be quite lame if same kind of roads continue. We went off of road some one and one-half miles to camp on river; best camp yet made, save mosquitoes. River very high, all had a fine swim and at night some are catching fine Blue Cat fish. Passed Bent's old Fort;[27] very large, made of sod etc.

FRIDAY, JUNE 17th. Camp No. 35. Fine morning and day not so hot as yesterday; roads better, more on bottom land. We had the finest scenery yet, being a succession of round Potato hills (as they are called) some two hundred feet above bottom lands. Roads lead through sage bushes as high as a man's head, wherein rattle snakes mass do congregate. I killed one, which had eleven rattlers, a bouncer; I shot it with my revolver. We saw lots of antelope but they are too wild to be shot at. Dr. Rose, while out on Potato hills, first saw Pike's Peak and when he got into camp and told us we gave him and the Peak three times three. We camped on the river, grass rather poor. My first watch; caught ten fine Cat fish.

SATURDAY, JUNE 18th. Camp 36. Got early start and all that could, left teams and went on to hills to see the snow-capped Peaks and we all saw it and the Spanish Peak and Sierra Mimbers range of mountains very distinctly, the latter lying immediately west and former northwest and southwest. It was a beautiful sight, the rising sun shining brightly on the perpetual snowy cap of these mountains made us all feel quite cool at same

(Breasts of the World), were landmarks on the Santa Fe Trail. They are immediately west of present Walsenburg, Colorado.

[27] For data on this most famous fort of the Southwest, see volume IX of this *Series*, page 101.

time we were delighted to know that the Auriferous Peak after so long and wearisome a journey, was at last in view, but how many long toilsome days we must travel before we get there. "Oh that I had the wings of a dove, etc." Spooner this day shot the first antelope we have yet had. Hilly, sandy and flinty alternately; grass poor. Camped on river, made fifteen miles.

SUNDAY, JUNE 19th. Camp No. 37. Started at six o'clock, traveled over high sandy roads six miles and camped for day and night in a very fine valley on bank of river under three very large cottonwood trees, at one-half past nine. Grass number one, river high. Went swimming, got back sunburned; washed shirts, socks, overalls, towels, hdkfs., etc. Read four chapters of Proverbs, part of "As You Like It," shot at mark five times, two hundred and thirty yards; ate supper and went to bed.

MONDAY, JUNE 20th. Camp No. 38. Started early, morning cool and pleasant but hot in middle of day as usual. Passed the big St. Louis train at noon, rather rough roads all day, one very high bad hill, bottom overflowed. Got our ox mired, jumped in to keep him out, got wet and muddy up to waist, got out without much trouble, made twenty-two or twenty-three miles, grass plenty all day. Towards night came to first habitation of man since Bent's new fort. It is a brush shanty or bower and one tent; they have some crops in. Two women and four men, camped on bank of river, best place to get rid of mosquitoes; fine grass and number one camp. Heard more favorable news from mines.

TUESDAY, JUNE 21st. Camp No. 39. It rained some, last night. Roads free from dust (a pleasant riddance of a great pest). We were this morning twenty-four miles from Fountain City or Old Spanish Fort Pueblo.[28] So Cutter and myself set out to visit the city and ride back to camp. We passed at five miles a ranch and blacksmith shop, and at sixteen miles two ranches, wagons, blacksmith shop, and at twenty-four miles we came to F. C. at one-half past twelve o'clock. It is located at the junction of the Fountainee Qui Boniat[29] with the Arkansas river in a very pretty spot, being protected on northwest and southwest and northeast by high hills or bluffs and consists of about four hewn log houses which were all or nearly all, empty – owners having gone to the diggin's. It will some day be a good point.[30] We started back to camp about half past three o'clock and reached it in six miles from the city; camp first rate.

WEDNESDAY, JUNE 22nd [1859]. Camp No. 40. Got early start, traveled six miles to Fountain City. Here the road leaves the Arkansas river and follows the Fountain Qui Bourat (pronounced Fountain Ka Bow you), nearly to the Peak. The creek is about as large as Stevens creek in Macon county, Illinois. Very rapid current and rich fertile bottoms on either one side or the other, easy of irrigation. Camped about ten miles from F.C.; poor grass on this side of creek; at a near camp, cattle fared slimly.

THURSDAY, JUNE 23rd. Camp 41. We hitched up, traveled six miles and camped near a ranch; drove stock across creek where they got number one grass, so

[28] Fountain City, on the east bank of Fountain creek, near its mouth, was founded by gold seekers in 1858-1859. The old Pueblo fort, built by the early trappers in 1842, was on the opposite side of the creek and on the bank of the Arkansas river.

[29] Fontaine qui Bouille, or Fountain creek.

[30] Now the city of Pueblo, Colorado, with a population of 52,162 in 1940.

we concluded to stay all day and the night. It rained a fine shower; it also rained some yesterday. We have a nice camping ground and it is now commencing to rain again, but it does not rain enough from tenth of june to twenty-fifth of december to avoid the necessity of irrigation. The cattle are on the other side of creek yet, and the watchers are over there and will guard them there.

FRIDAY, JUNE 24th. Camp No. 42. Traveled fifteen miles, very warm in the middle of the day, had a slight shower at noon, grass first rate. One of McMillin's oxen and one of Dr. Rease's gave nearly out and while I am writing this Mc's ox is kicking in death, a fine beautiful ox as one wants to see. It is a considerable loss because no other steer can mate the widower. We camped on the creek about to Denver City by way of the divide, grass very good. [Apparently, something omitted here.]

SATURDAY, JUNE 25th. This morning Dr. Rease's ox being unable to move, the train concluded to encamp about eight miles up the creek for four or five days. So Cutter and myself agreed to go to Denver City, and having filled a sack with bread, crackers, some tea and dried fruit, we set out, struck divide road and at noon stopped at Jimmy's camp to bait our horses and selves. This is a splendid camp, a very large spring is here almost equal to Diamond Spring,[31] we moved forward over a high but level road to Squirrel creek, where there is a large pine forest extending some thirty miles east and west. We encamped at Thelan's grove, [Fagan's Grave],[32] having traveled some twenty-seven miles

[31] For data on Jimmy's Camp and the crossing of the divide, see this *Series,* IX, 104-105.

[32] *Ibid.,* 105.

Denver City, Kansas Territory

From a contemporary wood-engraving of 1859

with a friend that had passed us. We slept under his wagon; he had no tent.

SUNDAY, JUNE 26th. We arose at two o'clock, rode twenty-one miles to head of Cherry creek by eight o'clock and breakfasted, cooking our "old Ned" on coals and making tea in a tin cup. At ten o'clock we rode down creek four miles and found some miners camped.[33] They told us they were averaging about two dollars to three dollars per day, not water enough to run sluices, with cradles being the only chance. They seemed quite cheerful. We went about four miles more and came to a saw mill in full blast – managed by N. J. Wyatt. It is a small rotary engine mill, but cuts some three thousand to four thousand feet per day, which sells readily for one hundred dollars per thousand in Auraria and Denver, or eight dollars at mill. It made me feel quite at home. We again mounted our ponies, having forty miles yet to go before we got to Denver. We overtook a man by name of Dewitt, who came out here last season, lives in Auraria. He gave us a full history of matters and things as he understood them. We traveled within five miles of Denver when Dewitt gave out and we encamped with a party and had good comfortable fare, bread and good fresh butter and cream in coffee.

MONDAY, JUNE 27th. We came to town at half past eight o'clock. We left the main road and came down Cherry creek bank and crossed to Auraria on west side. We were very much disappointed to find so large and flourishing towns, we saw lots of men, women and

[33] This was Russellville, near the head of Cherry creek. For its location and that of the road and camps over the divide from Fountain creek to the South Platte, see the map at the end of volume x of this *Series*.

children all busy and apparently as contented as people are in Decatur. What a great and sudden change, eight months ago not a single tent or habitation had here been seen on the town sites: now a moving, living and energetic people are building a great metropolis.[34] I broke for the post office; no letter. Went to Denver and at Coraville post office [35] found six letters, thirty cents each and four newspapers at ten cents each; so much for Jones and Russell's U.S. Mail contract.[36] Well I was glad to get the letters and I did not judge the money at all. I run all over the town, saw more gamblers and gambling than I ever saw before, and went to bed wondering what the Anglo-american race were approaching to, and concluded that a universal triumph and conquest was its destiny and went to sleep to dream of the dear ones at home.

TUESDAY, JUNE 28th. 1859. I forgot to record in yesterday's journal that on yesterday I wrote three letters, one to wife, one to father and one to or for Margaret. We got off for Peak at eight o'clock, took it moderately all day and got to within five miles of saw mill and for first time laid in the prairie without any cover save blankets, and I never slept better or more sound in my life.

WEDNESDAY, JUNE 29th. We arose early and reached Rocky Point, twenty-six miles at noon, found David Robinson and company and dinnered with them. They told us that our company had concluded to move up the

[34] The population of Denver in 1940 was 322,412. For data on the founding and progress of Auraria-Denver, see volumes IX and X of this *Series*.

[35] The name was short-lived. This post office is mentioned in the preceding volume, page 312.

[36] This first regular mail service was the Leavenworth and Pike's Peak Express, operated without government subsidy by Jones and Russell. For the route, see A. D. Richardson's account, later in this volume.

mountain road to the head of Platte and that our best way was to strike straight for mountains and we could there tell whether they had passed or not. So we put out due west and traveled over hill, dale and through forest where I presume no white man had ever trod, and reached the mountain base at sunset; but no road or even path was there so we followed down Monument creek without any guide or mark, dark as pitch and awful rough and steep hill sides. I went before and led my horse. At last I struck a bridle path and pushed forward down creek and at last saw what I supposed to be camp fire and then I struck a road running right across our path. We followed it towards mountains and it run out; then towards the plain and it run out. We could not cross a deep gulch and wandered up and down it trying to cross till eleven o'clock and laid down and went to sleep having rode and walked seven miles.

THURSDAY, JUNE 30th. We arose at day break and crossed the gulch and made for camp; traveled fifteen miles only to find the fire an old tree, but we found a notice written by Lemm, stating that on yesterday, they had started to Denver via road we left, so we were on a fool's errand. We breakfasted and rested until eleven a.m. and started in pursuit of the fugitives and came to Jimmy's camp at noon. Again rested and overtook a Missouri train at Squirrel creek at night and as our provisions were all gone we made their acquaintance and I found one of the men I got my horse of in the company, so we fared first rate.

JULY 1st. Arose early, got breakfast and traveled thirty-two miles. At one o'clock overtook our company all in good spirits.

THE PLATTE RIVER ROUTE

THE PLATTE RIVER ROUTE

Diary of E. H. N. Patterson

Editor's Introduction

It was not entirely a new adventure upon which E. H. N. Patterson embarked in the spring of 1859. Nine years before, he had responded to the lure of gold and had traveled overland to California. Now, on his way to the Pike's Peak country, he retraced much of his former route across Iowa and Nebraska.

By the time this diary was written, Mr. Patterson was well established as a journalist and was experienced as a traveler and miner. He had been born at Winchester, Virginia, january 27, 1829. At the age of seven he moved with his parents to Illinois. He attended Jubilee college near Peoria and Knox college. In the office of the Washington *Jacksonian,* owned and edited by his father, Colonel J. B. Patterson, he was initiated into the newspaper business. In association with his father he became editor of the *Oquawka* (Illinois) *Spectator*. Shortly after arriving in California, in 1850, he accepted an editorial position on the *Placer Times* of Sacramento. After a few months he became ill and returned to "the States." He had again resumed his position on the *Spectator* when news of gold near the front range of the Rockies induced him to take the prospector's trail once more.

The account of his journey of 1859 is long and detailed. In fact it is the fullest diary we have found of a trip to the mines of present Colorado. Being intended for publication in the *Oquawka Spectator,* it was filled with all the descriptions and observations that a newspaper reporter considered of interest to the home folks and the general public. He gives an especially complete and valuable account of southern Iowa as he crosses her second tier of counties. From Council Bluffs and Omaha he takes the direct road to Fort Kearny, and after crossing the Platte at this point he follows the south bank of this stream and its South fork to the foot of the mountains.

After visiting several mining camps he settled in Boulder county. From this district he went as delegate to the constitutional convention of Jefferson Territory (predecessor of Colorado). While at this convention in Denver he became acquainted with the local press. Presently his correspondence was appearing in the *Rocky Mountain News* of Denver and the *Western Mountaineer* of Golden over the name of "Sniktau." This Indian sobriquet, meaning "equal to any emergency," had been bestowed on him during his trip to California in 1850. He also continued to send long, descriptive and newsy letters to Oquawka, where they were published in the *Spectator*. His published correspondence of 1860 runs into many columns.

After a few years in Colorado, Mr. Patterson returned to Illinois. But the pull of the mountains brought him back. In 1873 he settled in the thriving silver camp of Georgetown, Colorado, and became proprietor of the *Georgetown Miner*. This paper he built into one of the leading journals of the state. Mr. Patterson died at Denver, april 21, 1880. His remains were interred at

Georgetown. Near that place, one of the prominent peaks of the Front range is named in his honor – Mount Sniktau.

There remains one episode of his earlier life that merits attention. While scarcely more than a boy he had corresponded with Edgar Allen Poe, and had, in 1849, proposed the publication of "a high-priced, and a correspondingly high-toned periodical, which would, without doubt, win a generous and extended patronage from a genius-appreciating public." [37] The plan was worked out, its originality and vision marking young Patterson almost as a prodigy. The date of the first issue of the magazine-to-be was deferred from january, 1850, to the following june, because of the illness of Poe. There intervened the tragedy of Poe's death, to shatter the dream.[38]

The Patterson diary, in possession of the State Historical Society of Colorado, is incomplete; in fact there are several large gaps. The publication in the *Oquawka Spectator* is complete, except for the entry of one day, and this fortunately is found in that part of the original diary that is preserved. So from the *Spectator* and the one entry from the original diary the copy was made for this publication.

Mr. J. Monaghan, a former associate and now with the Illinois State Historical library, located the Patterson account in the Illinois newspaper. Through his kindness and that of Mr. Paul M. Angle of the same in-

[37] Frances Higgins, "'Sniktau,' Pioneer Journalist," in the *Colorado Magazine*, V, 107.

[38] The biographical data given here was obtained principally from Miss Higgins' article, cited in the preceding note, and from the biographical sketch which appears in the *History of Clear Creek and Boulder Valleys, Colorado* (O. L. Baskin & Co., 1880), 528-529.

stitution, the present editor was enabled to procure a microfilm copy of the newspaper volume containing the diary.

E. H. N. Patterson
From a photograph, about 1860

DIARY

On Tuesday, the 15th day of march, 1859, a company, consisting of the following persons, left Oquawka [39] for the Pike's Peak Gold mines, intending to take the route through Iowa to Council Bluffs, and thence by the North Platte route to the crossing at Fort Kearny, or to Fort Laramie, as future events might determine: Wm. H. Phelps, Jos. C. McLinn, Eli Chase, James Collins and Wm. Carll, with one wagon and three yoke of oxen; Jos. S. Hand, W. W. Rice, J. R. White and the writer, with one wagon, two yoke of oxen and a yoke of cows; P. Murtogh, Thos. Hannegan, Timothy Miskell and Peter Hart, with one wagon and two yoke of oxen; F. P. Speck and Ed. Speck, with a peddler's wagon and one yoke of oxen.

We embarked at two o'clock, on board the steamer "Oquawka," and left the landing amid the farewell cheers of a large crowd assembled to witness our departure, and accompanied across the river [40] by a number of our friends. We were soon landed upon the opposite shore, where, at the very onset, we were obliged to pitch into what many would very naturally term a difficulty – as we had to wade through water several feet deep to reach the Plank Road. Once upon this highway, however, we rolled along very finely until we reached that part of the road lying between the Sand

[39] Oquawka, Illinois, is located on the east bank of the Mississippi, about twelve miles northeast of Burlington, Iowa.

[40] The Mississippi river.

Ridge and the Bluff, where we had some heavy wheeling. Lawrence City mud, like sticky dough, clung with a tenacity to our wagon spokes that caused many very sudden rises and falls of worthless real estate.

We reached the bluff about night, pitched our tent, built fires, and were soon enjoying a hearty meal. Speck's wagon stuck in a ditch alongside the road near camp; and the Lawrence City mud was a little too much for the Irish boys' team, so they were obliged to procure an extra yoke of cattle to go back and enable them to overcome the attraction of cohesion that existed between their wagon wheels and swamp land. They came up about eleven o'clock at night, and continued on a half mile further to the top of the bluff. Distance made today four and a half miles. Weather clear and pleasant.

WEDNESDAY, MARCH 16. Our first night under tent proved highly conducive to sleep and pleasant dreams, and we woke up this morning fresh and invigorated. The sun rose clear and warm – the roseate blush of the eastern skies betokening a fine day. Phelps took a yoke of his steers and assisted Specks out of the ditch; when we struck our tents and made ready for our departure. At nine o'clock we bid good bye to Mr. Zigler, "Dad" Hand, Will White and Hen Phelps, who had spent the night with us, and rolled out for the west. We ascended the hill without difficulty, and were soon entering upon the beauties of Iowa mud. The Irish boys joined us, but soon afterwards stuck in a lane – before they had come half a mile. Their wagon is too heavily loaded for the amount of team they have, and the probability is they will abandon the idea of proceeding further at present. We found several "bad places" but got over them all without much difficulty, and encamped in a grove near Mr. Taylor's, about two p.m. for dinner, and concluded to remain until next day, owing to the convenience of hay and a lot for the cattle. We find that our wagon requires another yoke of cattle to enable us to get along successfully – the cows can do but little in the way of pulling, and we have not a good lead yoke. Tonight the clouds are marshalling their forces, and the winds are driving the dark platoons from the southeast. Perhaps it may rain by way of variety. Distance today four and a half miles.

THURSDAY, MARCH 17. This morning we slowly awoke to the drowsy hum of rain-drops pattering upon our tent cloths. Without intermission a dull drizzling rain fell until the middle of the afternoon, rendering it necessary for us to dig trenches around our tents to prevent an inundation. For a pecuniary "consideration," Mrs. Taylor's poultry yard paid tribute to our appetites, and we dined off chicken soup and fried eggs. After dinner, Jo Hand and I went across to Mr. Crowder's to purchase a yoke of cattle; we found a yoke that suited our ideas, good leaders and well made up, and paid sixty-five dollars for them. About three o'clock this afternoon, snow commenced falling, and the weather to grow cold. Tonight the wind is blowing a gale from the north, and the snow is just "kiting" it. We care little for the storm, however, for we are comfortably seated in our tents, which shed rain and snow like a duck's back – (owing perhaps to the fact that they are made of "Duck") – a roaring fire in our stove imparts a genial warmth throughout our apartment, and the light of a star candle is reflected with a cheerful glare from the white walls of our cloth tenement. I must remark, for the benefit of those who are to "come after us," that the stove we purchased of Mel Fuller is the very "chalk"– it boils, bakes, fries, warms up the tent, does all that is required of a stove, in fact, to a T.

I heard today the particulars of a mysterious murder, the recital of which may prove of interest to our people at home. One day last week, a gentleman who was hunting pigeons in the timber, some five or six miles south of where we are encamped, came upon a spot where he observed that there had been a misplacement of the earth much in the shape of a grave; it had probably been dug and filled up before the ground froze, and since the thaw had settled down below the level. He communicated his discovery to a number of his neighbors, and a party of about thirty persons repaired to the spot for the purpose of ascertaining whether any person had been buried there. About five feet below the surface they struck upon a rough oaken box, which bore the appearance of having been hurriedly nailed together, and this being opened disclosed the corpse of a German, with two severe knife wounds in the left side, either of which, it is thought, would have caused his death. Great excitement prevailed in the neighborhood in regard to the matter. The deceased is supposed to be a German who worked in a cooper shop, in this vicinity, last fall. Suspicion rests, I am informed, upon a fellow workman, who has since left the country and whose whereabouts is unknown. This is one of those cases, probably, that will remain a mystery only to be solved when the great item book of the recording angel shall be opened to justify the final sentence that awaits the murderer at the bar of Eternal Justice.

FRIDAY, MARCH 18 [1859]. Snow covers the ground

to the depth of several inches this morning, and a keen, cold wind is blowing from the north. After feeding our teams we hitched up and drove over some heavy roads to Kossuth.[41] The weather being very disagreeable – the snow drifting sharply across the prairie – and learning that the prospect ahead is not favorable for a good camping place within reasonable distance, we concluded to lie over at Mr. Leonard's, in the suburbs of the town. We have here an excellent camping place – fine grove for our cattle to range in, excellent and cheap hay, a stream of spring water, wood in abundance, and dry hard ground for tent floor. We shall probably remain here until the snow goes off. Our new cattle "come up to the scratch" just right – no money thrown away when we bought them. Today we pulled Specks out of a mudhole that we came over without difficulty. We are not progressing very rapidly towards the Missouri slope; but, then, who could have foreseen the storm of yesterday? Distance today three miles.

SATURDAY, MARCH 19. Lying encamped. The boys are engaged in practicing with their firearms (Jo Hand making the center shot), rambling around, reading, lounging, and killing time to the best of their ability.

Kossuth is a small country village, containing two stores, a Presbyterian church and a college edifice of very creditable appearance. There are several students in the collegiate classes, and about sixty in the preparatory department. This settlement is, I take it, from appearances, composed of intelligent and prosperous farmers. Their crops have not been very satisfactory the past season, but their houses and farms denote thrift and

[41] Kossuth is in the north central part of Des Moines county, about two miles east of Mediapolis.

enterprise. All this section of country should naturally seek a market at Oquawka; the distance thither is not so great as to Burlington, and our prices generally range higher than those of that city. The soil of this section is much the same as our Illinois bluff lands – black loam and yellow clay.

SUNDAY, MARCH 20 [1859]. Today we might travel, but prefer to remain in camp, as it is the Sabbath. The church bell is ringing out its cheering invitation to the people round about to come up to the House of God, and worship at his shrine; and a large congregation are responding to the call. Two horse teams, Capt. Powell, hailing from Malta, DeKalb county, Ill., came into camp last night. They are bound for Pike's Peak! Like ourselves, they do not travel today. We have had an occasional patch of clear sky today, but an easterly wind threatens rain. It is eleven o'clock as I make this entry in my journal; the boys are all sound asleep beside me; an occasional gust of rain patters upon the tent; and the waters of the little brook that goes rippling along by our door are wooing me to slumber. In a few moments I will yield my senses to their sweet enticings, and upon the wings of the dream spirit visit the past and soar into the future – dream of those I've left behind me and of the "good time coming." So mote it be.

MONDAY, MARCH 21. The sun rose clear, with a fine breeze from the southwest. Left camp at half past eight o'clock, leaving Speck's team encamped; they having concluded to wait for better roads, as their team is not sufficient to cope successfully with the mud. Soon after starting we passed the residence of Wm. S. Campbell, Esq., formerly a resident of Henderson county, where we met a gentleman, who directed us to follow a ridge of prairie, in order to avoid some very ugly road. We took his advice, and found to our cost that, in so doing, we had been "sold," for the prairie ridge proved to be a wet, swampy sod, the turf cutting through before the wheels, making it a dead, heavy drag through it. After traveling about half a mile, we got back into the road, which we found bad enough, but not to be compared, in this respect, to the spongy prairie. Passed through a narrow lane known as "Wilson's" which had been held up to us as a bugbear for miles; but we were agreeably disappointed, as we found it fair wheeling. Crossed Flint creek [42] twice within a quarter of a mile, and began to look about for a camping ground. We were told to take the right hand road when we reached a small church in the woods; we did so, but, after crossing Flint creek the third time, found that we had been wrongly directed. We therefore retraced our steps, having lost a mile through the mistake of our informant. Crossing the Flint for the fifth time, we found, at Mr. Jones', a good lot and hay for our cattle. We are camped in a very pleasant place, and feel as independent as wood sawyers in a hard winter. Distance traveled today seven and a half miles, but we have only gained six on the road.

TUESDAY, MARCH 22. We were up this morning at half past four o'clock, and started out at seven. Crossed Flint for the last time at a steam saw mill, whence our road led up through a high wet prairie. I went about a quarter of a mile off the road, and persuaded a bushel of corn out of a farmer's crib for sixty cents, which I "toted" to the road. The Malta teams were just starting out when we reached them, about a mile

[42] Flint creek enters the Mississippi at Burlington.

in advance of our camp. For miles, today, our road has led over high beautiful vacant prairie. Mt. Pleasant was distinctly visible at a distance of twelve miles. Descending from this ridge we passed through two lanes in which the mud was almost bottomless, and as tough as could possibly be. By means of the skillful engineering of Will Phelps and Jim Collins, Joe Hand and Wallace Rice, our teams crept along through. We then passed Sponge prairie to Big creek,[43] here a beautiful swift prairie stream. Mr. Chase and I now started ahead to hunt a camping place, with hay and corn. We visited every house we saw, sometimes going a half mile off the road, but again and again failure crowned our efforts. The fact is there is scarcely hay enough in the country to keep the calves till grass comes – all the crops seem to have failed in Iowa except that which serves to swell the census lists. About six miles east of Mt. Pleasant, however, at Mr. Waters', we succeeded in finding a camping place, with every convenience except a lot for our cattle. Corn costs us seventy-five cents, and hay at the rate of six dollars per ton. We are now camped at Big creek, which is here fringed with willows. We have made ten miles today, a part of the distance being over roads to which Billy Carll says Darch's Lane, at its worst, can't hold a candle!

WEDNESDAY, MARCH 23 [1859]. Joe Hand woke us all up this morning with the startling announcement that not an ox was in sight! After a brief search, however, they were all found in a grove near by and driven back to camp. We struck tents at a quarter to eight, and found the roads to improve towards Mt. Pleasant. We

[43] A branch of Skunk river.

reached town [44] a little after noon, laid in some provision, and remained some time. Here we found a number of acquaintances, formerly residents of Oquawka – Rev. Mr. Linell, his sons, Phil and Jo (who, I am glad to learn, are about to become permanent citizens of Oquawka), Jonathan Perkins, and Saunders (Kelly's former partner). Ed Knowles is here attending court as an attorney, but I did not see him. We could find no hay in town, so we pulled out for the West. Passing over fine roads, we traveled a distance of a little over three miles from town and found excellent accommodations at Mr. Lusk's. Mr. Lusk settled in this country in 1833, and was the first white settler in what is now Henry county. He owns one thousand acres of land, all in one body, and is reputed to be worth fifty thousand dollars.

We were the "observed of all observers" in Mt. Pleasant today, as ours were about the first teams, except the Malta company, that had visited the city for some days. The streets and approaches thereto have been next to impassible for several weeks, and until today, I am credibly informed, all the dragging has been done with wheelbarrows on the sidewalks! Mt. Pleasant is a neatly built up city, containing about five thousand inhabitants.[45] Business is at a standstill, and the town is staggering from the effects of the hard times. What a little while ago was life and animation is now stagnation and inactivity. A number of fine churches and private dwellings adorn the city, but the Court house, which occupies a prominent position, is a shame and disgrace to the county. The State lunatic asylum occupies a prominent place among the surroundings of the city. It is not

[44] Mt. Pleasant is the county seat of Henry county and is on Highway U.S. 34.

[45] The population in 1940 was 4,610.

yet ready for patients, although two hundred fifty-six thousand dollars have already been expended upon it; and I am told one hundred fifty thousand dollars will yet be required to complete it!

Before camping tonight we crossed Big creek again, here a large stream with bluff banks and an abundance of timber. I saw a gentleman at Mt. Pleasant who passed the Duna boys eight miles west of Burlington; they were stalled and could proceed no further. Overtook Hen. Artley at Mt. Pleasant. Distance today nine and a half miles. Our cattle look fine, and the men all have great appetites. Roads improving fast.

THURSDAY, MARCH 24. Left camp at seven forty-five. Traveling four miles, we arrived at Skunk river,[46] which we crossed by means of a "rope ferry" to Rome, a small place containing from seventy-five to one hundred inhabitants – not much like its papal namesake, the "Eternal City!" Five miles further brought us to Coalport – a small collection of houses. The next town is Parsonville, another small place, one mile west of which we camped at Mr. Parsons', in the prairie. Our roads have been excellent, but a head wind has been sweeping against us all day. Grass is beginning to make the hillsides look quite green. Distance today fourteen miles. Corn is still seventy-five cents per bushel. Joseph Darnell overtook us at Coalport. He camps with us tonight, and will take the cars for the west tomorrow at Fairfield.

FRIDAY, MARCH 25. Left camp this morning at a quarter past seven. Pulled along over very good roads to Fairfield.[47] The streets of this place we found quite

[46] Skunk river enters the Mississippi about eight miles below Burlington.

[47] County seat of Jefferson county.

muddy and difficult to pull through. Nine miles from Fairfield we crossed Cedar creek[48] – quite a large stream – and camped four miles beyond it, at McIntire's. Roads today, "fair to middling" with an occasional patch of bad mud. We hope to reach Otumwa and get across the Desmoines tomorrow. The number of people in this section of Iowa who are going to Pike's Peak is astonishing – a company of over sixty will leave Fairfield next week, and nearly every man you meet is bound for the Peak in a "few weeks." The boys belonging to both teams are all well and cheerful – complain a little sometimes of being tired, but soon get over it – and generally lose their appetites after eating their bread and fat pork. Our teams continue in excellent plight, and elicit admiration in every town through which we pass. Distance today, eighteen miles. Corn is yet seventy-five cents; hay seven dollars to ten dollars per ton.

SATURDAY, MARCH 26.[49] Left camp at a quarter before seven. Roads not good until after we leave Agency City – I mean not good compared with the balance of the road this side of Mt. Pleasant, for they are excellent in comparison with what we had to encounter before reaching that place. Agency City is, at present, the terminus of the Burlington & Missouri River R.R. and is quite a stirring, old-fashioned sort of western town; lots of provisions are sold, and whisky "punished" and "lager" consumed here daily. I saw only three houses

[48] A branch of Skunk river.

[49] The diary to this point was published in the *Oquawka Spectator* of march 31, 1859. Dates from march 26 to march 30 inclusive, were published in the issue of april 7, 1859. The portion of the original diary in possession of the State Historical Society of Colorado begins at this date, march 26. The original diary, and the one published in the newspaper are almost identical for these entries.

here that I recognized as standing in the place when I went through it nine years ago on my way to California. Seven miles from Agency City we arrived at Ottumwa, a thriving town, the county seat of Wapello county, situated on the east bank of the Desmoines river. It contains a population of about one thousand five hundred persons; considerable capital is invested in business; the business ordinarily of a good class; and from all appearances, it will at no distant day become a city of considerable size and importance.[50] Our company were disappointed in not receiving a letter or paper from home, at this place. The view up and down the Desmoines valley, from the brow of the bluff where we commenced our descent, is a magnificent one – the opposite bluffs stretching for miles in the dim blue distance; glimpses here and there of the rapid stream, now quite high and wide, following its serpentine course; numerous tributaries threading their way through the bottom lands to the parent stream – all serve to make up a lovely panorama. We crossed the river at Ottawa by means of a wire rope ferry, and camped two miles from the landing. We have made fifteen miles, and camp early as it is reported we will not be able to find any hay within a reasonable distance ahead. We cannot get a lot to put our cattle in, and will set a guard for the first time since we left home. We left the Malta horse teams at Agency.

SUNDAY, MARCH 27 [1859]. We had a time last night with our cattle. Jo McLinn and myself had the first watch. While we were making a camp fire, the cattle, taking advantage of the darkness, gave us the slip, and we had to search in different directions for nearly two

[50] The population of Ottumwa in 1940 was 31,570.

hours (not being able to track them) before we found them. We brought them back, and by dint of close watching, kept them at camp until the new watch came on at one o'clock. Three times before morning they wandered off, and, finally, all of Phelps' cattle and one of our cows succeeded in getting away several miles, when Eli Chase finally found them in a dense thicket. Not being able to procure hay, for love or money, we could not remain here, so we rolled out at eight o'clock, and traveled over good roads until four o'clock, stopping a half hour at noon. Hay is very scarce; I tried a dozen places before I could find any person who could supply us with "roughness" of any kind for our cattle. We are camped at Mr. Trimble's, in Monroe county, where we get a lot for our cattle and some very good corn fodder. Distance today twenty miles. The Malta company passed along tonight; with them was a four horse team from Mendota. Our road from Mt. Pleasant thus far has followed the timber, generally, and has been almost as good as we could desire. We started at just the right time, for, by being delayed at Kossuth, we reached the clay roads just in time to find them settled. Three days earlier they would have been almost impassable.

MONDAY, MARCH 28. We were visited last night by a most furious thunder storm; the rain poured in torrents the whole night, drenching the face of the earth until every dry run became a foaming water course. Our tents did not leak a drop, but not expecting a storm of such magnitude when we went to bed, we had not taken the precaution to trench around them, and before morning the ground upon which we slept was saturated with water, which made its presence sensibly and disagreeably felt whenever a foot strayed beyond the protection of our oilcloth and rubber mats. The rain slacked up about nine a.m., and, as we were not able to coax any more fodder from Mr. Trimble, we left camp at nine thirty, our destination being "roughness" for our cattle. It soon commenced snowing and blowing keenly from the northwest; the roads were just muddy enough to render walking disagreeable; but we "leaned" along westward. In five miles we reached Albia, the county seat of Monroe county, containing about nine hundred inhabitants.[51] In pleasant weather we should probably pronounce it a pleasant little town, but the only "impression" left upon our mind today is that it is a scattered prairie town with – some evidences of a go-ahead spirit – more mud – and no sidewalks. Five miles further brought us to the banks of Cedar creek, which we found not bridged, and swollen to that extent which rendered it impossible for us to ford it. The road this side of Albia has followed a dividing ridge of prairie – the ravines dove-tailing, and rendering the road very tortuous in its course. The soil on the summit of the ridge is a sterile yellow clay, and the points of the ridges are gravelly – in an agricultural point of view fitted only for sheep grazing. Have seen no farms for several miles back. We find here some straw mixed with chaff and waste wheat, which our cattle eat with avidity. Our camp is a convenient one, with plenty of the best wood and shelter for the cattle. Huge camp fires are burning in front of the tents,and our stoves are dispensing a grateful heat within. Thus ends the most disagreeable day of the trip so far. Distance ten miles.

SUN – no, TUESDAY, MARCH 29 [1859]. I had nearly

[51] The population in 1940 was 5,157.

written sunday – so greatly has this "day of rest" resembled the calm and peaceful Sabbath. We have been encamped all day, the creek being still too high to be forded. Various camp duties have consumed the time today – drying clothes, greasing boots, refitting the "outer man" with clean garments and regaling the "inner man" with a savory game supper forming a portion thereof. The weather has been beautiful, although last night was "slightually" frosty. The stages met here this afternoon, and exchanged mails and passengers by means of a canoe. The water is receding rapidly, and we hope to get away by times tomorrow. Cedar creek is a misnomer, for it is said there is not a cedar growing upon its banks. The boys are all well except Collins, who had a touch of ague today.

WEDNESDAY, MARCH 30. This morning, when we were nearly ready to start out, the Malta and Mendota teams, which had been encamped near by since monday, came down to the ford and crossed without difficulty, although the water came near running into the wagon beds. We followed them and crossed without any accident. The owner of the straw pile then beset us for six dollars to pay him for the chaff the cattle had eaten! We offered to pay half his demand, although the stuff was not worth over two dollars, but he would not receive it, and we drove off without further ceremony. We passed through Staceyville – four or five houses – and Lagrange,[52] in which the *leg range* is very limited, as it contains only three or four houses. Twelve miles from morning's camp, we were waited upon by an agent of the straw proprietor accompanied by a justice. We talked the matter over and explained everything fully,

[52] Lagrange is just over the line in Lucas county.

when the magistrate at once advised the agent to take three dollars for the straw and chaff and consider it well paid for, and further advised him to charge at least one dollar for his long, tedious walk. We paid the three dollars, thanked the magistrate, and traveled on. Bought some corn today at seventy-five cents. The rain and snow have made the roads very bad for footmen, and the wheeling for teams is not very easy. Distance fifteen miles – over prairie, the surface of which is black loam. We are now in Lucas county.

THURSDAY, MARCH 31.[53] Camped last night just in time to escape the "pelting of a pitiless storm," which, however, was not of long duration. After hard coaxing, we succeeded in getting two hundred pounds of hungarian grass for our cattle, at fifty cents per hundred. This morning the ground was frozen, which rendered the traveling very bad. Roads during the day very heavy, owing to the recent rain and snow. Six miles from camp brought us to Little White Breast, a small stream of no importance. Four miles further we arrived at Chariton, the county seat, a place of probably nine hundred inhabitants.[54] It contains a number of business houses, where goods of all kinds are sold at very reasonable figures considering the distance they have to be hauled. The town contains also a very fine steam flouring mill. Flour is selling at four dollars to four dollars and a half per one hundred pounds; eggs, eight cents; bacon, hams, nine cents; sides, nine cents; shoulders, eight cents. We here met Mr. Robt. Wilson, who lived in Oquawka some ten years ago, with whom we spent some time in very agreeable conversation.

---

[53] The diary for the dates march 31 to april 3, inclusive, was published in the *Spectator* of april 14, 1859.

[54] This city had a population of 5,754 in 1940.

Visiting the printing office, I had the satisfaction of receiving some "exchanges," which served to post me up in the affairs of the outer world, as I had not seen or heard any "news" since leaving Mt. Pleasant. This side of Chariton we crossed a very beautiful and fertile rolling prairie for several miles, at which distance we reached the White Breast,[55] a stream of about the size of Henderson, upon the banks of which we are pleasantly situated in camp. Our cattle are in a secure lot, and have some hay,– not as much as we could have desired, but all we could possibly get of a man who only spared it because our cattle "ought not to suffer, he supposed." Never have I known or heard of an agricultural region in which there existed so utter a dearth of grain and hay as in Iowa at the present time. It is almost impossible to get either, and when we do secure a little it is at an exorbitant price. What the heavy emigration, now close upon our heels, are to do, I am at a loss to determine. Distance today seventeen miles. The horse teams to which I have before alluded (and which are beginning to look thin and jaded) are camped near us tonight – they can't get away from us!

While walking over the prairie today, Will Phelps picked up a piece of paper containing the "lines," which I subjoin in all their native simplicity, only suppressing the writer's surname. Kinzy is evidently a budding genius, and it is to be hoped he may receive the requisite amount of "edication" to develope fully the "faculty" that seeks by these premonitory spasmodic kicks to announce its advent. Kinzy is just the age that Patrick Henry was when his genius began to develop itself, so he need not despair.

[55] A branch of the Des Moines river.

My name is kinzy
i am twenty nine year old
    and four foot tall
and in case you should doubt it
i will tell you all about it
for i was measured with the square
my hat was off my feet was bare

and if you want to know the cause
of me being so little stature
i will try to inform you
for that was no small matter.

my mother she was making soap
and they supposed I was dry
so i just crawled up
and took a drink of lye.

if you want to know my weight
i can tell it pretty strait
for i was weighed in chariton
and i weighed just sixty one.

should it be the supposition
that this is a composition
i will just be a closing
for i am tired of composing.

FRIDAY, APRIL 1 [1859]. Left camp this morning at nine o'clock; bad roads for about seven miles, after which we found them very fair except a few mud holes. After crossing the creek we ascent a long hill, and a magnificent prairie country stretches away around us. We found only one small grove today, which was fourteen miles from our morning's camp. Passed through Ottowa, called by courtesy, "town," which consists of a small tavern, a vacant store, and one or two other houses. Bought some good potatoes at one dollar per bushel.

Corn varies in price from fifty cents to seventy-five cents per bushel. Passed through Osceola, the county seat, this evening. Could find no flour in the town, and the business houses, in other respects, appear to be pretty well "cleaned out." The number of stores is some evidence of latent enterprise, which requires only good crops to develope it satisfactorily. Osceola contains a population of five hundred and sixteen persons.[56]

This county – Clarke – so far as I have had opportunity for observation, is a splendid natural agricultural region – I have never seen finer; but it is as yet very sparsely settled. Lands have been held at exorbitant prices, but are now, I am informed, offered at reasonable rates. Land speculation has cursed this remote region in a still greater degree, it would seem, than in localities near the great thoroughfares of commerce and marts of trade. I had hoped to see the *Spectator* of the 24th ultimo here, but upon calling at the post office, learned that Mr. John Davenport, our only subscriber here, had taken out the paper, and that he lived six miles from town, off our road. We are camped near town, with a good lot for the teams, and hungarian grass at fifty cents per one hundred pounds. The weather looks threatening. Distance today twenty-two miles – the best day's travel we have yet made.

SATURDAY, APRIL 2. We were visited last night by a furious storm of wind, rain, sleet and snow. The storm continuing this forenoon, we concluded to remain in camp all day. Tonight the wind is in the northwest; out of doors the weather is bitter cold, and the ground is freezing very hard. Our tents, with stoves full of wood, in full blast, are as comfortable – nearly – as houses

56 Population in 1940 of 3,281.

composed of more substantial materials. The man of whom we are buying hay is one of that class who takes delight in squeezing an American quarter "until the eagle can be heard to squeal"– he refuses to weigh out our hay, and manages to "guess it off" so as to make it cost us at least seventy-five cents per one hundred pounds. We think of hunting up another stack, on ahead, tomorrow.

SUNDAY, APRIL 3. "Charity begins at home," and in obedience to the maxim we left camp this morning, to escape from the clutches of the extortionist at whose mercy our purses were suffering rapid depletion – our cattle meantime receiving no adequate compensation. He is a professing Christian – but heaven save the mark, if such men are to become our exemplars! Why, he charged us thirty-five cents for four or five sticks of cord wood and an armful of musty hay for a tent mat, and then came down this morning to carry back the hay – but that served us the purpose of a good fire before we left camp, a match not refusing, as the oxen did, to eat it. This old curmudgeon is quite wealthy, hence the contempt which his picayunishness engenders. Crossed the summit of the divide between the waters of the Desmoines and Grand rivers, about noon.

We are now fairly upon the Missouri slope. Scenery today one vast expanse of prairie, dotted here and there, at long intervals, with little groves of scattered timber. Soil along the road today not very good. Country very sparsely settled. Roads too rough before the thaw, and too slippery afterwards, to be called good. Made eighteen miles, and are encamped in a small grove, in a ravine, where we are sheltered from the wind which is driving a thin drift of snow across the prairie heights.

Good hay in abundance at thirty-five cents. The boys are all well – Collins having got rid of his ague. Passed a lone school house today where two venerable men, and two only, were conducting a prayer meeting, each praying alternately, and both joining in the good old-fashioned hymns. The Malta and Mendota horse teams are encamped a mile and a half in our rear. We are now in Union county.

MONDAY, APRIL 4.[57] Left camp at eight forty-five, and at the distance of a mile arrived at the ford of Grand river, which was crossed without difficulty. The road now, for nearly a mile, leads along the lofty bluff overlooking the valley of Grand river, and affords a magnificent view northward and eastward. Nine miles from camp we passed through Afton, the county seat, a small village, which will make a town whenever the country fills up; Union county being very thinly inhabited at present.[58] A mile from Afton we crossed the West fork of Grand river.[59] Two miles further brought us to Highland, where several buildings, two or three of them tenantless, add to the lonesome and dreary appearance of a vast wet, spongy, spouty prairie, that extends, seemingly without limit on every hand around us. The freeze of last night, which the cold wintry Norwester that has been blowing today serves to keep hard and solid, is a God-send to us on this swampy prairie, which otherwise would be very difficult to cross. Tonight we are camped on the prairie, with some little hay for our cattle. Corn today is very scarce, and what little we can get costs seventy-five cents. Have not been

57 The diary entries of april 4 to april 8, inclusive, appear in the *Spectator* of april 21, 1859.

58 In 1940, Afton had a population of 987.

59 Thompson creek.

able to buy any flour for two days. Distance fifteen miles.

TUESDAY, APRIL 5. Quite a hard freeze again last night. We now enter upon a long stretch of prairie, the monotony of which is only broken by one house and a small hickory grove, bordering Platte creek, which flows through the center of this sixteen mile reach of vacant land. Our road has led over high, flat, wet summit levels, most of the day; much of the time not a tree in sight in any direction. Camped at George's, where we got hay by paying enough for it. Distance sixteen miles.

WEDNESDAY, APRIL 6 [1859]. This morning Mr. Bradley, of Oquawka, came into camp. He is "footing it" through to the Missouri river, carrying with him only his gun and carpet sack. From him we learn that Scott and company's team, and Thompson and company's, were to leave camp, five miles west of Ottumwa, on friday morning last; also, that our friends, the Irish boys, took the cars at Burlington, and are now ahead of us. Crossed East Nodaway, quite a stream, just after leaving "French Colony." This is an Icarian village, containing a population of about sixty persons.[60] The community is a branch of the one at Nauvoo.[61] Their village is neat and compactly built – they own three thousand nine hundred acres of land, four hundred of which are in cultivation – are a frugal, industrious, moral and temperate people. Their industry and enterprise, to say nothing of their liberality in dealing with

[60] This village, shown as "Icaria," on the General Land Office map of Iowa (1878), was located about three miles northeast of Corning, county seat of Adams county.

[61] The Icarians occupied the Mormon city of Nauvoo, Illinois, on the east bank of the Mississippi, after the Mormons were forced to evacuate the city in 1846.

travelers, are in strange contrast with the want of thrift, the indolence, and the apparently instinctive disposition to swindle emigrants, that are dominant traits in many of their American neighbors. We bought of them flour at three dollars and seventy-five cents to four dollars; potatoes – as fine as I ever saw – at sixty cents; corn at sixty cents.

We next passed Queen City, containing three houses, and then, after crossing the West Branch of East Nodaway, ascended a long hill to Quincy, the county seat, a very small village.[62] Two miles and a half further we crossed Middle Nodaway, a fine rapid stream, at Walter's Mill, at which point coal has been discovered in large quantities.[63] Since leaving Grand river, our road has been following the general direction of the old Mormon trail,[64] which we will not leave very far at any time until we reach the Bluffs. This road was located by the Mormon scouts, and is probably the best natural road across Iowa. At the mill above mentioned we leave the Glenwood road – running westward through the second tier of counties – and strike northwest for Lewis, in Cass county.[65] We are camped tonight in regular plains style – night having overtaken us in the midst of a wide prairie far from timber or human habitation. White and Phelps happened to discover a few stunted burr oak bushes about half a mile from camp which will furnish us fuel enough – a neighboring slough supplies us with water – and our cattle are picking at the grass with avidity. Distance nineteen miles.

62 Quincy is about five miles northwest of Corning. The road is now to the north of Highway U.S. 34.

63 This was in the vicinity of the town of Carbon.

64 This was the route of the Mormon migration of 1846 between Nauvoo and Council Bluffs.

65 Lewis is on state highway 92, forty-five miles east of Council Bluffs.

THURSDAY, MARCH [April] 7. Left camp at seven fifteen. Traveled four miles, when Phelps' team stopped to get breakfast and feed the cattle hay. We, having breakfasted, and not liking the hay, pushed forward to the next house, a mile further, where we fed our cattle good hay all they wanted – for twenty-five cents. Set our host down for a "white man," pushed on three miles to Porter's, where we got corn at thirty-five cents, which led us to class Mr. Porter as both "white" and "human." Camped here an hour, waiting for Phelps' team to come up. They not arriving, we started at one o'clock across a high rolling divide – ten miles of prairie without a tree or improvement in the entire distance – to Seven Mile creek,[66] which we reached at five o'clock. All that the country we have passed over today requires is timber to render it equal to any in the land. We find the deep, narrow, crooked, rapid stream, upon the banks of which we are encamped, considerably swollen by the melting snow, and impassable on account of the bridge being under water. Our cattle find a little green grass in the bottoms tonight. We are now in Cass county. It is freezing hard tonight. Distance eighteen miles. Crossed West Nodaway at Porter's.

FRIDAY, APRIL 8. The creek having fallen several feet, we crossed without difficulty, and crossed another splendid divide of vacant prairie, between Seven Mile creek, and East Nichtenabotna [Nishnabotna] for the distance of seven miles to Lewis, the county seat of Cass county, a neat little town, handsomely located on the banks of the last named stream. This river we cross on a ferry, although it is not perhaps fifty feet wide. A mill dam covers the old ford, and a bridge was carried away

[66] A branch of Nodaway river.

last season by a freshet; so the county authorities instead of rebuilding the bridge, established this ferry for the accommodation of the citizens of Cass county, who pass over it free, and to swindle the traveling community who are obliged to pay very heavy toll. It is thought the collections of ferriage off the Pike's Peakers alone, will be sufficient to bridge two such streams. Passing Indian town and Iranistan,[67] two little one-horse hamlets, we traveled ten miles, along a crooked road across vacant prairie, to Walnut creek, where we are encamped. Two young men living here have fitted themselves out with a rough handcart, rigged up with a sail to assist them in pulling it, when the wind blows, with which they intend to start to the mines in a few days.[68] Distance fifteen miles.

SATURDAY, APRIL 9.[69] Traveled twelve miles, over a very fine prairie country, to Big Grove.[70] This is the title of a very fine grove of fine timber, situated partly on the bottom, on the east bank of the West Nichtenabotna, in Pottawotamie county. It is one of the finest sections of country I ever saw; the land is rolling and fertile, and there is timber enough to supply the wants of a large settlement for many years to come. We arrived here about noon, and camped near Reed's station, where we find corn at forty cents a bushel, and hay at very reasonable rates. Phelps' team drove into camp during the afternoon.

SUNDAY, APRIL 10 [1859]. Today is rainy and dis-

[67] This town is near the western boundary of Cass county.

[68] For description of a wind wagon at Westport, see the preceding volume in this *Southwest Historical Series*, 297.

[69] The entries for april 9 to april 12 were published in the newspaper of april 28, 1859.

[70] Big Grove is shown on the General Land Office map of Iowa (1878) and appears to be the same as the modern town of Oakland, on state highway 92.

agreeable. We are lying over, in company with Joseph Darnell, and some of our own company, we spent the day in visiting among our old acquaintances, who formerly lived at and near Oquawka. Living within the circle of a few miles are the families of Lewis Huff, Benj. Palmer, Miner Palmer, Mrs. Cousland, George Reed, Jacob Rust, Wm. Morris and Benj. Morris. They are all comfortably situated and appear to be prospering. A town has been laid out here which will become eventually the county seat of the new county that must before long be created out of the eastern portion of Pottawattomie.[71] The citizens of Big Grove appear to be enterprising and public spirited. Their farms are under a fine state of cultivation; their prices are fair and reasonable; their postal facilities are good, as a daily mail passes through; and their educational privileges are not surpassed by any other country settlement.

MONDAY, APRIL 11. This morning we crossed the W. N. river, traveled over a fertile ridge of prairie to Silver creek,[72] which we crossed at noon, and then passed over another handsome rolling prairie to Keg creek,[73] where we are encamped for the night. Distance sixteen miles.

TUESDAY, APRIL 12. Started early, and traveled over a broad prairie to Little Mosquito creek, whence we have a broken, hilly, rugged, muddy road to Big Mosquito, and thence to the city of Council Bluffs. Here we are camped, and shall remain long enough to recruit our cattle thoroughly – although one to look at them would not suppose they had been very badly used, for

71 The new county was not created.

72 A branch of West Nishnabotna.

73 A stream that flows by the city of Glenwood and empties into the Missouri river.

they really look to be in as good condition as when they left home. They have, however, a long trip before them, and the best thing that we can do is to give them every advantage that plenty of corn and hay will afford in fitting them to travel briskly along after we leave the Missouri.

We have now completed our journey through Iowa, in just four weeks from the day we left home. The time we selected for making the trip was, perhaps, everything considered, the most favorable that we could have taken. From Oquawka to Mt. Pleasant we encountered by far the worst roads that we traveled over. Between the Mississippi and Desmoines rivers we find the country generally well settled, well watered, and free from the gophers and prairie squirrels which increase in numbers as you proceed west until they become almost a scourge in some parts of the Missouri slope. Our road as far as Ottumwa passed through considerable of timber; after leaving the Desmoines the character of the country changes, and we enter upon a region of great plains – immense prairies, dividing ridges between long and narrow streams, with an occasional grove bordering the creeks, and here and there a clump of trees in ravines depressed below the general level of the country. Along some of the larger streams, it is true, there is considerable heavy timber, but, as a general rule, there is not enough in the country to supply the ordinary wants of even a sparse population.

As far as Quincy, we traveled along the line near which has been located the Burlington and Missouri River railroad. It is possible the road may be completed to the Desmoines at Ottumwa within a year, but I think its progress will then cease, at least for a long time to come. The facts which have led me to this conclusion must be apparent to the reader who has followed us day by day across the state, when he takes into consideration the general stagnation that prevails in real estate matters. The lands belonging to the company at the present time would scarcely sell for a song, if my information has been correct; but, should the company procure the necessary means for pushing the road forward, it will prove the great instrument of settling up a country that may, with good culture, become a fine agricultural region. Nine years ago, I passed through this section of the state, along the tier of counties adjacent on the north; at that time I found about the same evidences of settlement there, that now exist through Lucas, Clark, Union and Adams counties.

We have traveled, in all, twenty-three days and parts of days; the least distance made in a day was three miles, the greatest twenty-two miles – the latter being made with the least labor and being attended with less fatigue. The entire distance traveled over, from Oquawka to Council Bluffs (which I have been very particular to ascertain as accurately as possible), is three hundred and six and a half miles.

We find here a number of teams encamped, waiting for better weather before leaving. The news from the mines is very favorable. Numbers of the citizens here will go out this season for the purpose of mining.

In a day or two,[74] after I shall have had time to look about me, I will write more fully respecting the city and its surroundings. At present I will only add that everything is cheap here, and outfits can be obtained here as reasonably as on the Mississippi.

[74] He was to spend two weeks in Council Bluffs.

Council Bluffs, April 23d, '59.[75]

DEAR SPECTATOR: We are still "located" on the sunny slope of the ragged bluffs lying south of the city of Council Bluffs, and overlooking a broad savanna of bottom land intervening between the base of the hills and the Missouri river, on which our cattle have free range and excellent "picking." The weather, for nearly a week, has been warm, sunny and spring-like – the leaves are budding out, the grass beginning to carpet the bottom lands and tinge with verdure the upland lawns and sloping hills. The roads are hard and smooth and dry, and the emigrants are leaving us daily for the plains. On monday next we shall cross the river to Omaha City, and on tuesday we will be en route for the Mines taking with us nine bushels of corn meal and four bushels of corn. This amount, with the "picking" of new and old grass that we will be able to find along the route, we make sure will last us to Fort Kearny, where we will strike the "buffalo grass."[76]

"Council Bluffs and its surroundings" form the theme of what might be made a lengthy communication, but as my friend and fellow-traveler, Capt. White, promises me that he will preach from this text, in the columns of the *Spectator,* I will only pen a few lines in this connection. The city has impressed me very favorably. I have had the pleasure of forming a somewhat extensive acquaintance here, through the politeness of my good friend, Henry P. Warren, and it affords me great pleasure to bear testimony to the general intelligence, enterprising spirit and liberality of the citizens. We have had occasion to transact business with some of

[75] This letter was published in the *Oquawka Spectator* of may 5, 1859.

[76] The short, curly buffalo grass (Buchloe dactyloides), cured on the ground, was very nutritious.

the leading firms, in the mercantile and general outfitting line, and I must give it as my candid opinion that no city in the west contains more honorable or fairer dealers than Council Bluffs. There are two newspapers published here, which are well sustained – their advertising patronage being extensive, and reflecting great credit upon the sagacity of the business community. To Messrs. Babbett & Carpenter, of the *Bugle,* and to Messrs. Maynard & Provost, of the *Nonpariel,* I am indebted for many favors, in the way of good supplies of exchanges. Council Bluffs is an oasis in the desert of our Iowa exodus, which will not soon fade from the grateful remembrance of those who have been sojourners within its borders.

WHEREABOUTS OF THE BOYS

Tom Scott and Peter Hart visited us the other day, having walked up from White Cloud,[77] where their teams, in company with Caswell & Thompson's, are encamped. They will go by Plattsmouth, and may overtake us at Fort Kearny, as we shall probably lie over there several days. The boys inform us that corn and hay have risen in price fifty per cent along the route we traveled.

The other day, while in Omaha City, I met Ed Kean (who spent the winter in Oquawka). He had just come through Iowa, on foot, and was disappointed in not having overtaken some Mercer county teams which had gone on. He concluded then not to go on, and went down the river, intending to make his way home to Michigan.

Frank Dunn and company are with their team in

[77] White Cloud is in the extreme northeast corner of Kansas.

Plattsmouth; he was here today for the purpose of getting some articles necessary to their outfit. Speck's boys are camped at White Cloud.

We have not yet heard from Ray Simpson, Craig and company, but presume they must be near the river by this time. We will probably all be together at Fort Kearny.

Jo Darnell has joined us, and will go out in Wm. Phelps' mess.

The boys are all well and hearty. Good feeling prevails; and all are buoyant with hope and firm in the faith that Pike's Peak will pay.

THE MINING NEWS

I have conversed with persons who have returned from the gold mines. From their descriptions of the country and from their assurances, respecting the existence of gold there, I am fully persuaded that any industrious man can make it pay who will put in hard licks for it when he reaches the mines. The most of those who have returned here, have already gone back or will soon do so, some with their families and others with provisions to last them until fall. I have had an interview with a very intelligent young man, Mr. Courtright,[78] whose word is regarded as entirely reliable by his friends here; he is on the eve of returning with an outfit, and from his statements I am led to make more favorable deductions.

One or two men have returned (or at least reported that they had returned) from the mines, recently, who report not much gold there; with one of these men I conversed, and I learned enough to satisfy me that, with

[78] Probably the one referred to in volume IX, 196.

even my limited experience in gold mining, he could not enlighten me much. I presume it is in the new mines as it was in California – many have gone out; prospected a few days; lost much more gold than they saved, in washing; got discouraged; turned their faces homeward, and have come home poorer in pocket and no richer in experience than when they left it. It is just possible that these men are right, and that those who, with the same facilities for observation, have concluded to risk so much in going back with their families, are wrong; but I will not so believe until I have fully and thoroughly tested the matter by actual experiment. When I shall have done this, the readers of the *Spectator* may depend upon something that they may bet on as "reliable."

Mayor Brookfield, of Nebraska City, who, for some time, wrote rather discouragingly respecting the prospects in the mines, at a time when very little could be done in the way of prospecting, has changed his tune, and now writes most encouragingly to his friends.[79] Acting-governor Waters, of Nebraska, has received a fine specimen of shot gold from Mayor B. I saw it, when I was in Omaha, and find that it is the "pure stuff."

THE EMIGRATION

The emigration through this place, although considerable, is not so great as it was expected to be, not to be compared, in point of numbers, with that through some points lower down the river – as Leavenworth City and St. Joseph. At present, however, the tide appears to be changing, and teams are constantly rolling into the city. An impression prevails very extensively that the route

[79] See the preceding volume, pages 220, 242, 248.

from Plattsmouth and other places on the south side of Platte river is nearer to Fort Kearny (where most of the roads come together) than the Northern route; that such an impression is an erroneous one any person may satisfy himself by noting on the map the great bend which the Platte makes to the south between the mouth of the Loupe Fork and the Missouri, and the location of Fort Kearny, which is somewhat farther north than this place. The distance from the Bluffs to Fort Kearny is one hundred and eighty-four miles, while from Plattsmouth it is two hundred and thirty miles.

The great objection urged against the northern route, however, is that Loupe Fork must be crossed, and the Platte river forded at Fort Kearny. I have had some experience with Loupe, when it had to be forded and ferried both, and if it was then no obstacle to our progress and caused no detention, it cannot be much to be feared now, when three good ferries are established over it; while, as for Platte, I have seen too many teams cross it, and too many Indians wade it, to be frightened into taking a worse and longer road to avoid a cool, pleasant ford 18 inches deep. The average number of teams that have arrived at this place daily, during the last three weeks, is ten to fifteen.

As might be supposed, the emigration exhibits human nature in all its phases, and is marked by greater variety, as regards the manner of outfit, than any that has ever previously crossed the plains. We have opportunity here of seeing timorous, faltering, hesitating Indecision, which catches at every floating rumor that is wafted from the mines, and allows the temperature of its hopes to be elevated or depressed in the ratio of the favorable or unfavorable report – we behold, also, that defiant and unflinching Resolution which has determined to go through and test the matter, to "try all things and hold fast to that which is good," and which has adopted the motto:

> We know the worst, anticipate each ill,
> But have resolved to conquer, and we will!
> Then, comrades, onward – let us push it through
> And gain the Gold, our industry's just due.

Taken as a whole, I am satisfied that the great mass of the present emigration is composed of honest, industrious poor men – men who are accustomed to labor and who will not flinch at exposure and hardship – and who are impelled to the step they have taken by a determination to better their condition. Admitting that there is gold in paying quantities at the new mines – and I take it no reasonable man now pretends to entertain much doubt upon the subject – the fact that such a class of men composes the majority of the emigration is a guarantee of their ultimate success, and is a hopeful indication that far better times are about making their advent among us.

Without doubt, the great mass of those who will visit the mines are western men, and these men will bring the gold they may accumulate there back into the western states, which will assist materially in bringing forward the time when the west will no longer be crippled in every quarter by its dependence upon eastern capital. It is a melancholy fact that we are now too much at the mercy of the east. Eastern capital builds our railroads – or swindles us out of the value of our bonds; eastern capital makes speculative investments in real estate, which stifles enterprise and deters immigration; eastern capital sets up a false standard of commercial values for our products; and eastern capital floods the country with an unsound currency. Let the west become, pecuniarily, and by the actual presence of the gold among us, independent, and a system of exchanges which will produce reliable currency will be established, and our commercial relations will become more satisfactory.

INCIDENTS

In this connection, allow me to mention a few incidents that have fallen under my observation, and occurred within the scope of my information, touching the present emigration.

A day or so after our arrival here, a German arrived here on his way back from Ft. Kearny to Wisconsin. He had come to the conclusion that the mines were a humbug; this important mental deduction, at which he had arrived without personal observation he imparted to a company of twenty-four men who were here, with several teams, from a town above Chicago, and who had expended to the aggregate some four hundred dollars since leaving home, and upon receiving this "unfavorable news" they hitched up their teams and started upon their return home!

Whilst we were encamped at Walnut creek, we fell in with three Frenchmen, from Waukegan, who had a good wagon and two yoke of oxen. They had a good outfit, but one yoke of their cattle, owing to their mismanagement, were sore and lame, and they were very anxious to dispose of the whole "rig." When they got to Big Grove, they swapped off their wagon, cattle, and a thirty dollar gun, for an old carriage not worth fifteen dollars and two used up, blind and lame stage horses! This latter rig was sold at auction, the other day, in this city, forty-six dollars purchasing the entire establishment! The Frenchmen have, for twenty dollars each, procured board through to the mines, where they will be set down without anything. This is but one instance, among several, that have fallen under my observation of mismanagement. Allow me to say, *en passant,* that one of their men had more original wit and comical humor in his noddle than any other man I ever met; one of his odd sayings, in allusion to the cold weather that had attended us and the extortion to which we had many times been subjected, I shall never forget –"I wish zat hell pass through Iowa one month; it makes ze wezzer warm and ze people honest."

One or two instances there have been, where young men arrived here with good teams and money enough to purchase their outfits. Instead of doing the latter, however, they have permitted their footsteps to wander away into paths that lead to sin and defilement – gamblers have roped them in and stripped them of their all – and the result has been that their oxen have been transferred, at half price, to the butcher's pen, while they have themselves gone – who knows where? Let us hope that the parents and friends of these unfortunates may linger along in the delusion that those in whom they are interested "have not done well in the mines" – "where ignorance is bliss, 'tis folly to be wise."

We see on the road men on foot with packs on their backs – men with handcarts – men without anything but a blanket and a brazen face – all bound to Pike's Peak. Generally, however, the emigration from this point is provided with very good outfits. The majority of those going out are provided with oxen; while horses come next, there being only a few mules on the road. Of course, when we get started I shall have better opportunities to gather emigration items; at present, I shall turn to other themes.

TIME'S CHANGES

Nine years ago, as many of my readers remember, the writer came through Council Bluffs – then Kanesville [80]– on his way to California. Nine years have wonderfully changed the appearance of the Bluffs and its surroundings. Then there was only a small Mormon town, with scarcely a passable house within its limits, where now stands a city with three thousand inhabitants, many fine dwellings, costly business houses, and other indications of the existence and outlay of heavy capital. Eight miles below, where then only stood an Indian agency and a Mission school where a few Omaha children were taught, perhaps only enough to convince them that "a little learning is a dangerous thing," now stands the thriving town of Belleview, Nebraska. Immediately opposite us on the west, no house then marked the site of the present capital of Nebraska, where Omaha City now looms up proudly to view. Northward from Omaha, eight miles distant, where we crossed the Missouri in 1850, a few deserted huts then marked the site of the Mormon "Wnter Quarters," but since that time Florence money has rendered somewhat notorious the town which now occupies that beautiful site, but which, like the shinplaster alluded to, has waxed, waned and collapsed. All the places above named, and one or two others which have scarcely ad-

80 The Mormon town, named for Col. Thomas L. Kane, a friend of the Mormons. See Andrew Jenson, *The Historical Record,* VIII, 897; and O. O. Winther (Ed.), *A Friend of the Mormons* (1937).

vanced more than a hut or two beyond a paper existence, may be seen at one view from the summit of any of the high bluffs at the base of which nestles this handsome city.

I will not venture to transfer to paper the reflections which come, unsought, to the mind, as it dwells, even for a moment, upon the wondrous changes that are wrought by the hand of Time, which is never-ceasingly at work modeling the plastic material that humanity presents for the capricious designs of Fancy or the fixed and stern commandings of Destiny.

"Times change, and men change with them" – the footsteps of one race are not obliterated from their favorite paths, until the land passes under the control of the stranger, new customs and new landmarks bear testimony to the new manorship; and of the retiring race it may well be said, the places that knew them in their pride shall know them no more forever!

Even thus is it here; where once – and but a little time ago – the council fires of the Indian were lighted, and a race held sway with all the untutored dignity that native independence and untamed freedom engenders, now no traces of that race are seen except their pathlike trails worn deeply in the soil, and an occasional Pawnee who thrusts a begging paper into your hand, and, by his easily-learned vices, dispels the poetic fancies with which Cooper and Longfellow have invested the indian character.

ONWARD AGAIN! On monday morning, april twenty-fifth [1859],[81] we struck camp, after two weeks' pleasant sojourn in Council Bluffs, and again took up our

[81] The entries for april 25 to 28, inclusive, were published in the *Spectator* of may 12, 1859.

line of march towards the goal of our golden anticipations. After traversing three miles of rich fertile bottom land, over good roads, we reached the Missouri river, at this point a swift, narrow and remarkably crooked stream. The general points of difference between the Missouri and Upper Mississippi are well known to all my readers – the most distinctive feature characteristic of the former stream being its constant muddiness, the water continually washing down a chalky quicksand from its shores, which are composed of a soil that I shall have occasion to notice more fully in describing the Platte valley.

We cross the river on a good steam ferry boat – the charge being one dollar and seventy-five cents – and are landed on the Nebraska shore some half mile from Omaha city. Fronting the town is a low flat bench of land, evidently not many years ago the bed of the river, about a quarter of a mile wide. The second bench – upon which the town is built – rises abruptly some forty or fifty feet, and spreads out into a broad, level plateau, from which, at some considerable distance back, it rises by a gradual slope into a fine bluff, upon the summit of which and overlooking the city stands the yet unfinished Capitol building. This building is of magnificent proportions; it is of brick, is enclosed, but the interior arrangements and exterior ornamentings (including the twenty-four lofty columns) are in an unfinished condition, although eighty thousand dollars has been expended upon it already.[82] The city is built, for the most part, on the second bench, and contains a number of

[82] This was Nebraska's second capitol building, according to J. Sterling Morton's *Illustrated History of Nebraska,* I, 267, and was erected in 1857-1858 at a cost of about $130,000. It was located on Capitol Hill present (1941) site of the Central High School.

neat buildings, several brick blocks, two newspaper offices, a population of about two thousand five hundred, a hotel that cost seventy-five thousand dollars, a fine Court house, the Land office, the Treasury deposit office, and bankers, brokers, real estate men, saloon-keepers and lawyers without number. In point of business, although there is considerable competition, and prices are about the same as in Council Bluffs, I think the latter city is in the foreground; but then it is an older town.

An old friend of mine, A. D. Jones, Esq. (a brother of Brent and Thomas D.), informs me that, when he first came here in the late fall of 1853, there was only a small "claim" cabin on the site of the present city. In april, 1854, the treaty under which the Indian title was extinguished, was ratified, and Mr. Jones, who held a commission as Postmaster, erected a small office in may. The month following he laid out the town for the company who held the claim. The first permanent improvement was made the following fall, and the first election held in december. This has been one of the very "fast" towns, but it is "quiet" just now, and would be, I imagine, a very dull place, as to business, were it not for the Pike's Peak emigration passing through – notwithstanding what my friend Jones assures me is the fact, that three hundred thousand bushels of corn were raised in Nebraska last season. Stone for building purposes is procured within three miles of town, but coal and lumber are very expensive articles.

As the chambermaid of our mess – Capt. W. – will touch up Omaha, in his communication, I will leave the subject.

TUESDAY, APRIL 26. We had intended leaving Omaha today, but were visited last night by a heavy thunder storm – today the weather is cloudy, with occasional showers, and have thought best to wait until thursday.

WEDNESDAY, APRIL 27. The sun shines clear, the winds blow warm and balmy, the grass is springing upward with a new impulse, and everything evinces the advent of spring. Surely, the "long looked for" has "come at last!" The roads, which yesterday were very muddy, are dry and firm – so rapidly does this chalky clay absorb and drain off the moisture. I have made the acquaintance of two Messrs. Brown (brothers of Jas. F., who sold lumber in Oquawka last winter), who will start to the mines next week with a banker's safe and a load of goods.[83] J. F. will not come out until fall, being detained by business in Wisconsin. Four men were hung near Ft. Kearny, last week, for cattle stealing. This, we hope, will prove a salutary warning to all who may have been disposed to act the part of prairie marauders. We shall lie by a few days at Ft. Kearny, in the expectation that the Oquawka boys who take the Plattsmouth route will overtake us.

THURSDAY, APRIL 28 [1859]. This morning we left camp at seven o'clock. We soon lost sight of the Big Muddy, and pursued our journey over magnificent roads, the route leading over an undulating prairie, dotted here and there with a cabin erected to mark a "claim," for a distance of eleven miles, to Pappillon (formerly called Pappea) creek.[84] At the crossing we find a hotel. This stream is spanned with an excellent

[83] Samuel R. and G. W. Brown established their bank in Denver in june, 1860. See L. R. Hafen, "Currency, Coinage and Banking in Pioneer Denver," in the *Colorado Magazine,* x, 81.

[84] This stream flows southeastward and passes Bellevue. For another account of a trip from Omaha to Fort Kearny, see Appendix C in this volume.

bridge, and the same remark will apply to two other small streams respectively four and eight miles from Omaha. Our route up the Platte leads us along the line of the Great Military Road, and judging from the bridges we have crossed today, government has performed a good work in their construction, for they are built of the best of materials and in the most substantial manner. From Pappillon our road leads along a dry summit dividing ridge eleven miles to Elkhorn City.[85] This town site is beautifully located, contains a post office, and looks as though it would some day become the nucleus of a thriving farming settlement.

During our drive of twenty-two miles today, we regret to say, we saw almost no timber at all. The scarcity of good timber is bound to retard, in a great measure, and to a great extent the permanent settlement of the country. A tri-weekly mail is carried over the route of the Military Road from Omaha City to Ft. Kearny, in good post coaches. We have excellent hay tonight at twenty-five cents per one hundred pounds. Grass is already very good in the low places, and is springing up finely on the uplands. The only representatives of Flora's kingdom that have yet greeted my vision I saw today – the modest "boys and girls" tufting the slopes of a timbered ravine, and the lowly "lilies of the valley," with their pearly petals bedecking the green carpet of the lowlands. A number of horse, ox and mule teams are camped near us. Belonging to one of them is an old gentleman of sixty, from Ohio, who trudges along on foot, like the rest of us, being, he said, too proud and "limber" to be caught riding. Wallace Rice

[85] This town was located just a little east of Elkhorn river, a branch of the Platte.

shot two rattlesnakes in a slough near the road. We are now in Douglas county.

FRIDAY, APRIL 29. Started at seven o'clock, and descended the bluff to Elkhorn river, one mile distant, which we crossed on a fine bridge. This is a stream nearly twice as large as Henderson, and is now nearly bank full. Three miles further on we crossed Rawhide creek on a bridge, and then for eleven miles pass over an unsettled country to Fremont, a Massachusetts settlement, which was originally quite small, and has grown "beautifully less."[86] Some days ago much difficulty was experienced by emigrants on that portion of the valley comprising the bottom between the Elkhorn and Rawhide, which streams run nearly parallel to each other for many miles, their confluence being several miles below where the road crosses. Both streams were unprecedently high, and their waters ran down in one wide stream; after the water receded, the road was left in such a condition that heavily laden teams could not cross it without much difficulty.

Our wagon is laden with three thousand four hundred pounds, and for a few rods we found the pulling pretty hard yet. Four miles from Fremont we strike the sloughs bordering on the Platte – the road not approaching the river nearer than a mile. Proceeding up the valley, our road lying over level hard bench, bordered with lakes and spring sloughs, a distance of four miles, we found a good camp at Mr. .... where we get all the hay our cattle can eat for twenty-five cents. The timber along the Platte is principally cottonwood, with a skirting of willow, and an undergrowth of red cedar, but it is not nearly as abundant

[86] Fremont revived; in 1940 the population was 11,862.

as could be wished or as the necessities of the country will require when settlements become numerous. A great many "claims" have been taken along the valley, of which a number have been deserted, and which are now subject to be located upon by any who may feel disposed to cast their lots upon the banks of the Platte.

This valley, at this point, and for miles further west, contains as fine farming lands as ever were created for the handicraft of the farmer to be exercised upon, and the scarcity of timber is the only great drawback to their early development. The gentleman at whose "place" we are now camped has secured a strip of timber along the river containing some thirty acres, for which he has been offered and has refused some eighteen hundred dollars.

There are two Pawnee villages on the Platte, below this point, and the road today has been swarming with them; they are not so degraded as their brethren who hang about the towns, but have, nevertheless, lost much of the dignity and haughtiness that their tribe manifested a few years ago, when they sustained their reputation as being the most daring and fearless of the Missouri tribes. They will receive a payment amounting to about thirty thousand dollars during the coming month. All the teams that left Elkhorn City this morning are camped with us tonight, except three or four ox teams that we left camped a mile behind, and two four-horse teams that were floundering through the mud on the Elkhorn bottom when we last saw them. Our team (three yoke of oxen and one yoke of cows) is not eclipsed by any on the road, and we keep it in fine order. Two hand-cart men are camped near us tonight. Distance today twenty-three miles.

A gentleman who has kept a correct tally informs us that, since the first of february, the teams have ranged, daily, from one to sixty-six, going west over the route. The Platte valley is here some ten to twelve miles wide, and the river sweeps along its eastern verge – the south bank being an abrupt sandy bluff, in some places steep and naked, and elsewhere thinly timbered. Where we crossed the Elkhorn there is a steam saw mill, for the manufacture of cottonwood lumber. Nine miles further up the stream is the town of Fontanelle, the county seat of Dodge county, which we enter this side of the Elkhorn.[87]

SATURDAY, APRIL 30 [1859]. Left camp at seven o'clock; traveled over a low-land prairie for eight miles, on which the road, owing to recent rains, had been considerably cut up; here we struck the Platte river, at what is called the North Bend, where there is a steam saw mill and a small settlement.[88] For ten miles the road then runs a short distance from the river and over excellent ground to Shell creek,[89] which we cross, near its junction with the Platte, on a government bridge. We are camped at Mr. Albertson's, on the creek three miles from the eastern boundary of Platte county. The country along the road today may be termed well-settled.

We have passed through two very extensive cities – Emersonville and Buchanan – in each one of which stands one house! They were staked out a couple of years ago, and numerous "shares" changed hands at high figures, those investing being principally eastern

87 Fontanelle, on the east side of the Elkhorn, is now in Washington county.

88 North Bend is on Highway U.S. 30.

89 Shell creek enters the Platte a little east of Schuyler, present Colfax county (Schuyler and Colfax apparently named for Schuyler Colfax, national political figure).

capitalists, who, because they permit themselves to be diddled occasionally, lost confidence in all "Western securities," unless it may be water lots in some fabled Lawrence City. The principal crop raised by the claim-makers last summer was potatoes; these were "holed," and many of the settlers left to spend the winter in the States, while their absence proved most acceptable to the "poor Indian, whose untutored mind" was sufficiently well schooled to know that boiled potatoes could affright gaunt Hunger from their wigwams, and that hoes and spades could dig through even frozen ground. We got hay tonight at the usual Nebraska price. Visited a prairie dog town this evening, which covers eighty acres; we were too late, however, to make ourselves familiar with the inhabitants, as they had retired for the night to "their several places of abode."

Mr. Albertson came here in the spring of 1856, made his claim, erected his house and put in a crop – his dwelling being the first erected in the valley west of the Elkhorn on this road. At that time he had no white neighbors within a less distance than thirty-seven miles. The next season he removed his interesting family to his farm, where he now lives comfortably and independent of the "outer world." He keeps Buchanan Post office, and during the coming season a school will be established, which will make the settlement "right in town." Timber along Platte today all cottonwood, scarcer and principally on islands. Indians in the neighborhood are having good success in trapping beaver and otter, which appear to be quite numerous. There is good clay here for brick, which will soon supersede the logs as building material. Lime has now to be hauled from Omaha; but a quarry of good limestone has been discovered about three miles from here on the south side of the river. Weather still as it has been since wednesday – warm and pleasant; the mosquitos, for the first time this season, annoy me whilst I write. Distance, eighteen miles.

SUNDAY, MAY 1 [1859].[90] May day is ushered in upon us with a chill wind and a cloudy sky, accompanied with an occasional shower. Loupe Fork lies twenty-seven miles ahead of us, and we are informed that there is a bad slough midway, which we ought to cross before a heavy rain. Therefore, after partaking of a breakfast garnished with a mess of wild onions, of which great numbers are found along the road, we pulled out at seven o'clock to make the journey. For five miles we found the road pretty fair, but rather slippery, to Rattlesnake Slough, so called from the great number of these venomous reptiles that dwell along its banks; we counted twelve within about two hundred yards of the slough. Phelps' wagon not having left Omaha when we did, we found it necessary to "choose partners" for traveling company, and selected a team from Omaha, Messrs. Louden and Marstons – three very fine, agreeable, gentlemanly and accommodating fellows.

Four miles further, we came upon a slough which looked ugly – the sod being thin and the quicksand deep – but by doubling teams we snaked both wagons through. To this place we have given the name of Difficult Slough. The road for three miles is then passable, only, when we reach the Big Slough, bridged in the deepest part, but with a mile of bad bottom, where we had to double team for a short distance. This brings us

[90] The may 1st entry is missing from the *Oquawka Spectator* printing, but fortunately it is in that portion of the original diary owned by the State Historical Society of Colorado. From that source we reproduce it here.

to the river again where we found pretty good roads to Columbus, near which place we camped. Just after dark a heavy thunder storm broke upon us, and continued during most of the night, the surface of the prairie became a broad sheet of water, and at one o'clock we had to leave our beds, there being about three inches of water in our tent.

Making up a good fire, we made a platform of wood and boxes, which served to keep us on dry footing, so that we passed the balance of the night very comfortably. The writer experienced a terrific wind storm in this locality nine years ago, which was much more disagreeable than the one we have just passed through; altogether, we are having a much better time now than then, for the season, although backward is much ahead of 1850 – there being tolerable grass now where it was then a blackened plain. The new road from Shell creek to this point, however, although shorter, is, at this season, much worse than the old Mormon trail, which runs nearer the river over dryer ground. Timber along the river scattering – mostly cottonwood, as usual. The first live wolf we have seen left Platte river on the lope just as we arrived at it. Distance, twenty-two miles.

MONDAY, MAY 2.[91] Columbus is a little border village, containing ten or a dozen houses, including a tavern, store and post office.[92] A half mile further is Loupe Ford, which is crossed at this point by means of a rope ferry. Loupe is a wide, rapid stream, with a bed of treacherous quicksand; the channel is continually shifting – new bars forming, and old ones washing away almost hourly. The ferry boat conveys teams just across

[91] The entries for may 2 to 4, inclusive, are printed in the *Spectator* of may 26, 1859.

[92] The population of Columbus was 7,632 in 1940.

the channel, which is between four and seven feet in depth, and lands them in water three feet deep, about half way across the stream, and they then have to travel a quarter of a mile through the river and over sand bars to reach the opposite shore – a task which is not difficult if the wagon is kept continually progressing, but if it once stops, if but for one moment, the quicksand is whirled out from beneath the wheels, and down settles the wagon.

This ferry is considerable of a humbug, and is, I believe, charging more than its charter permits; in this I may be mistaken – but if I am, all I have to say is: "chartered privileges" are most valuable possessions in this territory. For a wagon and one yoke of oxen the charge is two dollars, and for each additional yoke fifty cents. This ferry is on the line located for the Military Road; there is another at the old crossing on the Mormon Trail, which we traveled in 1850 – one of the best roads I ever saw; and there is a ferry across main Platte, some twelve miles below the mouth of Loupe, known as Shinn's Ferry. Leaving Loupe we crossed a running slough (bridged), at the distance of half a mile, after which we traverse a high, level prairie, two and a half miles to a prairie slough, from whence the road leads over a low, flat bottom, where we found a good camp on the banks of a running slough which heads in a swamp several miles beyond.

On the last stretch we encountered two miles of awful road – for nearly a mile the wagon cutting through the thin, moist sod, and plowing into quicksand, nearly to the hub; but we doubled teams here, and got along very well – with our teams united we can pull through any place. The stream on which we are camped tonight

I shall call Beaver Run for there are no less than eight dams upon it, and the shores are undermined with the burrows of that "sagacious animal"; they would probably have built another dam, but for the fact that there was not another willow of any size left standing upon the "run." We have no hay tonight, and will get no more; but the cattle find a pretty good supply of grass. Distance, ten miles.

TUESDAY, MAY 3. At the distance of a mile from our morning camp, we arrived at a slough where we had to double team in order to get through; a mile further, ditto, when a half mile brought us to Prairie creek, a deep, rapid, but narrow stream spanned, near its mouth, by a bridge not made by government. The road then follows along between this stream and the Platte about a mile, when it leaves the creek and strikes off across a swampy prairie. Here we turned the "stock" out to graze an hour or so, during which period I improved the opportunity thus afforded to catch a mess of "chubs," and to navigate the winding stream for a considerable distance on a cottonwood log raft that I found drifted to shore.

A mile from this point we had to double team across a swamp. Two miles further brought us to Looking Glass creek, crossed by a low bridge, and one mile more to the bank of the Platte, where, finding a good patch of grass, we gave the cattle another "bait." The road then follows the river, over a hard, solid, sandy track to Eagles' Nest Island, which we have so named from seeing two eagle nests upon it. At this point we have our first view of the road up the opposite bottom of the Platte; several teams were traversing it this afternoon.

Still following the river, two miles, we reach Camp

Island, where a number of emigrants remained this spring for many days, storm-bound. Just below us is Beaver Island – until recently quite heavily wooded, but upon which the beavers have felled nearly all the trees, some of them fifteen inches in diameter. Above Loupe Fork we again find cedar growing upon the islands in Platte; on many of them it predominates. Today we have seen no timber except what is on islands – there being none on the main land. There is considerable of cedar, and a "right smart chance" of hard wood here – the balance being the inevitable cottonwood. The Platte today, is a wide stream; in some places a broad sheet of water, very shallow, and in others one wide expanse of islands and bars. It is nearly a mile across it here, but a man can wade it without difficulty. The weather today has been beautiful; the soil scarcely adapted to successful cultivation except for pasture; the road, on an average, not good. Distance, fifteen miles.

WEDNESDAY, MAY 4 [1859]. Left camp at six fifteen and drove over good roads three miles to a good spot for grazing, on the bank of the river, where we gave the cattle an hour on the grass. Driving on, the road is fair for two miles, when we encounter a double team slough, two miles further another of the same sort, and two miles still further, lies before us the "Big Slough," a deep running stream, some three feet deep, which, although its reputation is bad, we found not very difficult to cross, as the bottom is hard. Three miles further, over good roads, brought us to the river, where we have a good camp. High winds have prevailed all day. Met a solitary footman, ragged and forlorn, returning from Kearny, because he "had heard that only four bits a day could be made in the mines;" well, joy go with him on his homeward road – we are bound the other way, if there be an "elephant" there we wish to get a peep at the "animal." Platte river is rising rapidly; we hope, however, that it won't do much more of that till we get across it at Kearny. Today we have seen a few buffalo paths (old trails leading down to the river), antelope horns, – violets, and flowering beans.

LETTER FROM FORT KEARNY [93]

May 9, 1859

DEAR SPECTATOR: In advance of its regular place in my journal, I must give you information of the fact that we are now on the north bank of Platte, opposite Fort Kearny, in the midst of a wild panic. News of this homeward stampede of the emigrants will reach you long before this letter can, for the advance guard have gone forward down the south side of the river. We have not yet seen a team that has been all the way through to the mines. Some have been nearly there, others find the "turn-table" here. Five teams are going back to where one is going forward – except those that are going through to California. I call this a panic, because I cannot believe it to be anything else. Men can give no reason why they are returning, excepting that they are satisfied there is no gold there. When we ask the grounds upon which they found their belief, it is generally replied, "We have seen men who have been there and prospected at Cherry creek several days, and found nothing except the color – there is a little gold but not enough to pay." Now my theory of the matter is this: The footmen and hand-cart-men got there, or nearly got there, and ran out of provisions; they could get

[93] Printed in the *Spectator* of may 26, 1859.

nothing to do – there was no chance to prospect – and they had no recourse but to return; their stories of course turned many teams, these influenced others, the contagion spread, and now the panic is at its height; how long it will continue we know not.

We shall remain here a day or two, until some of the Oquawka boys come up. We presume that we shall carry out our original intentions – go directly to Fort Laramie, and then strike into the Black Hills. We find a number of others of the same mind. The most important object of this letter is to assure you that reports that may reach you concerning murdering, pillaging and robbing emigrants by hungry men coming back are not true. There is no danger. I say this to quiet any fears that may be entertained by our friends, arising from the wild rumors that may reach you. Don't be alarmed. The Indians are quiet, and white men, although they may beg, do not resort to violence to secure their ends; and, besides, the great rush of footmen is about over.

P. S. We are just over to the Fort. The turn-table has changed. The *Pioneer,*[94] published at Denver, says all is right, and gives nearly the same solution to the apparent mystery that envelops the panic that I have given. Two gentlemen, bound to the States after their families, have just gone down the river. The panic has wonderfully abated today.

E. H. N. P.

THURSDAY, MAY 5.[95] We camped last night in company with three gentlemen, two of whom had come

[94] The one and only issue of the *Cherry Creek Pioneer,* published at the mouth of Cherry creek (Denver), april 23, 1859.

[95] The portion of the diary for may 5 to 7 was printed in the *Spectator* of june 2, 1859.

down from Kearny with their team to meet a partner who was coming out from Omaha with a settler from Grand Island City, bringing with him sundry articles to replenish their outfit – they having started to the Peak last fall, but concluded to winter their cattle at Grand Island, on rushes and dry grass. They are clever boys – one of them is an excellent printer – and will probably travel in our company from Kearny to the mines. They have spent rather a secluded winter, up here, but have had considerable sport hunting buffaloes, of which they have killed twenty-three during the winter. Speaking of rushes, I would inform the reader that there are islands in the Platte covered with dense undergrowth, and containing immense patches of the sand rush (or joint rush), which keeps green all winter, affording excellent fodder for cattle.

Last night our cows were left loose, as usual, whilst the oxen were tied up, and this morning were nowhere to be seen. White, Jo Hand, Hen. and Wallace started out in search of them – all taking different directions. Artley discovered them about a mile from camp in a small hollow, his attention having been directed to that point by seeing two deer standing on a rise watching the movements of the cows. Not having a gun, he did not bring in a deer, but drove up the cows, and Capt. White returning about the same time, we took breakfast, hitched up at six thirty and drove six miles, when we turned out our cattle two hours on the grass – the other boys, meanwhile, having overtaken the wagon.

At this point is located a log hut, called the "Lone Tree Station" of the Western Stage company,[96] tenanted by the stage driver, his wife and child. This is

[96] This company operated a stage line from Omaha to Fort Kearny. See L. R. Hafen, *The Overland Mail*, 160.

the first human habitation this side of Loupe, thus far. Our road now leads along the Platte to a point of timber, ten miles distant; thence we travel three miles further, and camp on a slough near the river, at Dead Tree Point, which we so name because the cottonwood timber has nearly all been killed by fires. Very high head winds have prevailed again today, rendering pedestrianism rather a difficult and uphill business. Good grass for the cattle. All day the Platte has presented the appearance of being a broad, grand river, there being just enough water to submerge the sand bars. Islands stud the river thickly – at one view, today, I counted twenty-six!

We are camped near the foot of Grand Island, which is the largest island in the river, being about fifty miles long, and varying in width from one to three miles. We met six footmen returning from Kearny, who, being mostly with hand carts, had run out of provisions, and concluded to give it up; they ought never to have started without a requisite outfit. These men report that "lots of teams" are returning on the other side of Platte – not teams that have been through to the mines, but that have been within a hundred miles and thought they smelt the elephant afar off. This savors to me of the height of folly – that men should go to the trouble and expense of fitting out a team, with a season's provisions, and then turn back without any personal examination of the "diggings," after getting within a hundred miles of their original destination.

FRIDAY, MAY 6. Six miles from camp we enter a German colony of two years standing, known as Grand Island City,[97] containing thirty-five families, each pos-

[97] For further data on this project consult the Andreas History of the State

sessing a separate homestead. In course of time, when their farms are under cultivation and enclosed with good sod fences (the only kind they are making) this will be a thriving colony. Some unprincipled scoundrel as ever went unhung, out of pure malicious mischief, with a full knowledge of the results that would follow his criminal act, in january last fired a patch of prairie grass, left as a winter pasture for their cattle, adjoining the town. Many of the inhabitants were away from the place at the time, and the flames spread with such rapidity before a raging wind, that nine houses, with all their contents, having taken fire from the thatched roofs, were crumbled to ashes before the devouring element. The miscreant who did this atrocious deed was a wagoner, but he has not had occasion to travel this road since!

Seven miles from this "city" is Mendota, upon the east bank of beautiful Wood river; it contains two houses – in one dwells a family, but the other was securely locked up, whilst over the door appeared in fancy red and white letters "Spirit of the Times." What the house contains is left to conjecture. The Mormon trail of 1852 comes down off the highlands north of the rascally road we have been traveling from Loupe Fork, and both roads cross the river here together on the same ford.

We immediately ascent to a beautiful table land, which extends between the Platte and Wood rivers for many miles westward, its average width for the dis-

---

of Nebraska (1882), 921-934; and J. L. McKinley, *The Influence of the Platte River upon the History of the Valley* (1938), 38. The town site was abandoned in 1866, when the Union Pacific railroad was constructed. The site was a few miles south of the present city of Grand Island. The information in this note was kindly supplied by Mr. Edward A. Hummel of Omaha, the Regional Supervisor of Historic Sites, National Park Service.

tance of twenty-five miles being about five miles, with scarcely a perceptible variation from a dead level, except the narrow bench along the Platte. We continued up Wood river for six miles and camped, with excellent grass. Although too late in the day to do much at fishing, we caught over a hundred "chubs," this evening, which are excellent eating. Today we have seen the first prickly pears (or cactus) that become so numerous as we proceed further up Platte valley – increasing in number as the land diminishes in fertility, until it becomes almost master of the soil. Several antelope in sight today, but not within gun shot. Distance, nineteen miles.

SATURDAY, MAY 7 [1859]. Today we traveled up the banks of Wood river, over the very best of roads, and camped at the distance of eighteen miles. The country bordering on the opposite shore of the stream is fertile, not so elevated as the bench upon which we are traveling, and is covered with a carpet of living verdure. Far away upon the hills to the northward we saw six buffaloes, the first we had seen this trip. A company lying here encamped have buffalo meat in abundance, one of its members having killed a fine animal yesterday, fifteen miles from the road. An emigrant near Ft. Kearny lost a horse yesterday, which had been gored by a bull. We shall find them in abundance ten miles beyond Ft. Kearny. There are several fine settlements upon this stream – the only drawback being, as usual in this country, the want of timber; what there is on this stream is generally ash, but that is being cut off pretty fast by the settlers for fence posts. The Mormons have recently had a thriving settlement at Genoa,[98] on the Pawnee

[98] Genoa, about twenty miles west of Columbus, Nebraska, was founded

Reservation on Loupe Fork; they have recently been notified that they must remove, as the Indians are soon to take possession of their new home; the government will pay the Mormons for what prairie breaking they have done, but not for other improvements; – these people are now taking up many choice claims on Wood river, and have, in many instances, commenced to improve their new homes.[99]

SUNDAY, MAY 8.[100] At the distance of one mile from camp we arrived at a settlement known as Dr. Henry's Ranche, that gentleman – together with several relatives – having made a claim of nine hundred and sixty acres on Wood river. The doctor contends that the islands of the Platte will furnish cottonwood for the settlers in this country as fast as the timber is needed. I acquiesce in his opinion, provided that settlements do not become more numerous than I think they will; for a heavy settlement, however, the reproduction of cottonwood is rather a precarious dependence. At this point the road diverges from Wood river, and strikes across a prairie six miles to Platte Bottom. Finding some wood here, left by other emigrants, we concluded to camp until tomorrow. As we came across the prairie we met several teams returning, homeward, frightened, probably, at the prospect of crossing Platte; at any rate they were hopeful yesterday, but desponding today. Distance seven miles.

MONDAY, MAY 9. Two miles travel over a low bottom, brought us to the north bank of the Platte, opposite

as a Mormon colony in 1857, according to Sterling Morton, *Illustrated History of Nebraska,* II, 133, and was abandoned in 1869. In 1856 the Mormons had founded a Genoa in present Nevada.

[99] Morton, *op. cit.,* 133, says the Wood river settlement was founded in 1858 by Joseph E. Johnson. The Mormons moved on to Salt Lake in 1863.

[100] The entries of may 8 to 12 were printed in the *Spectator* of june 9, 1859.

Fort Kearny – the American flag being just discernible through the willows on the islands. When we arrived here, we found ourselves in the outer circles of the wild vortex of the panic which had overtaken the emigration, and to which I have alluded more particularly in a letter of this date mailed to the *Spectator* today. Near the landing place of the Ford, lies a dead squaw, enveloped in a blanket and buffalo robe, with moccasins on her feet, and head bare, upon the sod wall of an old house. She was the daughter of a Pawnee chief, and had left her home and lost her virtue. Several weeks ago her father came up here, got her across the river, and then rubbed out the dishonor she had brought upon her family by taking her life.

Being anxious to visit the postoffice, and prudence dictating the propriety of learning the ford previous to crossing with our teams, several of us started over. The first channel we found to be about half a mile wide, varying in depth from three inches to two and a half feet; the road leads then across a small island, and we cross the second channel, about fifty yards wide and averaging eighteen inches in depth; running up another island a short distance, the road crosses a third channel, one hundred yards wide averaging a foot deep; then crossing a small towhead, and stepping over the fourth channel, we are on the Grand Island; the road follows this island some quarter of a mile, when it crosses a narrow, shallow channel, after which we enter the sixth, which is nearly a third of a mile across, with soft quicksand bottom, swift current, and a number of holes waist deep then another island and channel No. 7, not more than one hundred yards wide, but with a swift current and some holes nearly swimming to an ox; crossing this you appear to have reached the main land, but after traveling a short distance find yourself mistaken by having to wade channel No. 8, which, however, is fortunately both narrow and shallow.

Half a mile from the shore stands Ft. Kearny[101] – a collection of frame and sod buildings, enclosing a handsome level square. The buildings are for the most part residences and stables – there being no blockhouse. Several hundred soldiers are stationed here. Our crowd received but little consolation at the post office – Jo Hand being the only man to receive a letter. Returning, we set our teams in motion about the middle of the afternoon. Our own team, Marston's, and a four mule team, clubbed together for mutual assistance. Blocking up our wagon beds, six yoke of cattle and a span of mules – the latter for leaders – are put in line, and, one at a time, our wagons are "snaked" along over the first four channels, and we camp for the night on the island.

TUESDAY, MAY 10 [1859]. This morning we finished up the arduous undertaking which we commenced yesterday – that of fording the Platte at this stage of water, the river being quite high – and at twelve o'clock were prepared to take up our line of march westward. The "stampede" is abating somewhat, today – that is to say, those arriving here from the East are not turning back en masse, but the larger portion are going on. The great rush is mostly over, but there are great numbers still on the road coming back. I have talked with a great many; most of those returning candidly admit that they

[101] For data on this fort, see the *Southwest Historical Series,* IX, 140. For a detailed study of the route from Fort Kearny to Julesburg, see A. B. Hulbert, "The Platte River Trails," in his *The American Transcontinental Trails,* I. See also Appendix B, at the end of this volume, and volume IX of this *Series,* pages 140, and 180-181.

started too early – before mining could be successfully carried on – provisions could only be had at high prices – and they were obliged to leave; many say that this was against their wishes, against their convictions, that if they had possessed a supply of provisions nothing could have induced them to return without giving the mines a fair trial, but under the circumstances they had no alternative but to return. Others again whom I have conversed with indulge in the coarsest invective against the country generally, and heap anathemas deep and profane upon Pike's Peak, and all who will persist in going on through to see for themselves; these men generally claim to have discerned the "humbug" before getting quite there, but some of them say they have prospected in the mountains and elsewhere, finding gold everywhere, nearly, but not enough to pay.

We have "rumors" of all kinds, but it is not necessary to repeat them – you can place but little reliance upon any thing you hear – everything is retailed second-hand, and the same original rumor reaches our ears with almost as many variations as there are persons to tell it. Today I saw Robert Graham and W. Martin, of Henderson county; they were here after letters, having left their team and companions some sixty miles back on the road. They intend going home, but will go by way of Kansas – where they will tarry a while. Leaving the fort, we traveled on slowly till evening and camped on the river bank, eight miles from the fort. Since crossing the river, we find the soil slightly impregnated with alkaline substances. Just at sundown a black cloud commenced rising in the west, and in about an hour a regular Platte river storm, of an hour's duration, swept down upon us. The lightning furnished an illumination for the scene – the rolling thunder beat the reveille and retreat of the clouds – the wind came in powerful gusts – the rain fell in torrents – and the hail beat down in fury; it took several of us to hold up our tent poles, and when a hail stone the size of a quail's egg would strike our knuckles, it left its mark.

WEDNESDAY, MAY 11. A clear sky after the storm – a glorious morning dawns upon us! We start early, and drive slowly along, for seven miles. Here we are in luck – we find encamped two teams from Oquawka, embracing the following persons: Buck McFarland, John Reed, W. Hensley, John Hensley, Bart. Tinker, John Simmons, Charlie Johnson, Horace Davis, Bill Davis, and John Smith. The boys are all well, and seem to feel confident of the future. From this point they will travel with us. We shall move along slowly, to recruit the cattle and afford the boys an opportunity to hunt. The best buffalo country is on the opposite side of the river, but they are said to be numerous on the south side about twenty miles ahead. The sand hills on the south of our road are alive with antelope, but they are very wild. A few miles above us, last night, hail stones as large as hen's eggs fell – a fact in vindication of which I have the word of the Oquawka boys and see the indentations in the clay. Traveled today fourteen miles, and camped near a patch of islands. We can get a few buffalo chips now for fuel, which burn well in dry weather, giving out intense heat, with the smell of burning dry grass. For wood we are obliged to wade the narrow channel between the mainland and the islands – no great trick.

THURSDAY, MAY 12. Today we are encamped. The tide of travel has considerably slacked off, and is about equally divided – the preponderance being slightly in favor of the "Westward ho!" It is a noticeable fact, that among all who are returning from Cherry creek, there are none who have been there all winter, except a few who are going home for their families. A man was carried down in a wagon today – one John Snyder, of Massillon, Ohio – mortally wounded, he having been shot near O'Fallon's Bluffs. The circumstances under which he received his wound are differently related; one report is that he was shot for robbing, whilst another is that he was shot and robbed. The weather is cool today, the result of another violent storm which broke upon us just at dark last night. I have talked with several men today, who are returning. One man, from Davenport, thinks it all a humbug – another, from Iowa county would have staid until fall if he had had provisions to keep him till june, when he could have gone to the mountains.

This whole matter of gold in the Black Hills may turn out to be a delusion and a cheat – if so, it will be the most stupendous humbug ever known, the fabled Atlanta of the olden time "was a fool to it." But, as yet, the whole matter is in a nut shell, and the shell is not yet cracked. We calculate to go through, and, if Providence permits, will sift the matter thoroughly. My faith, I may as well say, is not shaken, that there is gold in large quantities in the mountains. I can only be satisfied that there is not when I go out and prospect for myself. It is a good deal as a verse on the wagon cover of Mr. G. W. Lucas, of Fremont county, Iowa, reads:

We're "humbugged" if we stay at home,
  Or "humbugged" if we leave;
There's few reports that come or go
  But what will some deceive.

Mr. Lucas is a son of old Governor Lucas, and I am happy to say, is "Pluck" and going through.

FRIDAY, MAY 13.[102] Today we traveled sixteen miles, over a beautiful road, and camped on what is termed Plum creek[103] – a deep valley running through the bluffs, with here and there a pool of standing water, except during a heavy rain, when it becomes a raging torrent. The banks are fringed with plum bushes, and scattering box-elder, ash and elm timber. We had, today, several exhibitions of the mirage – to many a novel and remarkable phenomenon. It is, indeed, difficult for anyone who has never before witnessed these freaks of refraction to convince himself he does not see lakes of water here and there with islands interspersed on the open prairie, which, in reality, is an arid waste, whilst it is provocative of some surprise to see white wagon covers in the distance magnified in size, and apparently lifted up into the air, floating along like sloops at sea.

SATURDAY, MAY 14 [1859]. We are camped today on Plum creek. Having excellent grass, a good range, plenty of wood and water privileges here, we naturally enough have plenty of company. The day has been cold and drizzly, rather uncomfortable and decidedly disagreeable. Although the weather was anything but propitious, I took my gun and went back on the plains, like many others, in search of game; saw two antelope, three wolves and eight wild turkeys; I made an unsuccessful attempt to shoot one of the latter, but all the other game was too far off to be reached even by a Sharp's rifle ball. I traveled some seven miles due south, and had a good opportunity to look at the country.

[102] The *Oquawka Spectator* of june 16, 1859, carries the diary entries of may 13 to 20.

[103] This was in the extreme northeast corner of Gosper county.

The valley of the Platte, since we left Kearny, on the south side, has averaged from three to five miles wide – the soil is not by any means fertile, although covered with tolerable grass, and the bluff range, which at the fort consists of low sand hills, with a flat arid tableland beyond, gradually increases in height, changes in the character of its soil and becomes more abrupt in its elevation, until, at this point, the summit ridge is nearly two hundred feet above the level of the river; the soil is a light, porous, chalky clay, or sand grit, which is capable of being reduced by the fingers to an almost impalpable powder, and which is easily acted upon by the water and winds.

The table land stretches far away to the south, towards the Republican fork, affording good pasture for buffalo, but it contains no water, and the whole face of the country is scarred with deep gulches running up from the valley in every direction through it. These gulches have been formed by the action of the annual rains, and are of all lengths and sizes; their valleys are level from side to side, with a very gradual ascent, and covered with good grass, the walls are abrupt and sharply defined, and the naked, weather-beaten clay presents many fantastic shapes.

These ravines, as well as the hills, are traversed in all directions by buffalo paths, deeply worn in the soil. Wherever the sod is once broken the soil rapidly washes down into the valley – there, by degrees, the waters of the Platte convey it to the Missouri whence it is carried onward, until it finally reaches its destination, and being deposited along the shores of the Gulf, becomes in time fertilized and capable of being of service to man. Seriously, it looks as if the great Creator had made this vast desert region as a sort of storehouse of materials from which he is day by day transporting them to other regions, where they can be made more available for the use and to the benefit of man. This vast region is destitute of timber, save a stray cottonwood on the side of a ravine, a few trees on the banks of a dry creek, and a little grove now and then on an island in the Platte. The uplands are covered with buffalo grass, and with patches of a species of flowering pea, exactly resembling the sweet pea of your flower gardens except that it grows in low bunches and is destitute of fragrance. The hunters are all in –nothing killed.

SUNDAY, MAY 15. We are still in camp; the weather is still foggy and unpleasant. On friday last, whilst a gentleman who is camped near us was out hunting on the bluffs, he stumbled upon the skeletons of a man and a buffalo; near the bones of the man laid his "trusty rifle," which bore the appearance of having been exposed to the weather for several months. It is supposed that some person while out hunting has wounded a buffalo, the infuriated animal has turned upon the hunter and slain him, whilst the wolves have made a banquet on their dead bodies. Speaking of game, I may as well mention here on the north side of the Platte there are plenty of buffalo – there is better grass there, the country is better watered, and it is their favorite range. A hunter who spent the winter in this neighborhood last winter killed a great many buffalo for wolf bait – he poisoned the meat and the wolves became an easy prey; and the hides netted him a fine return for his trouble.

MONDAY, MAY 16. Today we traveled twenty miles. The character of the country has not materially changed, save that the bluffs are becoming more rough and elevated. Took a long tramp over the hills for game, but saw nothing save a stray antelope or two, wild and unapproachable. We had to turn off the road to the river for a camp. For several days we have met very few returning emigrants.

TUESDAY, MAY 17 [1859]. The road continues today nearly parallel with the river, and about two miles distant from it. At noon we had to drive our cattle to the Platte for water. The team has traveled, today, twenty-three miles. At two o'clock, being very thirsty and considerably ahead of the train, Jo Hand, Capt. White and the writer undertook to walk to the Platte for water. This high up the Platte the air is very clear, and objects at a considerable distance appear much nearer than they really are. We had become somewhat familiar with this optical illusion, and making all due allowance supposed the distance to the river to be about a mile; upon walking it, however, we found it to be more than twice that distance; but we put it through, quenched our thirst, laved our head, hands and feet in the cool, muddy stream, and started on up the river bank.

When we reached the appointed camping place it was late – the teams were not there, and we concluded they had camped several miles below us. As we never take the "back track," but two alternatives were left us, either to lie out on the prairie in our shirt sleeves, without any supper, or go ahead until we found the Oquawka boys – Davis and company – whom we knew to be somewhere up stream. Pushing on, we arrived at their camp about dark, partook of their hospitable fare and shared with them their comfortable couches. Heard from Ray and company today – they cannot now be far behind us.

By the way, on sunday, whilst lying over at Plum

creek, Capt. Powell's Malta team came into camp, and there we left them; I have said before, and I may repeat it now, "they can't get away from us." A returning Pike's Peaker came to us for a few crackers to allay his hunger. We have very few such applications – as nearly all have provisions to last them to the settlements – and it is needless to assure our readers that no one in our train would refuse a hungry man so simple a request. I am glad, however, for our own sakes as well as theirs, that the returning emigrants are not so destitute as rumor has represented the case.

In camp is a Wisconsin man, returning to the states with his team; he has been up to the mines, sold off his provisions at a very high rate, and had eighty dollars in gold dust, which he had received in exchange for goods; he says there is gold, in that region, and thinks it will pay. I think he has gone down after another load of provisions. A train of thirty wagons, four-mule teams, laden with goods for Salt Lake is camped near us.

WEDNESDAY, MAY 18. Traveled today in all fifteen miles. Drove first about seven miles and camped on Platte, where we procured wood and baked up "lots of grub," as we understood that wood would be scarce for some fifty miles ahead. We then traveled on eight miles, and turned down a mile from the road to the river, where we found both grass and wood. Nine miles from our morning's camp we reach Cottonwood Springs,[104] where a never failing stream of water wells up in a ravine and flows towards the Platte. At this place, there is a trading post. Two miles further is Ash creek – a

[104] Here Fort McPherson was later established. For a description of Cottonwood Springs and comment on its importance, see Root and Connelley, *The Overland Stage to California,* 208, 499.

dry run fringed with ash and box-elder – where there is a trading house, a stage station, a dwelling and a carpenter shop. These buildings are all constructed of cedar logs, procured from the ravines, which furnish cedar logs of large size in considerable quantities; we noticed a number of fine hewed logs, the destination of which we learn is O'Fallon's Bluff.

The upper bench of the bottom lands, today, has been covered with fragrant clusters of a handsome and delicate flower, much resembling in shape and perfume the tube rose. Upon the sides of the most precipitous bluffs, today, I have found a number of fine specimens of the *Agare Amiricana,* a very singular and beautiful plant, and one that is very rare in this latitude. I took a two mile jaunt from the road this evening for the purpose of climbing to the summit of the highest pinnacle of the bluff range, which has presented all the abrupt characteristics of a mountain range, half-grown, all day.

From the summit of this peak – nearly three hundred feet above the level of the river – the view was truly enchanting. Southward, for ten miles, appeared a waste of abrupt bluffs, peaks and backbone ridges, with scarcely an acre of level land in the entire distance – westward the bluffs suddenly change their character at this point and become more depressed, presenting the appearance of rolling table land, still, however, presenting the same features as to soil and vegetation – to the north lie the high bluffs on the other side of the river, restricting the view in that quarter – while to the right and left sweeps the Platte, with its panorama of islands and sand bars, a birds eye view of the stream being presented to the beholder, for thirty miles of its course below the junction of the North and South forks. I had a pencil and paper in my hand, but could not gratify my desire to sketch the magnificent landscape, simply because the hand had not been early trained to be skillful in this most practical branch of education.

It is a shame that in respect to drawing our schools should be so far behind those of Prussia, where it is made an elementary branch of every boy's education. In this "land of ours," where every man is a traveler, and where so much splendid scenery abounds, it is of great importance that the art of delineating objects from nature with the pencil should be imparted to every child. It is not a valid objection – that which is usually made to teaching drawing in common schools – that not every person has a talent for drawing; we admit this, but it is a fact that applies with equal force against imparting any branch of learning, if the argument be sound. Because every man cannot excel or become proficient in any art or science is no good reason why he should not become as skillful as he can.

Tonight our crowd, which have been traveling together from Plum creek – comprising our team; the Omaha boys: Messrs. W. H. Falkner, Albert Tuttle, S. Fletcher, Geo. Dickey, Henry Battles and J. M. Squires (a Massachusetts company); Messrs. Jno. Bailey, Jno. Davis, Geo. Bailey, Jno. Wells, F. S. Pressgrove, and C. Maxwell (a Missouri company); an Iowa company; the rest of the Oquawka boys whom we met a few days ago; and two Swedes from Galesburg – organized ourselves into a company, elected the writer keeper of the guard roll, and mutually agreed to travel twenty miles a day, more or less. Davis, Hensley and the Swedes have mules – all the others oxen. The mules stampeded tonight, but were caught after a short race. Two men –

one of them from Canton, Illinois – came to our tent last night, asking for their supper. They started from Cherry creek down the South Platte in a double canoe, having on board their provisions to last them down to the states, but in passing over a beaver dam their craft was upset and they lost their all. We gave them some bread and meat and Hensley's crowd furnished the coffee; they ate their supper and went on their way homeward, intending to get lodging and breakfast somewhere else.

THURSDAY, MAY 19 [1859]. Today we traveled twenty-seven miles. The road leads along the valley, near the base of the bluffs, for about sixteen miles, sometimes crossing a small foot hill of the range. At the point where we left the road last night to go down to the camp, it would have been advisable for us to have taken in a supply of dry cedar, of which there is abundance in the ravines, to last us for several days, as we are now soon to enter upon a timberless region. As we failed to improve the opportunity, however, we had to supply the deficiency with dead willows at this camp. Before reaching the point specified above, sixteen miles from morning's camp, we passed three prairie dog towns, one of them covering perhaps sixty acres, where we saw large numbers of the lively little creatures. These animals always live in communities, digging deep holes, with considerable mounds at their entrance, at the top of which they sit and bark with their feeble voices at the approach of an intruder, but generally manage to dodge into their holes in time to escape a stray rifle ball that may be sent after them; but they are not always so lucky, and a bullet gave our party an opportunity to inspect one closely. They are about eighteen inches long, in shape closely resembling a ground squirrel, with short tail and long black claws, and of a grayish brown color. About their towns they keep the grass eaten off very closely.

About these villages, moreover, you may frequently see owls and rattlesnakes; some persons have an idea that they all live happily together, in the same hole; but I hold to a different theory: I think the rattlesnake takes possession of a deserted hole, or becomes a trespasser merely to obtain a residence; while the owl not only trespasses upon their homes but preys upon their young. After traveling sixteen miles, we reach fork roads; the road to the right leads by Fremont's Springs,[105] where excellent water can be obtained – the other road takes up over the ridges and is destitute of water for miles. Two miles from the springs is the junction of the North and South forks of the Platte,[106] but the road does not approach the river nearer than a mile.

Six miles further on we pass a spring slough on the north side of the road, but finding no grass we traveled up the slough one mile farther, where we had poor water but grass, whilst our dead willows furnished us firewood. Just at dark a heavy storm passed around us, but we escaped with only a few flashes of lightning and a few dashes of rain. Better roads than we have now-a-days man ought never to desire. The first stone that has come within the scope of my observation on Platte river, I saw outcropping from the sides of the bluffs during our forenoon's drive; it is a species of soft porous limestone, occuring in arbitrary masses, which

105 For the location of Fremont's Springs and Fremont Slough, see A. B. Hulbert, *The American Transcontinental Trails,* II, map number 8.

106 The city of North Platte is located near the junction, on the neck of land between the two forks of the Platte.

would indicate that it is drift rather than a regular formation. This morning we saw something that resembled a bunch of feathers floating from a pole on top of a high bluff, and in company with some of the "Boston boys," I climbed the hill to see what was there. We found a new made Indian grave; the banner proved to be a fantastic but handsomely wrought feather cap – a pipe and a sack of tobacco lay upon the grave – and the whole mound was so thickly covered with prickly pears, gathered and placed there, that no wolf would ever dig into the sand. The boys are all well and in good spirits; our team keeps up and we are all right. We have met very few "stampeders" today.

FRIDAY, MAY 20. Left camp at six o'clock; one mile brought us to a point where O'Fallon's bluffs strike the South Platte [107] – where there is considerable brushwood and timber (the latter being on Shanghai Island), and the scenery is rough, rugged but romantic. The road now runs over the bluffs for three miles, to the stage station,[108] where there is a trading post and some Indian tents; two and a half miles further we arrive at another trading post and another Indian encampment.[109] A mile and a half further we turned off to the river, where we could procure wood, thinking it better to rest the cattle the balance of the day and prepare, by baking bread and boiling beans, for the timberless

107 O'Fallon's Bluffs are just south of Sutherland, Nebraska. Data from Mr. C. M. Rolfson of Julesburg, Colorado.

108 This was a station on the Salt Lake mail route. Soon the Leavenworth and Pike's Peak Express was to move its line to this road. See volume IX of this *Southwest Historical Series*, pp. 139-143, for the Oakes and Smith description of the route and a table of distances on this Platte river trail.

109 Apparently, this was newly established. The Oakes and Smith description (of the fall of 1858) refers to O'Fallon's Bluffs as the "last settlement and trading-post" to be passed until Fort St. Vrain is reached.

stretch before us. Our friends at home, who are accustomed to see us all pick our way carefully across mudholes on a rainy day, would be amused as well as surprised, could they see us, at the *sangfroid,* the utter indifference, with which we seize our axes, and, all clothed as we are, plunge into water waist deep and wade to an island where we cut our timber and "toat" it back over the stream.

Wading the channel – the water gradually [generally] not more than eighteen inches deep, however – is almost of every day occurence with the emigrants, along this portion of the route, and I have yet to hear of a single instance in which such exposure has caused ill health. The morning, until we arrived at the first station, was showery; it then cleared up and the remainder of the day was beautiful. At the station we met one of Major & Russell's Utah wagon trains, numbering thirty wagons, with about three hundred head of cattle; these wagons are monsters in size – they are going down empty, but will return laden with sixty hundred pounds each! We met a train of army wagons, drawn by mules, at the same place, numbering twenty-five teams. The Salt Lake mail stages pass this point each way once a week. They are drawn by six mules, and each coach is accompanied by an outrider.[110]

The Indians we saw today, were of the Sioux family, and they compare favorably, indeed, with the Pawnees. The braves are now all off on a war trail against the Pawnee Loupes, and but a few men are left about the encampments. The women are generally cleanly in appearance and neatly dressed – the interior of their large

[110] Hockaday and Liggett had been operating this mail service. They sold out to Jones and Russell in may, 1859. See L. R. Hafen, *Overland Mail,* 150.

wigwams very conveniently arrayed, and decorated with Indian gewgaws, beadwork and finery. The children are all remarkably bright, sprightly, good looking and intelligent – some of them "dressed to kill," and others *in puris naturalibus*. One fine handsome little fellow was clothed in a suit of white buckskin, the skin being almost hidden beneath the wealth of beads which his doting mother had worked in handsome pattern upon it.

I entered one wigwam where I was received with cordial greeting by an elderly Indian, who was quietly and meditatively smoking his kinnekinaick, and who invited me to be seated and dispersed the hospitality of his mansion (to the extent of making me feel perfectly at ease and a welcome visitor) with a native grace and dignity that would have done honor to the noblest gentleman of the land. His wife was braiding the hair of their dark but handsome little girl, and a few expressions of admiration on my part, of the child's personal appearance, convinced me that the way to obtain the good will and respect of an Indian mother (as in the case of her white sister) is through the avenue of her affection for her children.

The Sioux construct their wigwams of tanned buffalo hides, which are sewed together and stretched into the shape of a cone, upon long poles which are fastened together at the top where an orifice is left for the escape of the smoke that arises from the fire that is built in the centre of the lodge. The mites (a very small, shiny winged gnat, scarcely larger than a poppy seed) have been very troublesome for a couple of days, their bites having given some of the company the appearance of an attack of the measles. I never saw any other insect whose bite is so venomous in proportion to its size. We have concluded to make today our Sabbath; and the Oquawka boys who have mules have thought best to go ahead; this is well enough, for their teams can greatly out travel ours.

SATURDAY, MAY 21 [1859].[111] Left camp early, as we have a big day's travel to make. Twelve miles from camp we passed a slough of sulphur water and a prairie lake of brackish water, near which we nooned. The cattle we drove to the river – a mile and a half distant – rather than let them drink the mean water of the sloughs. Six miles further the road passes alongside of an alkaline bottom, where the slough water is impregnated with alkali, and the ground covered in many places with a considerable efflorescence of nitrate of soda – such being the only name I can apply to a composition of nearly equal parts of saltpetre and soda.[112] Camped on the bank of the river, with buffalo chips (*bois de vasche*) and weeds for fuel.

The South Platte, thus far up, where the stream is in one body, is about four hundred yards wide, and can be waded anywhere; the current is rather swifter than the main Platte, but the general features of the river are the same – both are floating beds of quicksand. The river washes the base of the bluffs on the north side, and the ridge is rather steep and broken, with occasional ledges of rock outcropping from the surface.

The river bottom on the south side commences at the Stage station at O'Fallon's Bluffs, and is about a mile

111 The entries for may 21 and 22 were published in the *Spectator* of june 23, 1859.

112 Alkali was common in a number of places along this section of the trail. Alkali Lake was later a "home station" on the stage route. It was located fourteen miles west of Elkhorn (near O'Fallon's Bluffs), according to Root and Connelley, *The Overland Stage to California,* 102, 212.

and a half wide; the bluffs are low ridges, resembling in appearance the sand ridges below Oquawka. We met a lieutenant of the army today, on his way from Fort Laramie to Leavenworth, who stopped and chatted quite freely for some time, and imparted to us considerable information respecting the mountains; he assured us that the probabilities are all in favor of our not being disappointed in our search for gold in the Black Hills. Met two of Russell & Major's trains, each containing twenty-eight wagons, six yoke of oxen to each wagon. One-half of the cattle are driven loose.

Met some Indians today traveling; they pack their ponies in a manner that looks a little singular to one who has never before seen the process – the long tent poles are tied on each side of the pony, and fastened with a breast strap, dragging along behind, the pony walking as it were between shafts; a platform made of willows is laid across the poles and the baggage and children are thus conveyed from place to place.[113] With this train of two families came Red Plume, an Ogallalah Sioux, who was very friendly ineed; he exhibited a letter given him in 1855 by Gen. Harney, certifying to the fact that he was one of the ten friendly Indians who performed good service to the whites by delivering up the five hostile Indians who attacked the mail train near Ash Hollow.[114] Red Plume told us that, although he had meat enough, the papooses had not tasted bread for a week; and Red Plume took away a number of biscuits as the proceeds of his interview. Distance, twenty-two miles.

---

[113] This was the well known Indian travois.

[114] Colonel W. S. Harney led the campaign of 1855 against the Sioux to punish them for the Grattan massacre and other depredations. See Hafen and Young, *Fort Laramie*, 221-245.

SUNDAY, MAY 22. Our road runs all day only a short distance from the river, affording a good opportunity for watering both cattle and men. The day has been extremely warm, albeit is quite chilly at night. Scenery today rather monotonous, and not particularly striking, presenting no new feature whatever. Fourteen miles from camp we reach the ford, where the road to California, via Fort Laramie, crosses the South Platte;[115] there is an encampment of Ogallalah Sioux here, a blacksmith shop, and a trading post.

The distance from this point to Laramie is one hundred and fifty miles. Ash Hollow, where the road strikes the North Platte, is eighteen miles distant. Here we saw Fred Stuck, a young German from Oquawka. He started from St. Joe with a hand cart, but at Kearny concluded to pull it no further, and so hired his passage through to California. The hard, solid roads, in conjunction with the warm weather, have contracted and hardened the shoe leather of many of the company so much that they have been going barefooted in preference to wearing their boots, but they improved the opportunity offered here to trade with the Indians for moccasins. No bargains can be had for money, all must be barter. For two pints of sugar I procured an excellent pair of rawhide soled moccasins plus fifty cents.

A number of teams cross here en route for California. A gentleman who resides here says that not a great

[115] This was later known as the Lower California Crossing. It was about four miles southwest of Brule, Nebraska. According to Patterson's figures, this was forty miles west of the station at O'Fallon's Bluffs. This corresponds to the distance given by Oakes and Smith in the *Southwest Historical Series*, IX, 142. Oakes and Smith in 1858 called it the Upper Crossing. After the crossing near the mouth of Lodge Pole Creek (present Ovid, Colorado) was developed and used in 1859, the other crossing, near Brule, came to be called the Lower Crossing.

many teams have passed this place from Cherry creek; he thinks, and I entertain the same opinion, that the four great turn tables have been located at Kearny, Cottonwood Springs, O'Fallon's Bluffs and the Crossing. The same gentleman informs me that the emigration toward the mining region is now settling in pretty strongly again. In anything that I may have heretofore written that might be deemed disparaging of the "stampeders," I do not wish to be understood as intentionally unjust or uncharitable; in fact we cannot but admire the zeal and enterprise which sent them here whilst the roads were so bad and the weather so forbidding. Yet at the same time they certainly can all see now, with regret, their great mistake in coming out so early unprepared to remain.

We here find the Malta teams again – they will join our company tomorrow, and we shall travel together probably the balance of the way. Two miles above the crossing – we found the other Oquawka boys, with the mule teams; they had laid up and were waiting for us. Here we camped, having green willow brush for fuel, which we procured upon an island. We will probably not have an opportunity to send you another letter for several days – perhaps weeks – and I will merely say, as we bid you a temporary good-bye, that our destination is into the mountains; just where we will strike them I cannot positively say, but the general intention, at present, is to cross the river at the mouth of Lodge Pole creek, forty-four miles [116] from here, and follow up that stream on Bridger's Pass road. I will write again as soon as I have an opportunity to send a letter to Laramie.

[116] The distance between the crossings was usually given as about thirty-five miles.

Several teams bound for the mines, who have been in company with us more or less for several days, have women and children with them. I must here reiterate the fact that we are all remarkably well – no one has been ailing except one man and he is a physician – he had a "shake" and we told him to "heal himself." Wallace Rice, Buck McFarland and myself – if I must single out any three who have been particularly benefited by the trip in health and robustness – have improved "some." John Reed killed an antelope today. We have just met Messrs. Oakes & Street with their saw mill. They had turned back, but one of their party – Mr. Oakes – has just returned from the mountains, his teams having been camped here three weeks, while he went out to prospect, and he has turned the teams again.[117] This is the gentleman who has been reported killed so often by the stampeders. Mr. Oakes assures us that in the Jefferson diggings ten dollars a day can be made to the man. He is going to the neighborhood of Boulder City with his mill. He tells me to state what I do on his responsibility; he is a gentleman well known, from Pacific City, Iowa. Hurrah for the mines!

MONDAY, MAY 23.[118] Traveled twenty-two miles. For twelve miles the road follows along the river bottom the soil being strongly alkaline. We next strike a dry creek – a ravine with pebble bed – the beginning of a series of sand ridges and gravel banks, which continue for three miles; thence three miles further brought us to a point where a few cottonwood trees used to grow, and where some of the "guides" advise emigrants to lay in a

[117] For a fuller account of the Oakes trip with the sawmill, see D. C. Oakes, "The Man Who Wrote the Guide Book," in *The Trail,* II, no. 7, pages 7-15.

[118] The entries for may 23 to 30 were published in the *Spectator* of june 30, 1859.

stock of wood to last for eighty miles – there being, say they, no timber for that distance. There are now only a few stumps that serve to mark where the trees were, however, and we pass on four miles further to the river bank, where we camp in the midst of most excellent grass, with buffalo chips for fuel. There is a Cheyenne village near us, and a number of the men are about camp eating up scraps and seeking to gratify their curiosity. I produced a new sensation among them by giving them a lively tune on the jewsharp and excited great wonderment by showing them the likeness of my children. They had seen watches and fiddles and revolvers, so that these, although they interested them, did not excite and gratify their curiosity to the same extent as did the jewsharp and ambrotypes.

The river is here nearly a half mile wide, with low banks; cactus has nearly taken possession of the surface of the earth except along the river shore where we find grass patches here and there. From the summits of the bluffs the country can be overlooked, with the aid of a glass, and presents for many miles the same desert waste. The reader can easily understand that this country can be nothing else than a sterile waste of territory, when he remembers that the road has not crossed a single running stream since we left Fort Kearny – not even a spring branch. We have passed one or two springs, it is true, but they were between the road and the river, and the extreme length of the brooks is not more than two miles. We met two small flat boats today going down the river with returning emigrants aboard.

TUESDAY, MAY 24 [1859]. Six miles along the river bottom, road pretty fair, brought us to sand hills again. The bottom on the other side of the river widens in proportion to the narrowness of the bottom on this side – the ranges of bluffs being nearly parallel, and the river winding alternately from bluff to bluff. Two miles further the road strikes the river at a point of rocks, where we find a thicket of brushwood – rose bushes, choke cherries, currants and young cottonwood. Here we saw a mound of earth purporting, from an inscription on a buffalo skull, to be the grave of Samuel Curtis, of Council Bluffs. Mr. C. gave favorable accounts from the mines last winter, and when we left the Bluffs was making preparations for coming out again in a few weeks.[119] Many of those who first turned back, whom we met near Fort Kearny, threatened to kill Mr. Curtis if they met him; but whether they would have carried their threats into execution is another question.

A mile further is a point of bluffs, gray sand stone base, with a cement of cobble stones, sand and pebbles, overlying. Seven miles further the road leads over bad, sandy roads, and crosses numerous gravel gulches. The land is getting more and more sterile, cactus and desert lizards abound, and here and there we find little patches of dwarfed wild sage. The day has been very warm, and sufficiently windy to be disagreeable. At noon Capt. Powell, of the Malta team, and Jo Hand, shot an antelope between them, which furnishes the whole company with an abundance of excellent meat. The flesh of the antelope is more tender and juicy than venison, partaking something of the flavor of both venison and mutton. The antelope's head is shaped more like a sheep's than a deer's, and Jo says that if they were wooly he would pronounce them sheep on long

119 For data on Curtis and two of his letters, see the preceding volume, pages 147 and 171.

legs. They are numerous in the bluffs on both sides of the river; they are timid, but their curiosity often gets the better of their fear, and the most successful method of hunting them is for the hunter to hoist a flag made of a red handkerchief, and await patiently their approach; for they will be sure to come up to ascertain what the flag is, when they may be easily shot. A thunder shower came up just at dark, and threatens to continue all night.

After dark Mr. Wm. H. Long, of Montgomery county, Ohio, came into camp, on his way back to the States, thoroughly drenched with the rain; a warm fire and a warm supper did him a great deal of good. He started, with three others, from Denver City, ten days ago, with a boat; the second day out their boat capsized, their arms and provisions were lost, and one man was drowned;[120] the other two he left some one hundred miles above here, down with ague. He started to the mines from the States with a load of passengers, taking what is known as the Smoky Hill route. This was a new route – a mere experiment – and a most disastrous one indeed it proved to many. He had to leave one team, and was obliged to feed flour to the other, in order to get it through, agreeing to replace his passengers' flour thus used, at Pike's Peak prices. This absorbed nearly his entire outfit, when he got through, and left him "strapped." He tells me that a number of persons were lost on that route during a violent snow storm, and about sixty persons are still missing.

He gives us what we presume is an authentic account of a particular case, which we have heard related with a variety of details. This is the melancholy narrative of Daniel Blue, of Whitesides county, Illinois. He started

[120] Quite a number of disappointed goldseekers tried to make their way homeward by boats on the Platte. Many of these crafts were wrecked.

on this road with his two brothers early in the season. They all got lost and bewildered; they were without food and could find no water, and wandered about in vain endeavors to regain the road and to find wherewith to quench their thirst; finally one of the brothers died, and the survivors lived upon his flesh for several days; at length another brother died, and from this period Mr. Blue's memory is defective and incoherent; he was found however by some friendly Indians and carried to a station on Russell's Express road from Leavenworth to Denver city. When they found him he was lying within a rod of water, without sufficient strength to reach it. He had opened the skull of his brother and devoured the brains. Mr. Blue is now in Denver city, where he is being cared for, but it is feared that, owing to his horrible memories and terrible sufferings, his reason is tottering on its throne. And what wonder! The imagination of the reader must depict for him the distress and sufferings of the emigrants on this route [121] – they remind one vividly of the perils incident to the first travel on the new and untried "cut off," into California and Oregon, during the first few years of the emigration.

Capt. White and Harry Faulkner waded across the river at noon for the purpose of hunting. They saw a number of antelope and buffalo – the latter were too far off to render it prudent for them to go after them, as the teams were going ahead, and the precursors of a storm gave them warning to return. They found the average depth of the water to be less than two feet. The country they traveled over had the appearance of being more fertile than the bottoms on this side of the river –

121 The Smoky Hill route and Daniel Blue will be discussed later in this volume.

the bluffs are more rolling, not cut up into gulches, contain ledges of rock, and springs gush up at their base. We camp on the river bank, with buffalo chips for fuel, of which we gathered a number of bushels before the rain.

WEDNESDAY, MAY 25 [1859]. The weather is cold and rainy, consequently we are lying encamped. It is fortunate for us, for it will soften the roads without making the wheeling difficult, and our cattle's feet were beginning to get quite tender, traveling over the hard gravelly roads. All hands except the drivers, had purposed going out to hunt antelope today, but the weather will not admit, so the boys are occupied in cooking antelope meat, mending clothes, reading, writing, singing, telling yarns, arguing politics, discussing religious topics, and the like. We joined teams, generally, on stoves today, some of the messes being without stoves, and it being impossible to cook with a camp fire. Our stove served to do up the "culinary arrangements" of ourselves and the Massachusetts company, they furnishing lots of buffalo chips, which burn well in a stove. Our cooking was about half done, when we found that our stock of fuel was nearly exhausted. I started out, in company with Tuttle, on a prospecting tour, hoping to find a little drift wood, as wet chips will not burn, and had the good fortune to find a patch of thrifty wild sage, which supplied the whole camp with abundance of fuel.

Capt. Powell having the largest tent, and there being but three persons in his mess, he has shared the hospitalities of his household with Mr. Long, who will remain in camp until the weather clears up, and will take our letters to Ft. Kearny. We had an addition of a young heifer to our cattle last night, and the cow we got of George A. will materially enhance our stock of provisions by a supply of fresh milk. As I write tonight the wind is blowing cold from the north, and a settled rain is steadily falling. Not far from camp is a mound purporting to be the grave of Mr. Oakes, and near the same place, alive and disposed to be kicking the perpetrator of the fraud, is Mr. Oakes camped, on his way back to the mines.[122]

THURSDAY, MAY 26. We have ascertained that we are just above the mouth of Lodge Pole creek, which comes into Platte from the north. Bridger's Pass road to Utah runs up the valley of this creek.[123] It is located in most of the "guides" as being twenty-nine miles from Cottonwood Springs, mentioned on monday, when in reality it is only about twenty. Dr. Davis and Capt. White, who were on the last watch last night, report that there was a heavy fall of snow between two and three o'clock, which, however, melted almost as rapidly as it fell. The lofty bluffs ten miles north of us were covered with a robe of glistening splendor, but the fingers of the sun's ray tore away the mantle before noon.

After traveling about four miles over sand ridges, we struck a bottom road, rendered somewhat muddy by the recent rain, for six miles, where the road again takes over the sand ridges, which it follows for about eight

[122] Oakes, in *The Trail, op. cit.*, 10, says the epitaph read:

Here *lie* the remains of D. C. Oakes,
Who was the starter of this damned hoax!

[123] This was apparently written in the morning of may 26, as the mileage in the next sentence indicates. At the mouth of Lodgepole creek was the "Upper Crossing" of the South Platte. The Bridger Pass road which followed far up the Lodgepole, was never extensively used. The generally used road to Oregon, California, and Utah followed the creek a few miles and then turned northward to the North Platte river.

miles. Two miles further on we camp with chips and willow brush for fuel. The grass, which is luxuriant and very nutritious, is along the margin of the river, in patches of a few acres in extent – from ten to eighty – in the bottoms intervening between the points where the sand ridges extend into the river. The bottom on the opposite side has been very extensive all day, and the bluffs present a fine appearance, being lofty ridges, with towering mounds, steep slopes and naked ledges.

Nearly opposite our morning camp are two pyramids of rock – cobble stones united by cement – rising some one hundred and fifty feet above the level of the surrounding plain, and about one-fourth of a mile distant from each other. Saw several handsome flowers peculiar to these sand ridges, on which, by the way, the "sand burr" flourishes; a purple flower, growing in clusters upon a stem six to eight inches high – resembling the "blue bell" in shape and the "lilac" in color; a species of vine milk-weed, with clusters of white flowers; and a blue blossom which we call the Desert Forget-me-not. All these are without fragrance. Just as we camped at noon and were about to spread our dinner table, a six year old rattlesnake slowly uncoiled himself under our wagon-tongue and received his death stroke from one of our canes. We met Mr. Weidner, of Keithsburg, and his son, John Weidner; they were on their way back from the mines – said they had been there three weeks and had prospected everywhere, and were satisfied that there was no gold there in paying quantities. Weather very cold all day; at noon we sought the "sunny side" of the wagon, instead of carrying our dinner into the shade thereof as we have lately been doing. Distance twenty miles.

FRIDAY, MAY 27 [1859]. The road follows the base of the sand ridge, and over barren rolling table land, parallel to the river and not far from it, for seven miles; we then encounter a mile of bad, deep sand hills, then follows a bottom for two miles, when the road becomes fair for ten miles, with, however, occasional sand patches. We stopped at the river bank, at a point three miles from our evening camp, and cut willows for fuel. Very few "chips" are to be had in this section – the pasture is only such as would support buffalo that are passing through the country. Met a physician from Fulton county, whose name has escaped me, who assured us that some men had claims that paid as high as ten and fifteen dollars a day; but, having tried mining, he found that it was hard work – he never had done a hard day's work in his life – and he'd be d—d if he wasn't going back where he could practice medicine for a living.

Met several Smoky Hill emigrants; they report the road as being very "hard," but think the sufferings on that road, although very great, have been exaggerated somewhat. Bluffs considerable distance from the river today. During the day's travel we have noticed two creeks coming into the river from the opposite side. Distance twenty miles. We had a heavy white frost this morning, but it mercifully spared what little vegetation this poor country manages to foster into a feeble vitality.

SATURDAY, MAY 28. Our day's travel has been somewhat monotonous and tedious, being over a broad plain covered with little else than cactus and wild sage of a dwarf variety. The bottoms on both sides of the river are short and narrow, with a wide table land, or second bench. About noon we passed a cluster of eleven trees on the opposite side of the river – a welcome sight, these lonely cottonwoods! Saw a number of boats – four or five – going down the river today; they make pretty good time, averaging three men in each, the current being about five miles an hour, and a channel of two or three feet being easily found. If they meet a rise in main Platte, they may make a successful voyage down, otherwise the shoal water in that stream will occasion much vexation and delay.

At twenty miles distant we reach Beaver creek [124] – a running stream very much resembling the Platte, on a much smaller scale; the banks are steep, but the crossing is not difficult. Up to this point we have found no very good grass, except a small patch at noon camp. Dr. Davis brought in an antelope at noon, and very generously shared it with all the company. The reason why more of these animals are not killed by our hunters, is because it requires patience and time to hunt them successfully, and the time cannot very well be spared, when one has to make the regular distance traveled by the team in addition to extra distance winding about the bluffs. Leaving Beaver creek, we traveled one mile and camped on the bank of the river, with good grass and green cottonwood for fuel, which we obtain by wading to an island. It is poor stuff to cook by, though, and I trust that none of my lady readers will ever have their patience tried by it. The weather has been very warm. Some of the boys have an idea that they saw the Rocky mountains this evening – perhaps it was only a cloud. Distance, twenty miles.

[124] Beaver creek runs through Brush, Colorado. There is an error in the mileage given, or in the locations, as it is more than sixty miles – the distances given for May 26, 27 and 28 – from the mouth of Lodgepole to the mouth of Beaver creek.

SUNDAY, MAY 29. Sunrise reveals a peak of the mountains, covered with snow, standing out in bold relief against the sky, far off in the West. We only traveled twelve miles, and camped on the bank of Platte, with an abundance of wood on an island – water only waist deep in spots. The patch of grass we are camped on is quite extensive, being over a half-mile in width, and extending along the river two miles or more. The uplands present the same waste of sand and gravel characteristic of most of the country this side of the Crossing. We camped about ten o'clock, and had a pleasant afternoon's rest.

MONDAY, MAY 30 [1859]. Five miles over hard gravel roads brought us to a handsome little creek of clear, sparkling water, slightly impregnated with sulphur and alkali; just before we reach it, we pass a saleratus lake, whilst yet above its mouth we saw a large spring of the same kind of water. So far we have not had any trouble about this water, as we have been very careful not to allow the cattle to have access to it when we could possibly avoid it.

As an alkaline region, however, this country will not hold any comparison with the plains of Sweet Water and the Humboldt, where I have seen great lakes, acres in extent, covered by evaporation, with an incrustation of nitrate of soda, from three to six inches thick. Authorities differ as to what is the name of the stream we just passed, whether it be Kiowa or Bijou; I will therefore call it Kiowa.[125] After crossing it, we ascend to the table land again, where we have, for five miles, a hard gravelly road, very trying on the feet of the cattle, which are already quite tender. We strike then across

[125] It was undoubtedly Bijou creek; Kiowa is farther west.

five miles of desert – deep sand – and reach the brow of the hill, whence, by taking the right hand road, we strike the river in a short distance, at a Cottonwood grove, known as Carson's Point, an excellent place to water. Two miles further on, still over deep sandy roads, partly, brought us to Fremont's Orchard,[126] where we have lots of wood, but no good grass. There is excellent pasture two miles above, but our cattle were very much fatigued with their long, hot, dusty trip that we had to traverse today, and we have concluded to start at four o'clock in the morning and drive to grass before breakfast.

Fremont's Orchard is a lovely grove of young thrifty cottonwoods and occupies a nice level area of some eight acres, entirely destitute of undergrowth, whilst the trees present the appearance of having been set out with almost the regularity of an orchard. I send this letter to the Crossing, to be mailed, by a Mr. Hazen, of Ohio, who is now on his way to Shokokou, where he has relatives; he was not prepared to remain at the mines, owing to the fact that he had not a supply of provisions.

We shall, in all probability, strike first for Boulder creek, but will take Denver city on the way. I gain favorable news every day, from gentlemen who assign various motives for going back; at any rate, we shall soon be in a position to test the matter for ourselves. The lofty range of mountains, covered far down with snow and far up with dark forests, have loomed up

[126] Fremont visited the grove in july, 1843. Fremont's Orchard was east of the present town of Orchard – named for the famous cottonwood grove – and south of the town of Goodrich. A few of the old trees were still standing when I visited the site in 1928. Most of them had been cut down and used in making boxes.

ahead of us, all day, like some Titan sentinel set to guard this sterile waste, against the kindly influences of any angel messenger that mercy might send to bless the land and make it productive.

TUESDAY, MAY 31 [1859].[127] This morning we started early – four o'clock – and commenced our journey en route for grass. We ascend a long sand hill, and the road follows the ridge nearly two miles, when it branches – the left hand fork following along the hill, while the other turns down the bluff; the latter we followed, and soon found a splendid patch of grass, and plenty of dry wood with which to cook a breakfast to which our appetites (sharpened by our early drive) enabled us to do the most ample justice. We grazed the cattle a couple of hours, and drove on over sandy and gravelly road to the noon camp, on a high ridge, with grass on the bottom, a distance of twelve miles from the "Orchard." A mile further we descent to the lowland again – road still gravelly; another mile brings us to a point of rocks, with a cliff of sandstone overlying marl outcropping, and large masses of the same formation lying in scattered fragments on the hill side. I ascended to this cliff, when the first object that met my view was a grave, neatly covered with stone slabs, immediately under the cliff, and bearing the inscription:

W. PROBASCO, of Careyville, Ky.
Died May 11, 1859.
Meet Me in Heaven!

His comrades had chosen a romantic spot to entomb the remains of him whose journey had ended. As I stood looking upon the tomb and admiring the neatness

[127] The *Oquawka Spectator* of july 28, 1859, carries the diary entries of may 31 to june 3, inclusive.

with which the legend had been engraved upon the soft marl at the head of the grave, I could not resist a feeling of sadness in sympathy with the mournful emotions that must have wrung the hearts of the travel-worn men who stood around the grave of their companion, who had passed from earth in this dreary and lonesome waste, as I remembered that those who had known him would know him no more – that his bright hopes of golden treasures in the snowy peaks upon which his dying glance may have rested, had been nipped by the chill fingers of Death, as the flowers of spring are withered by untimely frosts.

I spent some time on the summit of the peak (which, though not lofty, is as elevated as any of the surrounding points), in surveying the surrounding country with a glass; and the future traveler who may follow my footsteps will be rewarded for his trouble by finding on the table rock at the summit a very good knife, which, by accident, I left lying there. Two miles from this point the road strikes the river, where there is a good camping ground; thence we ascend to an elevated table land, or level plain. This broad prairie is now chiefly occupied by prairie dog communities and prickly pear plantations, but it has been the scene of many a sanguinary conflict between the Arapahoes and Utahs. *En passant,* I may mention that the pronunciation by which the names of these tribes is generally known here is "Rappahoes and Utes."

Night overtook us on this broad plain – there being no convenient or suitable camping place under eleven miles from where the road leaves the river; but we "made camp" at nine o'clock and soon had supper cooking over a blazing brush fire, the fuel being obtained on an island. This makes our travel, today, foot up twenty-seven miles. Faulkner, Battles and Rice went across the river at noon for the purpose of hunting.

Faulkner has just come into camp, but the other boys are not with him; he got tired of hunting and crossed the river, leaving them on the other side, but he afterwards saw them on this side the river, so we presume they are safe. Faulkner had a serious time getting back, having to swim and carry his gun and clothes for some distance across the swift current. I found a dwarf species of phlox (or Sweet William) growing on the barren sand-hills, which, for fragrance excels any wild flower that I am acquainted with. Judging from the dry stems and seed pods, the Platte valley, late in the season, must be covered with a variety of handsome flowers. Met a number of men returning – most of them say they did not undertake mining; others tell us that we will find some few men making from five dollars to fifteen dollars a day, but as for themselves they could have no luck.

WEDNESDAY, JUNE 1 [1859]. Summer is ushered into our presence this morning in no pleasant humor; the season that we are wont to represent as a lovely maiden strewing flowers along our pathway, came upon us, after midnight, like a waspish shrew, in a passionate tempest of wind, fierce and cold, which would have been more in season during the reign of March. Every tent in the encampment was thrown down except ours, and that would have gone with the rest had not Jo wakened up in time to strengthen its fastenings. This morning the wind still blows a gale. Battles and Rice have just got into camp. They laid out last night in a little ravine, and must have had a "good time" of it, for B was as wet as a rat, and Wallace had no coat. While crossing the river, B got in over his depth, lost all his clothing, but managed to get ashore with his gun; he then accidentally saw his bundle of clothes boil up to the surface, and plunging in recovered them all except his boots. His long barefoot walk among the prickly pears has left his feet in a "sore" condition, but otherwise the boys are both uninjured in health – not even having caught cold – and are stowing away a very large amount of "grub" to make up for lost time.

Our camp is just opposite the mouth of Crow creek. The road now follows a gravelly ridge as far as we proceed on it. Seven miles from camp we pass opposite the mouth of Cache la Poudre river (pronounced Cash la Poodare; contracted into Cash la Poo; and signifying the stream where the powder was buried.)[128] Five miles further brought us to Douglas City[129] (where there is nary house, only a trader's tent, where he keeps a squaw and a few traps), and here we found a number of teams about to attempt fording the stream. The river is rising daily, and as no delay is admissible, we commence our preparations immediately; the wagon beds were blocked up, the teams united, making of all only two, and we started across; the crossing follows a circuitous route, but all the wagons went across safe and without accident, except Esq. Powell's – his wagon upset just as he was leaving the stream, but he had the good luck

[128] There is some uncertainty as to when and by whom the powder was cached. The generally accepted story is that some trappers on their way to the Green river were snowed in beside this stream in november, 1836. They cached powder and other supplies to lighten their loads. This information came from Antoine Janise who was in the party, and was published in the Fort Collins (Colorado) *Courier,* feb. 8, 1863, and reprinted in Ansel Watrous, *History of Larimer county, Colorado,* 161.

[129] This paper town did not materialize.

to save everything except a little sugar, which came out of the water molasses. We all camped on the west bank, leaving no team on the other side.

Mr. Oakes came up on the other side this evening with his steam mill, and passed along up towards Denver city, not wishing to risk the ford with his heavy load. Distance, including crossing, thirteen miles. Today Fletcher had the good luck to kill the first deer that has been brought into camp. He made a center shot, through the heart, and this was the first shot he ever made at a deer – pretty well done for Massachusetts. The traveler along this route will observe scattered over the plains everywhere, this side of Laramie Crossing, what I do not remember to have ever seen elsewhere, or to have read a description of; little hills, in the shape of regular perfect cones, generally two feet in diameter at the base and two feet high, formed entirely of gravel about the size of rice grains. These rise out of the center of a circular space about five or six feet in diameter, which is entirely free from gravel and grass, and are the work of the red ant of the plains. The millions of pebbles of which one of these hills is composed are carried up and fitted to their places by these little artisans, one by one. The entrance is generally at the base, and by cutting down through one of these hills, and removing one half, the remaining section will exhibit a wonderful labyrinth of avenues, chambers, streets and store-rooms – the latter even now well filled.

THURSDAY, JUNE 2. This morning several of us started ahead, to Thompson's creek,[130] which, at the regular ford, we found impassable; we hunted some miles

[130] The next principal fork of the South Platte south of the Cache la Poudre. This is known as the Big Thompson, which rises in the Estes Park region.

up the stream, but found no better show, and concluded to await the arrival of the teams, and start across the uplands, in search of a ford nearer the mountains. At length a company – Williams' from Michigan – came up and informed us that our teams had started westward across the great divide between Thompson's and the Cache la Poudre. This company then took the same track, and we started across the country to head the teams, passing over a dry barren waste, destitute of grass, but prolific in prickly pears and prairie dogs. We traveled until noon, when we found the teams encamped on the banks of the Cache la Poudre, which runs through a beautiful and fertile valley, and is now a deep rapid river, being swollen by the melting snows.

A village of Cheyennes is just opposite us, and about a thousand ponies are grazing on the rich buffalo grass that carpets the valley and hill slopes; several of the "bucks" have been crossing the stream – swimming their horses – and trading; for four half dollars, Esq. Powell bought one of the finest painted buffalo robes I ever saw. After dinner we traveled about ten miles, alternately on the upland and along the valley, towards the mountains, and made a fine camp on the river bank at night. The banks of the stream are well wooded, with cottonwood, box elder, elm, and thickets of underbrush.

FRIDAY, JUNE 3. Today we traveled along the river about twelve miles, when we halted for dinner at the base of the foothills of the Rocky mountains. Along the table land at the base of the mountains we saw great numbers of antelope, but they were very wild; John Bailey came into camp with one, which was the only one killed. After dinner a number of our party started out into the hills. The scenery along the river is wild and romantic; huge piles of sandstone and trap rock are piled up promiscuously, presenting many fantastic shapes to the view. The escarpments nearly all face the west, and are steep and bluffy, sloping off gradually, towards the east. Crossing the first range of hills we find a beautiful valley, covered with superior grass, to which, by a steep descent, we brought our teams, where we can have grand quarters, for some days, whilst we are "prospecting" in the mountains.

SATURDAY, JUNE 4.[131] Today we formed a correll of our wagons, for the greater security of our cattle at night. A few words, now, descriptive of our camp – north of us, and only a few rods distant, runs the Cache la Poudre, roaring and surging along over its rocky bed, with a current running at the rate of ten miles an hour; westward rises, successively, four distinct ranges of hills and pine-clad mountains, before the great snow-clad range, towering above all, is reached; the latter is not visible from camp, but for several days it has formed the background of the magnificent mountain scenery that has greeted our vision, standing out in bold relief above the plain as we journeyed westward. On the opposite side of the river is a town called Colona,[132] and a large collection of Cheyenne wigwams. A company of traders, from Glenwood, Iowa, are stationed here. A number of the boys, including the writer, prospected the country adjacent to our encampment, but, as was to be expected from the geological formation, no gold was

131 The diary entries of june 4 to 16 were published in the *Spectator* of august 4, 1859.

132 Near La Porte, about six miles northwest of Fort Collins. Colona was started in 1858 by the Janise brothers – Antoine and Nicholas – and other mountain men. A number of these traders had Indian wives. Some gold seekers joined the mountaineers in founding the town.

Prospecting for Gold in Pike's Peak Region
From a contemporary wood-engraving of 1859

found. Some of the party are cooking the provisions for the use of two prospecting parties, who will leave here on monday, one taking each side of the river. Found a ledge of quartz rock today, imbedded between two strata of trap; no granite in the neighborhood, except in the form of boulders.

SUNDAY, JUNE 5 [1859]. A Sabbath in camp.

MONDAY, JUNE 6. A busy morning is this in camp. Eighteen men are to prospect the north side, and sixteen the south side of the river, while the remainder stay in camp. The party on the south side have one pack animal – that on the north three – these being kindly furnished by Capt. Powell, and Mr. Hopkins of Glenwood, Iowa.

The Northern Prospecting Party consisted of the following persons: Esq. Powell and Case, of Malta, Ill.; Dr. Marston and Louden, of Omaha; the writer and Jo Hand, of Oquawka; Hopkins and Whipple of Glenwood, Iowa; John and Wm. Crow, of Centerville, Iowa; Cohenour, Cain, Nokes, Tucker, Long, Kindheart, J. and W. Maltby, of Mt. Sterling, Ill. We were divided into three messes, of six men each, and provisions calculated to last ten days for each mess were packed upon three ponies. Each man carried a pack comprising a pair of blankets, a coat, a mining tool – pick, shovel, or pan – or a rifle. Thus equipped, we set out to the river; the stream being at too high a stage to admit of being forded, it was determined to effect a crossing, if possible, by means of a raft.

Esquire Powell, Jo Hand and several others went to work and a strong pine raft was soon constructed. Geo. Case swam across on a pony and attempted to convey a rope over, but the strain was so great that he could not accomplish the feat. Mr. Whipple then made the attempt, on another pony, and succeeded; but the terrible strain of the current soon parted the rope, and the attempt to cross by means of a line was then abandoned. The raft was then poled out into the stream, when it was found that the surging current waves would wash it under, and render it entirely unmanageable. Opportunely, word was just at this time brought to us that the mountaineers living at Colona had completed a ferry boat and were ready to transport us across the river; we started for the landing, and had to wait and work several hours, trying to rig a rope arrangement by means of which the boat could be managed, but all such efforts were finally abandoned as futile, and it was determined that oars must be brought into requisition; in this way the crossing was finally effected, with difficulty, but no accident, and at an expense of only a half dollar per man.

Several teams bound for California by the Bridger Pass road[133] (which follows up the stream) were ready to cross immediately after us; the boat had been manufactured of whip-sawed lumber, and was of such small size that two trips were required to bring over one wagon. We started at two P.M. for the head waters of the Cache la Poudre, by the Bridger road, intending to push our exploration, if possible, into the North Park. Before leaving Colona, however, we called to see the traders; conversed with Nick Jness [Janise] (pronounced John-nees), an old mountaineer, – his brother, Antoine, being absent in the mountains with a small prospecting party; the latter is said to be the most celebrated mountaineer of the times – and as courteous as

[133] In this area the road was better known as the Cherokee Trail, traversed by several California-bound parties of Cherokees in 1849 and 1850.

he is intelligent. The crowd that surrounded us, filled with native curiosity, was indeed a motley one – Indians, squaws and children; blooded and half-breeds; neat and slovenly; of all grades and conditions, – an unusual number of wolf dogs swarmed about the town, and just as we were departing, one of them suffered death on the gallows, preliminary to his preparation as Indian food, and in concert with his dying struggles rose an universal howl from all of his species in the neighborhood.

Two miles from town we dined on the banks of the river; then, turning around a high bluff of sand stone, our road leaves the river (which comes down from the mountains through a narrow canon) and crosses a small drain which bears the evidence of sometimes being a raging torrent, and travel in a N.W. direction about eight miles,[134] through a pass bounded on the N.E. by a range of arched bluffs, presenting abrupt escarpments of naked sand stone (colored by the red oxide of iron) on the side next the road, and on the S.W. by a range of pine-clad mountains that rise to a considerable elevation. This pass rises with a gradual but constant elevation to our camp, which is on the banks of a small spring branch, the seventh of the sort we have crossed today.

The valley is about a mile wide and covered with fair buffalo grass. The soil is red (partaking of the color of the sand stone from which it has been formed by the decomposition of the latter) and with an abundance of rain it might be coaxed to produce a few harvests of small grain. The sand stone composing the perpendicular bluff near our camp is chiefly of two kinds

[134] The road was along the general course of present highway 287, leading from Fort Collins to Laramie, Wyoming.

the ferruginous (colored with iron) and igneous (changed and hardened by intense heat). The cliff is about three hundred feet high, the first one hundred feet from the top being a sheer precipice. In a niche in the rocks, about six feet square, a pair of large eagles have built a nest which now contains a young eaglet. It is ten feet from the top, and some of the boys have been amusing themselves by trying to dislodge it with poles and huge rocks, but it is too securely fixed – the poles could only play around the edge of the nest, and the rocks only knock off some protruding sticks; rifles were then put into requisition, but the breastwork of limbs and twigs protected the young inmate from danger. Slept in our blankets on the ground, without a tent or other shelter, comfortably and soundly. Prospected some but with no success – which was no disappointment, however.

TUESDAY, JUNE 7 [1859]. Rose early; had breakfast over by five o'clock, and were on the road. The character of the country and scenery is about the same as yesterday for five miles, when, still following the same general direction, the road crosses a plain several miles in extent, and again strikes the river. We stopped at a small stream about a mile before reaching the river, about nine o'clock, and partook of a lunch; a cottonwood tree under the shade of which we sat was barked five years ago, and contains several inscriptions made at that time in lead pencil marks, still plainly visible. Sunk a hole down to the water here; when we had to abandon it, having no pump or other convenience to bail it out.

At the river we again sunk a hole eleven feet deep, but the water again prevented us from reaching the bed-rock. While we were here the teams that crossed at Colona yesterday came up. Several prospectors and several hunters here left our train, intending to come up again, during the afternoon. We traveled on, and camped for dinner on the banks of a fine little stream, a tributary of the Box Elder, which at this point runs through a wild canon of rugged granite rock, rent and seamed in a thousand fantastic forms. Just as we commence our descent into the canon, on the road, a point of rocks attracts the attention of every traveler; it is a perfect representation of an old lady's head – the features and cap being very marked and distinct. We prospected here as thoroughly as we could for the water, but although we obtained plenty of black sand, we got no gold.

We waited several hours for the hunters; but as they did not come in we took it for granted they were ahead, and started on; we had crossed ten spring branches and did not apprehend any trouble about water, but we soon found ourselves on a great plain – the divide between the Cache la Poudre and Lodge Pole creek – which for a distance of ten miles contains no living water. After traveling five miles, and night coming on apace, we kindled a huge fire from a pine log which we opportunely discovered upon the very summit of the divide, to call in the stragglers, and leaving a note for them to come ahead, we pushed slowly on, occasionally firing signal guns to let them know our whereabouts.

About ten o'clock they overtook us, and we soon afterwards reached a little stream where we found the Californians encamped; we had to go a mile further up stream for wood, where we camped at a quarter before eleven, and made a fire out of two large dry cottonwoods. All were in good spirits, though some were very tired.

Across the divide the road bears nearly west. This morning Joe Hand called to me from the top of a high bluff, nearly three-quarters of a mile distant, on a straight line, to "come there with the spy glass." I was surprised at the distinctness with which I heard him – for at home one could scarcely have heard at that distance a shout at the top of a person's voice. I went up, and was amply repaid by the magnificence and grandeur of the scene. From the eastern slope of the divide we had a magnificent surrounding landscape; ahead of us the gradual elevation obstructed our sight of the bluffs in the distance, making the plain appear one grand limitless prairie; on our left rose high mountains covered with pine trees; to the right was a range of sand stone bluffs, some of the most remarkable shape – one resembled a colossal fortress, as neatly arranged as military skill could have devised – another, jutting out into the plain, resembled most perfectly a steamboat, wanting only the chimneys to render the image complete; the hull, the water line, the bow sprit, the wheel house, the cabin with its green blinds, the texas and the hen coop were all there. This I named the Steamboat Rock, and the company acquiesced, in the propriety of the name. Near this great landmark which is in sight for many miles, looms up a circular mountain which, from its shape and its ribbed surface of ridges, renders the name given to it by Jo Hand – Crinoline Hill – eminently appropriate.

WEDNESDAY, JUNE 8. Fourteen years ago today a great light went down in our national firmament – the hero of New Orleans breathed his last at the Hermitage! The resemblance of Old Hickory awakened new determination and firmness in the hearts of his admirers in the party, and we started out early with our hearts and hands ready for the tramp and the work. We enter the mountains again and commence making an elevation which renders itself very perceptible to our lungs, which are obliged to inflate to their utmost capacity. The scenery for four miles is a fine panorama of picturesque mountain slopes, and hills of rugged granite, piled up in confused masses all about us. At this distance from camp, we met Antoine Jness returning with his party; he had been prospecting among the foothills surrounding the head waters of the Cache la Poudre, and reported that the water was so high as to interfere entirely with successful search for gold.

He advised us to proceed to the Park, and gave us an outline map of the country and the road by which we could reach the pass opening through the Medicine Bow mountains from the Laramie plains to the Park; he thought that if we could find the trail of his party and follow it some distance, it would save us considerable travel. After some further conversation, Mr. J. enquired if we had any fresh meat, and learning that we had not, generously supplied us with the ham of a mountain sheep, which we ate at dinner time and found to be very much like venison. Bidding him good bye, we crossed several streams, and halted at a small quaking aspen grove to engrave our names upon the bark of the trees among thousands of others.

We pushed on, keeping a sharp lookout for the aforesaid trail, which we found about six miles from where we met the party. The road from our encampment to this point is a very good one, generally smooth (though gravelly, and hard on cattle's feet) with occasional steep pitches and rough ledges of rock. Near where we strike northward into the trail are a number of pure hard quartz mounds, rising above the level of the granite debris of which the surface level of the whole country is composed.

I may as well mention here that the plains and the valleys between the mountains are composed of rotten granite gravel – all about you, the gradual decomposition of the granite is going on, plainly perceptible on every hand – hills and boulders all giving way before the corroding fingers of decay. Traveling along the trail five miles we camped for dinner, on a small stream of calybeate water. Here some of our hunters started out to look up some game, a rendezvous being appointed which we all thought was on our road; a difference of opinion then arose as to whether we should here leave the trail and bear off to the road, or hunt the former and follow it further; those following the latter plan prevailed, and two hours and a half were then occupied in hunting for the trail, which we had accidentally lost in a meadow of grass; following it some eight miles, we found ourselves wandering through the forest a long way south of the rendezvous. Some of us then, it having been deemed prudent to camp, ascended a lofty mountain and built a fire, which served to guide the hunters all into camp. We prospected here with our usual success. The brooks are too high for either gold or trout to be found. Had a very pleasant evening – nights are cold, but our blankets and fine fires protect us. The hunters killed several antelope, but the distance was so great (and at any rate uncertain) to camp that only the hams of one of them were brought in.

THURSDAY, JUNE 9 [1859]. Started about nine o'clock, and followed the trail through the forest for some miles, when, about noon, we lost it in a swamp, where the hunters saw much bear sign. We then struck off in a direction we thought calculated to bring us out right, passed over a few acres where fallen pines obstruct the passage at every step – the timber having all been prostrated by some violent tempest – and camped for dinner in a small glade, where we were hailed and rained upon for an hour; but a blazing fire of pine knots soon made us all right, and we proceeded on our route.

Passing over hills and vales, through woods and across glades, and over snow drifts that were slowly melting away, we at length came upon the rim of Laramie Plains, near the eastern extremity, and some miles from the point where the road crosses it. We now crossed the plain, at this point some three miles wide, and as a thunder storm threatened us, and several hunters were in the adjacent timber, we selected a camping place. The storm blew over, and we soon heard the welcome announcement that Jno. Crow ("Old Buffalo," as we call him) had killed an elk. Half the men went out to assist in bringing his elkship in, and the rest set to work preparing a scaffold and gathering in dry quaking aspen wood for the purpose of jerking so much of the meat as was not needed for immediate use. The huge animal weighed, net, about five hundred pounds – supplying the whole company with an abundance. At sundown, Hopkins went down into the dark woods and shot an enormous turkey which he had seen fly up into a tree. The night threatening to be cold, we cut down a large pine, and taking the branches built a neat correll or hedge around our sleeping place, which protected us from the wind. No gold prospects in our immediate vicinity. Ascended a lofty hill, and found that to the southward of our camp lies an interminable forest, more dense than any we have before seen.

FRIDAY, JUNE 10. Trouble in camp this morning. Part of the company – more than half – are afraid they will not have provisions to last them to the Park and back. It looks like rather an abortive trip, this going home to camp now, when within a day and a half's journey of our original destination, but, while some of us are willing to allowance ourselves as to flour, the greater part say they cannot consent to risk starving (!) and we all conclude to go back to camp. We will remain here today and finish jerking our meat; some of the boys will hunt, and others put in the time as best pleases them. With Messrs. Powell and Marston, the writer took a ride some nine miles down the plain, along the base of a spur of bluffs which juts down into the level and forms a divide between the two branches that unite some fifteen miles lower down and form the main Laramie river.

From the lofty bluffs at the point of this range, we have a fair view of the plain, which stretches out apparently without limit before us; of the two Laramies; of the snow-clad mountains that hem in the wonderful Park (which we hope yet to see under more favorable auspices – when the water is low, and with a crowd all of one mind); of the line of the Bridger's Pass road; and, nearer to us, bearing directly for the park, through which it passes and again joins the main road beyond the Platte, of the Cherokee trail. Scanning the horizon with a glass, we discover a drove of ponies in the distance, belonging to some Arapahoes, but their lodges are hidden in some ravine where they are safe from the scrutiny of the predatory "Utes"; in another direction we think we see teams bound eastward – a second look assures us of the fact, and yet we were not prepared to see two wagons going in this direction; but, hold, behind these are two more driving a yoke of oxen – this may explain the matter, perhaps they may have met some obstacle to their further progress westward; they are going our road, now, and we will find out tomorrow, perhaps.

SATURDAY, JUNE 11. Three hours' travel this morning brings us to where we took dinner on wednesday. Our night camp is at the small creek at the eastern verge of the divide that we crossed on tuesday night. A storm coming up we camped early. About dark three Arapahoes rode into camp, and remained with us during the night. They came from the west and their horses show marks of severe travel. An antelope was killed today which affords us plenty of fresh meat. Soon after leaving camp this morning we ascended a high hill, from the summit of which we had a view of Steamboat Rock in the far distance, through a gap in the mountains.

SUNDAY, JUNE 12. Started early and retraced our old road to Colona. Saw Antoine Jness, and received a promise from him of his company whenever we saw proper to make a trip to the Park, which, he suggested, might better be postponed until the waters were down. He also informed us that the Indians we saw were in pursuit of some Utes, who had stolen the night before one hundred and fifty-five ponies that Cheyennes were herding some twelve miles from town. They recovered one hundred – scattered along the road – found that thirty had been killed, but lost twenty-five entirely. The Arapahoes who camped with us last night brought down full particulars; five Utes were the robbers – they had learned from some white emigrants that the Cheyennes were at Colona, and had they not happened upon the drove they did, Jness says they would have come on down and driven off all their ponies.

The Cheyennes have raised the war whoop, and are gathering in for the war trail. Jness says that the Utahs are friendly with the whites who need apprehend no danger whatever from them; in fact, there are no hostile Indians upon our route or about the mountains, at present. The teams we saw on Laramie plain had been out as far as the North Platte, but could not ford it, and were returning to pursue their way to California by way of [Fort] Laramie. Some of these California bound emigrants have a long and dreary road ahead of them – that's certain; for many of them have not sufficient teams for the trip, and are not fully advised of the road over which they have to travel.

The men we saw driving a yoke of oxen are a couple of Irish boys who lost their wagon and outfit in attempting to cross Medicine Bow creek. We ferried the river, and were soon in camp, where we sat down to an excellent supper – the writer and Jo finding in store for us a luxury for this country, excellent fresh butter. On tuesday last, Mr. Squires and Mr. Augustine, started down to Denver city. Messrs. Byers and Gibson, the gentlemanly publishers of the *Rocky Mountain News,* sent me a full file of their paper and a late copy of the *Missouri Republican,* from the perusal of which I derived much satisfaction. We find the news is exciting from the mines. Tomorrow we shall set tires on some of the wagons, and make all other preparations for an early start on tuesday for the south.

We will first, however, take a glance at

THE SOUTHERN PROSPECTING PARTY

Which was composed of the following persons: Dickey, Fletcher and Battles, of Mass.; White and Artley, of Oquawka; Watson, Rodgers and Goodrich, of Mich.; Piper, Huddelson and Stokes, of Illinois; I. Baily, Micksell, Wells and Pressgrove, of Missouri; and R. Conquest, of Iowa. From different members of the party we have obtained information relative to their trip, which enables us to make up the following journal of their travels and adventures:

MONDAY, JUNE 6 [1859]. Started about eight o'clock, and traveled in a S.W. direction; by noon they had crossed the first range of mountains and reached the head waters of Thompson's creek;[135] here the party prospected, but without success. With some difficulty they then succeed in crossing the next range, accomplishing the task by sundown. Whilst crossing this range, the party encountered a very large brown bear; they were ascending the mountain by two different ridges; when about half way up, White, who was on one ridge, discovered the bear coming down the other in the direction of the party ascending it, who were sitting resting; he ran about a hundred yards down, to give them the alarm, but before he could notify them, the bear was within forty feet of them before they discovered him.

Although there were two rifles and four revolvers in the crowd, bruin escaped without having a shot fired

[135] This was probably the Buckhorn branch of the Big Thompson.

at him, the boys appearing to be terror struck at the "grim monster," who, when he discovered the party, stopped short, took a deliberate survey of matters and things, and then, with a parting groan, beat a dignified retreat across the ravine towards the other party. When about half way, his progress was impeded by a formidable array – White with a rock in each hand and Huddelson with an old shot gun, the only available weapons within their reach. The bear fled, closely pursued, but made good his escape, to the disappointment of one party and satisfaction of the other. Camping, at sundown, the boys had a good time, and boasted of the valorous feats the sight of another bear would call forth.

TUESDAY, JUNE 7. The party slept well, and, after breakfasting on grouse, commenced their line of march towards the snow-capped mountains, stopping at every favorable looking place to prospect; there were three old Californians in the party, and upon them devolved the selection of places to be prospected. While nooning, the party observed a black bear about a quarter of a mile off, but failed to get a shot at him.

Two miles from noon camp, when passing around the point of a ridge, another very large brown bear was seen in a small open valley about three hundred yards in advance; several shots were fired at him, without effect – the bear sitting on his haunches, facing his pursuers, and wondering, no doubt, what such a cracking meant. To gratify his curiosity, perhaps, he then advanced a few paces toward the party, when White threw down his pack, and unstrapping a pick, put it on a handle and called on the boys to meet the bear half way. Bruin, for fear of being "picked" up, fled about a quarter of a mile, where the pursuing party found him "denned" and had to abandon the chase.

Proceeding on about a mile, they encamped about four o'clock – the party dividing, one portion going back to watch for the bear, and the other "prospecting." The camp was in a beautiful valley of about six acres, in which three springs center, and form one of the tributaries of St. Vrain's creek; the spot is surrounded by lofty, rugged mountains, except a narrow pass to the northwest. The boys have built them a cabin of cottonwood, to protect them from the heavy frosts – as they had arrived at an elevation where ice formed every night. Four men can, of cottonwood or quaking aspen poles, construct a shelter in half an hour that will protect them from frost, which, with a good fire, renders a night's repose in the mountains quite comfortable.

WEDNESDAY, JUNE 8 [1859]. After breakfast, the party proceed on, and about three o'clock struck the head waters of the Cache la Poudre,[136] at the eastern base of the snowy range of the Medicine Bow mountains. Here they came to a halt, as their duty was now performed, having prospected as thoroughly as circumstances would permit, every available spot upon the route. The party went to prospecting on the banks of the creek, which here runs at the rate of about twenty miles an hour, rolling large rocks along in its course. At night they build a large correll of pine timber, set it on fire and went to sleep in the ring.

THURSDAY, JUNE 9. The party rose early. Divided into three parties – two to prospect around camp, while the third were to proceed as far as the snow would permit into the mountains; the latter party, headed by Captain White, was composed of the following persons: Artley, Fletcher, Pressgrove, Micksell, Wells, and

[136] The identity of the streams here is uncertain.

Huddleson. They proceeded with great difficulty, about five miles, when their further progress was cut short by snow and ice. Fletcher hauled from his knapsack a fine lemon and a quantity of sugar, which he had brought for the occasion, and with one of the gold pans made a "bowl" of ice-cold lemonade, which was drank where never lemonade was drank before, each one of the party in turn drinking a toast. This may appear strange to some – that the boys should take it so cool in this region of snow, but the wonderment is diminished when we add that, although their feet were in the snow, their bodies were in a broiling sun, the temperature being eighty-five degrees.

The days are very warm, but the nights are frosty and keen. The snow is going off fast, but from some of the peaks it never disappears. A heavy storm coming up, the mountain party, having finished their spirited but not spiritual spree, returned to camp amid a considerable shower of rain and snow. Arriving at camp about noon, they found the rest of the party awaiting their return, and, after taking a hasty lunch, they set out on their return. After several incidents, but no accidents, they all arrived safely at the general rendezvous on friday evening, where they were cordially greeted by those in camp.

The mountains through which the party passed are exceedingly rugged; between the ranges there are narrow passes, which are smooth, and which render access through the ranges easy. Wild animals abound in this region; the ground is tracked over with bear, elk, deer, mountain sheep and other animals, but bear appear to predominate, the party having seen four brown bears and one black bear; they saw no grizzly bears, but plenty of his tracks. The party informs us that there are thousands and thousands of acres of the finest pine, fir, cedar, spruce, and other timber growing on the mountains which they traversed, but of course only a little of it could be available for the use of man.

The party did not discover any gold whatever, in all their prospecting. As Captain White very truly remarks: "men endowed with less energy and perseverance would give up in despair, but men who could come up here through all the tide of returning emigration are not to be bluffed off so easily." The Captain speaks in the highest terms of all the party – there being, he says, only one who showed that he had better be somewhere else than in the mountains gold-hunting. When the party were ready to return, Capt. White and Artley, who had been cradled in the Alleghenies and arrived at manhood in their wild recesses, headed the train, and the Capt. being a practical surveyor, brought them by a bee line (so far as circumstances would permit) right into camp, a distance of forty-five or fifty miles, without calling into requisition even a pocket compass.

EN ROUTE AGAIN

Part of the teams that were correlled with us started yesterday (monday) – the Brown county teams among the number. Nokes and Tucker, and Dr. Davis of Missouri started home. Three miles from camp we came through a rough, rocky, hilly pass between the foothills into the plain, where a small creek runs out. Five miles further is a small creek that will soon be dry. We then have a long stretch of ten miles without water, to Thompson's creek. This is a swift, deep stream, the water coming about half way up the wagon beds, but we had everything raised up so that no damage was done. We all crossed without accident, and camped for the night.[137] The road today, has been good, except the gravel and hills – short, steep pitches.

WEDNESDAY, JUNE 15 [1859]. This morning, I went up the creek, a short distance, washed two pans of surface dirt, and obtained three small pieces of gold. This is the first that any of our company have found. Traveled eleven miles without water to a small creek;[138] six miles further brought us to St. Vrain's creek,[139] an impetuous mountain stream, which we forded as we did Thompson's. Camped with good grass. The mountains are not so far off – the snowy ranges, I mean – the foothill ranges not being so numerous.

THURSDAY, JUNE 16. We have traveled nine miles this morning, and arrived at a small creek [140] where we found good grass. Here our teams have stopped. A portion of our party will go tomorrow to Boulder and Jefferson Diggings; Capt. Powell, Hopkins, Battles, Augustine, Pressgrove, Marston, Porter, and myself start at one o'clock, to Denver city, and Gregory's Diggings, to test the truth of the reports we hear from there.

Auraria, K. T., June 17, '59.[141]

Seven miles [from Lefthand creek] brought us to Boulder city, which we found pleasantly situated at the foot of the mountains, just where Boulder creek bulges impetuously out of a gorge in the grand old hills.

137 This was probably a little west of present Loveland.

138 Little Thompson creek.

139 A little east of present Lyons.

140 Lefthand creek.

141 This letter was published in the *Spectator* of july 28, 1859.

The city contains about fifty-nine log houses, a few of them completed and occupied – the remainder awaiting roofs and tenants. We called on Mayor Brookfield, formerly of Nebraska City,[142] from whom we had the satisfaction of learning that a discovery had only the day before been made of rich quartz leads (similar to those at Gregory) at "Boulder Diggings," twelve miles northwest from this place, and where a number of our party will be tomorrow.

Crossing Boulder creek by raising our wagon bed, we turned eastward across the plains. The mountains here are more rocky and abrupt, steep, broken, seamed, and shattered by convulsions, than at any other point where I have seen them. The second branch of Boulder creek we drove into without raising our wagon bed, thinking it was but a little thing – but we found the water deep enough to run over the top of the bed! Camped seven miles from Boulder city. Hopkins caught an antelope fawn, but let the little fellow go again as he was too young for veal. This morning we had fifteen miles to travel to reach the "Consolidated City." [143] A few miles from camp we met a drove of three hundred and ninety cattle, en route for California. Many of them were sore-footed already, and the road they have before them is "awful" for gravel and rock.

We reached here at noon, left our team on the west bank of the Platte (which is here a small stream not swimming to a horse) and crossed the ferry for five cents each – the usual price for footmen being twenty-five cents, but competition having reduced it. The

[142] See the preceding volume in this *Series*, pages 220, 242, 248, for letters of Brookfield and descriptions of Boulder city.

[143] Auraria and Denver, on opposite sides of Cherry creek, at its junction with the South Platte.

Platte is here a mountain stream, and its shores are thickly studded with cottonwood trees. Denver and Auraria are situated on the eastern bank of the river, on opposite sides of Cherry creek – Denver on the north and Auraria on the south. Cherry creek is sometimes a clear, beautiful stream, but this morning the water suddenly ceased running, except a small rivulet at the upper part of the city. Considerable business is going on – the saloons are flourishing – the bakeries making money – the cattle market down.

Horace Greeley, the editor of the *New York Tribune,* is stopping here at present, nursing a sore leg, which he received by being upset in the stage coming out. I called to see him, and learned that he would proceed to California by way of [Fort] Laramie on monday next. He has been up at Gregory's Diggings, and fully endorses the high colored picture of rich strikes reported there.[144]

I am indebted to Henry Allen, Esq.,[145] and to Messrs. Byers and Gibson,[146] for many courteous favors.

I send you a list of the prices current here:

Flour – States, $14 to $16 per 100 lbs.; Mexican, $10 to $15 do. Corn Meal, $12 per 100 lbs. Bacon, sides and hams, 35 cents per lb. Sugar 20 to 25 do. Coffee, 25 do. Saleratus, 35 do. Salt 15 do. Beans, 15 do. Onions, 25 do. Potatoes, 25 do. Butter, 75 do. Cheese, 50 do. Lard, 50 do. Crackers, 25 do. Bread, 15 do. Fresh beef, 12 to 15 do. Venison, $1 per quarter. Milk, 10c per qt. Molasses, $2.50 per gal. Whiskey, $3 do. Lumber $100 per 1000 feet. Nails, $25 per 100 lbs. Glass, $16 per box. Oxen, $30 to $50 per yoke.

---

144 See Greeley's report, published in volume x, pages 376-382.

145 Data on Allen may be found in volume x, 175 and 183.

146 Publishers of the *Rocky Mountain News.*

I go to Gregory's tomorrow, whence I will write you again.

I can hear nothing of the rest of the Oquawka boys, I rather think Davis and the boys with him have started for home. I shall keep a good look out for the rest of them, however.

Yours, &c,
Junior.

MY IMPRESSIONS OF THE NEW EL DORADO AND ITS SURROUNDINGS [147]

We left Auraria on saturday, june 15th [18th], for Gregory's Diggings – situate forty miles from the city, and twenty-five miles from the base of the mountains. The road to the mountains leads over rolling prairie, which is for the most part covered with short scanty grass, prickly pear in abundance, agaves in full bloom, and a thousand varieties of more ordinary flowers. The soil is poor; it might produce the small grains – wheat, barley, rye and oats; but I do not think the crops would be abundant or the yield large. In fifteen miles we reach the foot of the mountains at Vasquer's Fork (or, as it is more generally known here, Clear creek). The mountains are very lofty, with small spurs taking the place of foot hills. Thousands of cattle, hundreds of wagons and tents, and people innumerable throng the valley of the stream.

We find representatives from nearly every state in the Union; there are gaming tents, restaurants, stores, little doggeries where poor whiskey is retailed at "10 cents a nip," itinerant gunsmiths, extempore blacksmith shops; and a general paraphernalia of business is

147 Published in the *Spectator* of august 18, 1859.

ostensibly going on. The hardest sight, however, is to behold four or five females with families of little children, washing and cooking in the broiling sun, and obliged to gather and cut their own wood. They all appear, however, thanks to the trip and this salubrious air, to be endowed with excellent health.

We find many here who have been to the mines and are returning to the States discouraged; others, again, are going up; and so it continues – a constant flow and ebb – every wave, however, leaving its deposits in the mines. We here cross the river on a rough bridge – toll for team and eight men, one dollar and seventy-five cents. Here we find a few little garden patches enclosed; down the river for miles may be found stock ranches, where oxen are taken care of at a charge of seventy-five cents to one dollar per month. We concluded to leave our wagon at a ranche, and pack up our provisions on our animals, so we set about making pack saddles, and were ready to enter

THE MOUNTAINS

late in the afternoon. The first mountain over which the wagon road passes is over a mile high, and the road runs up the steepest part of it – making the very entrance to the "rough and rugged road" that leads to the mines the most difficult part of it. We, however, take the packers' trail, which leads along the sides of the high mountains that fall off with a slope of seventy-five degrees – traverses deep valleys – runs over lofty hills – winds about through pine woods and among rocky ledges – until, at the distance of seven miles from the valley, it joins the wagon road.

Never have I been so forcibly impressed with the

presence of silence as during our tramp along some of the deep gorges that our trail led through; it was twilight – not a zephyr sighed – not a leaf rustled – not a twig cracked beneath our tread – not the hum of an insect nor the twitter of a bird was heard – and the muffled tread of the mules in the dusty path only served to render the unnatural stillness more startling – to make the silence audible! When we reached the point where the path intersects the road, it was quite dark; but several camp fires were blazing on the adjacent hill sides, which served to light us to a suitable place to add another to the number. A little mountain stream supplied us with water – of which we consume enormous quantities – and, after supper, as there is no grass for the pack animals, we "hung them to pine trees," and visited some of our neighbors, whom we found to be chiefly from Illinois.

EARLY on the 18th [19th] we continued our journey. The mountain ranges are in succession becoming more and more elevated. The road is thronged with wagons and carts and packers going and coming – for vehicles it is a difficult one; now steep, now sideling, now running over boulders and steep ledges of rock, and leading through deep mud holes, and winding about among dense groves of aspen and pine; two hundred pounds to the yoke is all the load that oxen can haul, and pack animals are preferable for the transportation of supplies over the route. The mountain slopes are covered with groves of yellow pine, spruce, fir and quaking aspens; none of the timber, however, being very large or growing to a very lofty height. In the ravines, between the ridges, down which generally ripples a little spring branch, we find a profusion of rank and luxurious vegetation – dense thickets of gooseberry, currant, service berry, raspberry, huckleberry, and wild cherry bushes; clumps of birch and alders; fringes of flowering willows; great patches of rose trees (the wild rose growing ten feet high); columbines and other flowering shrubs.

Among all this mountain vegetation, however, we find neither laurel nor wintergreen. As we progress, dense forests lie before us; among those forests are raging fierce fires, the smoke of which rises and entirely obscures the sun. All through these mountains we see thousands of acres of dead pines – sometimes whole mountain slopes, with but a green bush to break the monotony of the scene. Among these dead pines the fires spread rapidly, and communicating to the fallen leaves and dry cones under the green trees, the devouring element sweeps upward in its wild fury, licks up the resinous leaves, and sweeps along over the tree tops with the speed of a racer, filling the atmosphere for miles with a dense and suffocating smoke. Three men lost their lives in the midst of one of these fires, a few days ago, and prudence dictates to us that we should camp at a small prairie, or open glade rather than venture to run the fiery gauntlet of the road before us.

After dark, the lurid glare of the burning forests – the curling eddies of flame – the illuminated clouds of smoke rising above the mountain tops, make up a picture terrible in its sublimity! Camped with us tonight is D. R. Carlton, of La Salle. On the next morning, the fires having swept on past the road, we continued our journey, and after crossing some tremendous hills – over some "rough and rugged road" – we descend a long hill and find ourselves, after we have crossed a small branch of Clear creek, twenty-four miles from

Gregory Gold Diggings, Colorado
From a contemporary wood-engraving

the base of the mountains, and in the very heart of

GREGORY'S DIGGINGS [148]

A busy scene now presents itself to the eye; for, where a few weeks ago the solitude of the mountain wilds was unbroken save by the occasional howl of the wolf, the whirr of the grouse, or the growl of the bear, we now find a throng of men, three or four thousand in number, actively engaged in building houses, washing gold, butchering beeves, bartering goods, prospecting, and loafing – the latter class, however, being largely in the minority. Upon crossing the creek we beheld a carpenter building sluices, and in a tent near by hear the groans of a man who has had his foot shot to pieces by the accidental discharge of a gun.

Below us, along the stream a number of claims have been taken, and men are busily engaged in turning the water into a new channel that they may work the old bed, which, as far as prospected, promises to pay well. The Diggings, as at present defined, embrace an area of some three miles in length, by a mile east and west. They were discovered early in may by Messrs. Gregory and Allen – Mr. G. having discovered the first "quartz lead." At first, and for several weeks, only one gulch was opened or thought to be a paying one, but within a few days a number of others have been opened, and thoroughly "prospected," and in nearly every instance afford rich enough dirt to pay remunerative wages. The gulch I speak of as having been first opened [after that of Gregory], lies two and a half miles from

148 The vicinity of present Central City and Black Hawk. The Gregory Lode, first vein of gold found in the region, was discovered by John H. Gregory of Georgia on may 6, 1859. The lode was located between present Central City and Black Hawk. A historical monument marks the site.

the ravine where most of the houses are located, and was discovered by the celebrated Georgian, Green Russell; his claim pays very largely – from sixteen dollars to twenty dollars per day to the hand – and is daily growing richer, the gold getting more abundant and coarser as he goes down.

The quartz leads are the most striking feature of the new mines, and I will now proceeed to describe them. Let us cross the summit of that high hill, keeping a good look out for auriferous indications. Do not, however, as you would in California, watch to see white and crystallized quartz – for that is no particular "sign" here; but look – what a singular ledge or outcropping of sharp hog-backed rock is this, jutting up from the surface some twelve or fifteen inches generally, and running in a southwest and northeast direction – it appears to have been upheaved edgewise, and its color is a deep purplish red; upon close examination it turns out to be quartz – but the fires have changed its color, so that you would scarcely have recognized it, and it is no longer a solid but a porous, spongy stone, comparatively hard on the surface but soft and honey-combed as you dig down into the "vein."

We have a pick and shovel with us, so tracing the "lead" along to a favorable point, where it is distinct, and where we are not liable to be deceived by the "drift," which is often the case on side hills, we commence unearthing the "blossom" and loose rock immediately beneath it. Varying in depth from two to eight feet, we will strike upon a hard, flinty rock, several inches thick, known as the "guard rock," through which we have to work our way; beneath this we find a crevice from six to twenty-four inches wide, and this crevice is filled with a soft clayey dirt – decomposed quartz – which yields from the start from fifteen cents to twenty-five cents to the pan, of fine gold.

As you go down the gold increases in quantity, and the particles become somewhat coarser. Having now determined that our "claim" will pay, we will take our axes and cut out a path down to water, where we can set our "sluices." If the hill be very steep, and the distance not over a quarter of a mile, we will rig a track down which to slide the dust in raw hides, or we will get some hand sleds and hire men at two dollars and fifty cents a day to drag the dirt down; if, however, the dirt be very rich and situated a mile from water, we will try to open a wagon road, and haul the decomposed quartz to the sluice – albeit there is scarcely sufficient grass within several miles of the "diggings" to afford sustenance to our cattle. Having overcome the difficulty intervening between our "claim" and the "sluice," we will commence "washing."

The gold is so fine that great care must be exercised in the construction and operation of the sluice – but this being properly attended to, we commence work with assurance of success. The gold readily separates from the clay – what cannot be otherwise saved is caught with quicksilver – and the chunks of burnt quartz which remain are carefully thrown into a heap, which will be preserved until a quartz mill is in operation, for it is fully as rich as the clay. Sometimes, however, a lead which has opened well, after we get down fifteen or twenty feet "runs out" – that is, there is no longer a crevice.

A question then at once arises – has the vein run out entirely, has it slipped off the original vein, or has a hard rocky shelf been thrust across the vein? Generally it is found to be the latter, which is cured by blasting; sometimes, however, it is found that a "slide" has occurred, which is remedied by drifting up the hill ten or twelve feet; but it is not often that the vein is entirely lost. A great many claims have been opened in these diggings, and nearly all of them are paying well. I have seen sluices cleaned up, which gave, as the proceeds of twelve hours run, from one hundred to three hundred dollars; but occasionally, owing to some mismanagement, the yield is very small, whilst the "tailings," being run through a rocker, will yield good wages.

The reader will not suppose, however, that all the "leads" pay largely, for some of them are "bogus" – that is, the "indications" are all right, but the gold lies too low to make it profitable to open leads; but it is now being suggested that a tunnel through the hill will reveal the leads in all their richness, and a company will commence one of these great enterprises in a few days. In some instances the yield from these claims is much greater than I have stated above. Many who have made claims do not work them, but have sold them to companies who proceed at once to open them, paying weekly installments, one-half of the proceeds of their mining, until the claim is paid for – the price ranging from five hundred to forty thousand dollars. Many of the miners are working two sets of hands – running their sluices night and day.

We were in the Gregory Diggings three days; when we first went in, we learned that all the claims were taken – that the only show for us would be to buy. We kept our eyes open, however, and succeeded in securing several claims which I think will open well; these we secured without purchase, and left four of our party to watch after them. The water privileges at Gregory are not first rate, for it is thought that all the gulch streams will dry up by the first of august – but it is to be hoped that the anticipation may fail of realization. In reference to every word I have written in regard to the yield of these mines, I wish it to be distinctly understood that I am not mistaken and have not been deceived. In future letters I shall have more to say in regard to the auriferous resources of this region; and shall now content myself with a brief allusion to the different mining localities, and a general view of wages, etc.

THE SPANISH DIGGINGS

Are situated about seven miles south of Gregory, are all gulches, are occupied principally by Mexicans, and are rich.[149] The Mexicans are now selling out, and hunting new diggings. Here the coarsest gold is found that has yet been discovered.

THE JACKSON DIGGINGS

Are ten miles south of Gregory. Lead and gulch claims are in operation, some of which are paying well.[150]

THE JEFFERSON DIGGINGS

Are situated six miles north of Gregory, on the south fork of Boulder, or Nebraskus, and are quite extensive. There are not so many people congregated here yet, but

149 On the South fork of Clear creek, near present Idaho Springs.

150 The original discovery in this region was made by George A. Jackson on january 7, 1859. See the Jackson diary in the *Colorado Magazine,* XII, 201-214.

every day adds to the number that are crowding in. The claims here are of the lead, gulch and river character, and some of them are paying well. Our company – the "Rocky Mountain Union Mining Co." – have a large number of claims here, of each kind, all of which prospect well. We have just put in a sluice one hundred and thirty feet long, and will be able to give you a report of our operations by the time I write again.

THE TWELVE-MILE GULCH

Is near Boulder creek, at the above distance from Boulder city. Some of the claims are paying well; quite a number are mining here, and I have seen considerable gold which has been dug in these gulches. It is of excellent quality, both coarse and fine.

BOULDER CREEK

Where it leaves the mountains, yields an excellent prospect, of the finest quality of coarse gold. We have just completed a big dam across the river, which drains one thousand feet of the bed, and we will soon know what is in it. Three more dams are now under process of construction – draining more than a mile of the creek. I will now give you a brief statement of

PRICES AND WAGES

In my last letter I gave you the prices current at Denver and Auraria. The rates are about thirty-three and one-third per cent greater in the mines for all ordinary goods and provisions. The price for shoeing horses is one dollar per shoe; half-soling men's boots, two dollars and fifty cents a pair; crowbars are worth twenty dollars; drills, eight inches long, six dollars – there being only a few in the country; day laborers are getting from one dollar and fifty cents to two dollars and fifty cents per day; whip sawyers wages are from three dollars to five dollars per day; lumber is worth twenty-five dollars per hundred feet, and very ready sales; the use of a whip saw is worth four dollars and fifty cents per day – but steam saw mills will soon be in operation in different parts of this region which will reduce the price of lumber, it is to be hoped very materially.

ST. JOSEPH TO FORT KEARNY ROUTE

ST. JOSEPH TO FORT KEARNY ROUTE

Diary of Edwin R. Pease

Editor's Introduction

This diary came into the hands of Professor C. L. Camp of the University of California and from him was procured by the State Historical Society of Colorado. Dr. Camp had no data on Pease except a letter recommending him as a teacher.[151] Accompanying the diary was the tintype of a man, presumably Mr. Pease. But we cannot be sure of this, as there is no definite proof to sustain the assumption.

If Mr. Pease was "qualified properly to teach the English branches of an education," as the recommendation asserts, his strong points were not punctuation and capitalization. We have made the necessary alterations

[151] The recommendation reads: "Mc Henry Co., Ill. Dec. 10, 1859

"We the undersigned, Directors and patrons of the School taught by Mr. Edwin Pease in dist. No. 1, town of Seneca, Do hereby certify that he is qualified properly to teach the English branches of an education, and that he sustains a good moral character and has given good satisfaction both in government and mode of teaching and therefore can consciensiously recommend him to any who wish to employ a good and competent teacher

Hiram Huff	Lewis Hubbell	Ambrew Cowe (?)
L M. Woodard	D. B Sanborn	C L Clark
Morris Dickerson	P K Sanborn	James Randolph
Silas Dickerson	John Rairdin	Crawford Weaver
Frederic Fulton	Andrew A Weeks	Charls Rairdin
Michael Harmon	John Ackerson	A W Pike
	Orramus Turner	

in the diary, especially by insertion of periods, to make the construction and typography conform to that of the other diaries and of the *Series*.

The diary is written in ink in a leather-bound book which measures four and three-fourths by seven and one-eighth inches. The first page carries this title: "Edwin R. Pease Diary."

There were hundreds of persons who set out for the reported gold fields of the Pike's Peak region who turned back before reaching the Rocky mountains. Pease was probably one of these, for the diary ends abruptly after recording numerous poor reports and after his party decides to sell its supplies and divides.

Pease started from his home near Woodstock, in the northeast corner of Illinois, with cattle and wagons. These he loaded on the train near Elgin, Illinois, and took this outfit by the railroad which ran through Mendota, Galesburg and Macomb to Quincy. Here the stock and wagons were carried by boat on the Mississippi to Hannibal, Missouri, and thence by the newly-constructed Hannibal and St. Joseph railroad to the Missouri river. After crossing from St. Joseph to Elwood, the teams took the direct road west and northwest to Fort Kearny. Most of this route is along the well-known Oregon Trail. It was also the route, with slight variations, of the overland stagecoaches and the Pony Express.

Richard F. Burton took the stage over this route in august, 1860, and left us a good account of the trip in his *The City of the Saints, and Across the Mountains to California* (New York, 1862). His itinerary is reproduced as Appendix B in this volume.[152]

[152] For a detailed identification of this route, see A. B. Hulbert, "The

DIARY

MONDAY, APRIL 25, 1859. Start from home[153] this morning at nine o'clock. Many a tearful eye in our company this morning. Drive about seven or eight miles and feed our cattle. Start after dinner and drive about seven miles, passing through Woodstock and camping near Chrystal Lake. Pleasant and cold. Our first camp; all sleep in our wagons.

TUESDAY, APRIL 26. Had a heavy shower this morning and start at eight o'clock. Rather slippery this morning for our teams. In a mile's travel we pass through Chrystal Lake, a fine village. Pass through Algonquin in five miles more travel. Five miles to Dundee,[154] feed for noon between the two places and feed poor hay. Some rain today. Pass through Elgin at six o'clock, a nice city.[155] Drive four miles and camp. Poor hay tonight; late when we halt.

WEDNESDAY, APRIL 27. Leave camp at six thirty, a.m. Pleasant this morning, Leathermans station our camp. Two teams take the wrong road, hire a boy to bring them back, arrive at eleven fifty at the junction. Get our stock and baggage aboard at four o'clock and the

Platte River Routes," in his *The American Transcontinental Trails,* I. See this *Southwest Historical Series,* IX, 140, 180-181, for short descriptions.

153 There are no indications as to the location of his home, except in the distances and directions given to Woodstock and Chrystal Lake, in northeast Illinois. His home must have been about eight or nine miles north or west of Woodstock.

154 Algonquin and Dundee are on Highway 31, running north from Elgin, Illinois.

155 The population of Elgin in 1940 was 38,333.

trains leave at six o'clock. Ride all night in the cars; lay over from eleven p.m. till two a.m. at Mendota.[156] All pretty tired tonight.

THURSDAY, APRIL 28. Find ourselves between Galesburg and Mendota. Arrive in Galesburg at nine o'clock; feed our stock and have a good breakfast and Egg and myself take a walk. See two fine female colleges and one male. We start at eleven twenty-five a.m. After two miles' travel we come to Henderson grove, as fine a grove as I ever saw. Pass through Henry and McDonough county and find a fine farming country, some prairie and timber, some uneven country, but generally level. Everything is in blossom and grass looks fine around McComb and Tennessee stations. One car run off the [track] two and a half miles east of Plimoth [Plymouth]. Get our stock in to another car. Met an old school mate here, have not met before in three years. Leave here at eight forty-five p.m. and arrive in Quincy at one o'clock, a.m.

FRIDAY, APRIL 29. Commenced unloading our stock, which looks rather bad. Get some yards and feed them, after which we go to the Virginia house. Arise and find ourselves somewhat fatigued. After breakfast E. [?] Wells and myself go out in search of hay, find some at sixteen dollars per ton. We also saw some fine dwellings. We were informed that there were twenty-one churches and about twenty-two thousand inhabitants.[157] R. Allen Hill, E. Wells and myself go on to a very high mound where we get a fine view of the beautiful city, which we call a splendid sight. We load our stock this afternoon on board the "Fannie" [?][158] bound for Hanible [Han-

[156] Mendota is on Highway U.S. 34, 78 miles from Chicago.

[157] Quincy's population in 1940 was 40,469.

[158] The "Fannie" was operating between Quincy and Hannibal in april, 1859. See the preceding volume, page 299.

nibal], Missouri. This boat is very heavy loaded today with Pike's Peak trains. Arrive in Hanible in the evening. Here our stock, wagons and provisions were put on board of the Hanible & St. Joseph railroad.[159] Some rain this evening.

SATURDAY, APRIL 30. Leave Hanible at seven thirty a.m. and have to take second class cars from here. Beautiful timber and a fine country; pass men [?] and then a plantation with their slaves to work on it, pass through Palmyra at eight o'clock a.m. Here the country is mostly prairie after leaving this place, and but little cultivated. We occasionally pass through small towns building up. Honeywack [Hunnewell] is a small town on the prairie without a fence in sight. After leaving this place we pass through a fine grove and then come again to a fine prairie on which is a fine town called Shelbina; after going a short distance we come to a rough mountainous country, stop at five for supper. We start on and go fast. We go to sleep in the car and have a fine rest. Cars run fast and some are very much afraid that the cars will run off.

SUNDAY, MAY 1, 1859. Arrived in St. Joseph at four-thirty a.m. Find our stock all alive. Take them from the cars and feed them some hay, eat our breakfast at the Willow Grove house. Go and unload our supplies and wagons, during which time we had a fine shower and it cleared off fine. Go up in the city, write a letter home. Today watch the stock part of the day. Hitch up our teams and drive out on the green and camp. Build up a big camp fire, and rest well.

MONDAY, MAY 2. We arise this morning in good season. Go up to the city and finish our fit out. Went to the

---

[159] This road, completed in 1859, was the first railroad to reach the Missouri river.

ferry and Pike and myself go over on to the Kansas side in search of feed. Here is a nice place called Ellwood, in which is a printing press, some nice stores, and so forth. We go up a piece and find some rather light feed, return and find our teams on the move. Pay fifty cents for crossing our team over the Missouri river, which is a muddy, deep and swift stream. Drive two miles and camp in the woods.

TUESDAY, MAY 3. This morning some of us return to the city and on our return find our teams have gone on from the river. We find four miles of heavy timber on the border of which is Wathena.[160] Have about six miles travel to find our teams, some hungry I guess. Along here are some nice farms. Drive over an uneven prairie this afternoon and camp at night with poor feed, make about ten miles today. Leave Weeks and Fitch behind. Pleasant weather.

WEDNESDAY, MAY 4. Get a usual start this morning and drive over an uneven prairie, yet fertile and rich. Camp at nine a.m. on the prairie, have tolerable grass. W. Smith and myself took a stroll about three miles from the wagons in search of game. Find a small stream with little timber. Several go out hunting this afternoon, find no game. Have a pudding for supper, which is considered quite a rarity. Drive about three miles today, weather good. Singing and oudling [?] tonight.

THURSDAY, MAY 5. Start from camp at seven o'clock a.m. one mile west of Cottonwood spring and drive over an uneven prairie partly settled and in about eight miles drive we come to Wolf river,[161] which is a nice stream about seventy feet wide and a stony bottom.

160 Wathena is due west of Elwood and St. Joseph.

161 Wolf creek flows east and then north into the Missouri river.

Eat dinner here and move on over an uneven prairie about four miles and camp with good feed for cattle and water also. Eat in a claim shanty. Some timber on Wolf river. Drive about twelve miles, weather good.

FRIDAY, MAY 6. Leave camp this morning at eight o'clock, drove over a rough country, bad mud in low places, which makes hard traveling. Camp a short time at noon. Pike and I go on in search of camp, pass a nice spring and at the left of Hibans [?] go on to a small creek and camp. A very heavy shower, after which we have some supper and get our stock in. Drive about ten miles today, rains hard tonight, which gives us wet beds.

SATURDAY, MAY 7. Arise early this morning and have a hard time to get breakfast, everything is wet. Some time before we find our stock. Hitch up late and go one mile and a half and come to Hiawatha,[162] a nice town, the county seat of Brown county. Go on about three miles and camp. The country still continues rough and sloughy, feed a little better. Go some ways after water. Get bad news from the Peak. Weather good, drive about four or five miles.

SUNDAY, MAY 8. It being sunday morning we conclude not to travel and so we take a wash and I make my first attempt to make some bread, have tolerable success. A great many emigrants pass today. Have good news of gold at Pike's Peak. Pike and myself go out for

---

162 Hiawatha is on Highway U.S. 36, about forty miles west of St. Joseph. Pease is here following a more northern road than was taken by R. F. Burton and the overland stagecoach in 1860. See his itinerary reproduced in Appendix B of this volume. For a map of the stage route, see Root and Connelley, *The Overland Stage to California*. See the diary of Edward J. Lewis (edited by H. E. Pratt), recounting a trip from Bloomington, Illinois, to the Colorado mines, in 1860, published in the *Colorado Magazine*, XIV, 201-212. Lewis left the Missouri river at Nebraska City and traveled up the south side of the Platte.

stock and see some nice farms yet some distance off the road. Nice warm weather today, grass poor yet.

MONDAY, MAY 9. Start in good season this morning, cross a small stream early, go on about seven miles and come to a spring grove, go on about three miles and halt for our dinner. Today cross several small streams, a nice rolling country today. Some go on to look for camp, but we stop and camp in a slough, have very poor water and grass today. The boys return to camp in good cheer saying they had a good camp. Drive sixteen miles, weather good.

TUESDAY, MAY 10. This morning get breakfast in good season and two start after the stock. They find one yoke missing. We were afraid they were stolen but we find them and soon start on. Go on to Harris creek and water. Some timber here. Go on one mile to Nimehaw [Nemaha],[163] a fine stream on which is Richmond, the county seat of Nimehaw county. We drive on five miles to Wildcat and camp early. Drive today fourteen miles, very good roads and nice weather.

WEDNESDAY, MAY 11. This morning we have some wet things on account of the violent rain storm which we had last night. Rather tegeous [tedious] finding our stock this morning, but get a tolerable start. Drive on a mile or two and have to put six or seven yoke of cattle on one wagon to get out of the mud. Go on to Ash Point,[164] roads rather slippery. From Wildcat to Ash Point about four miles. Make about ten miles today and

[163] This was the south fork of Nemaha river, which here flows northward through the middle of Nemaha county.

[164] Here, or in this vicinity, the road Pease is taking intersects the route followed by Burton. See Appendix B. Ash Point was seven miles west of Seneca, Kansas, according to Burton.

camp early on Clear creek.[165] Meet a man on his return, given bad news. Weather clear.

THURSDAY, MAY 12. Had a very violent hail and thunder storm last night. We hear of wagons being blown over and cattle killed in it, but we meet no accident at all. We start this morning in rather wet circumstances, go on five miles and cross the Vermillion,[166] a rapid stream. A good country in Marshall county. Broke Fitches' wagon and he goes on to have it fixed. Make today about fifteen miles. Cross some nice streams and camp on one. Have a cold night. Meet forty-eight wagons going back.

FRIDAY, MAY 13. Stood watch last night till one o'clock. Very cold. Get an early start, drive about four miles and cross the Big Blue on a ferry,[167] a deep stream. Go two miles and eat a cold dinner. See an antelope today; some go out a hunting. This afternoon make seven miles. Today make thirteen miles. A new road and a poor one.[168] P. Wells goes hunting and does not return. Tonight cold and damp, camp near a spring. Hear bad news and see many returning.

SATURDAY, MAY 14 [1859]. Rains this morning and we conclude to start. But it rains all the time we travel. See lots of returning teams, hear all kinds of news. Go

165 A branch of the south Nemaha.

166 A branch of Big Blue river. Guittard's, at the principal crossing of Vermillion creek, became a famous stage and Pony Express station.

167 This may have been at or near Marysville, Kansas. The distance from the Vermillion to the crossing of the Big Blue as given by Pease – fourteen miles – is the same as that given by Burton from Guittard's Station (on the Vermillion) to the crossing of the Big Blue (at Marysville). But it seems strange that Pease does not mention Marysville. He may have taken a more northern route after crossing the Vermillion, such as the road that went by way of Oketo (shown on the Root and Connelley map).

168 This may indicate that he is taking a new road to the north of Marysville.

about seven miles and camp on Camp creek.[169] Pike and I go walking around and find in one of the camps lots of milk. Have a good fire built when we camp, built by Tige and Smith. See a wolf chase this afternoon. Make some bread and biscuit this afternoon, very good for me. Rainy and cold.

SUNDAY, MAY 15. Did not drive today, but stay in camp. See the wolvereens play ball and from them return and make bread and have pudding and milk, after which we have a heavy shower, wetting our covers through. Go over to Pike's wagon and read a long time, and go home and make my bed and E. T. Allen sleeps with me. Hear bad news again today from Pike's Peak.

MONDAY, MAY 16. Start this morning in good season and get into a bad mud hole the first thing, have a job to get out. Drive about two miles and on account of the rain we lay off till tomorrow. See today one hundred and twenty-seven teams on their return; hand carts, and all the bad news that could be told was. See some specimens of the gold. Clears off today, have a heavy mist tonight.

TUESDAY, MAY 17. After a cold night we hitch up and start. Go to Rock creek,[170] where gold has been discovered. We are now in Nebraska country, rough here. Rock creek is a swift running stream with high stony banks. There is a trading post here. Grass all gone on account of the hail storm on the twelfth and on this account of which our stock get no feed. Hear bad news today again.

WEDNESDAY, MAY 18. Start this morning in good

[169] This may be the stream which Burton (Appendix B) calls Walnut creek, and says was seventeen and one-half miles from the Big Blue.

[170] Burton calls it West Turkey or Rock creek. The crossing was about three miles northeast of Endicott, Nebraska. For a description of this route by W. B. Parsons, see volume IX of this *Series,* 180-181.

season and have a cold wind, go on about ten miles and E. Wells shot a fine antelope. Y. Dickerson, E. Knudtson and I go a hunting. Today cross the Little Sandy near where it enters into the Big Sandy. Camp on the Big Sandy,[171] a nice stream, where we have good grass and water and some fine antelope meat. Make about seventeen miles today. Good roads, make seventeen miles.

THURSDAY, MAY 19. Arise early this morning and have a fine antelope stew. Cross the Big Sandy, see as fine residence here as we have seen west of the River. A Pawnee Indian shot here a day or two ago. Go on to the Little Blue, a stream six or seven feet deep and sixty wide.[172] Good water and some fish, none got, though. Drive our stock across the river for feed, weather fine. Make about eighteen miles today.

FRIDAY, MAY 20. After a heavy rain we arise and get a good start, roads slippery. Go about seven miles and camp for dinner. See a large drove going ahead and a great many returning; hear very bad news. Pass a large Salt Lake train loaded with merchandise for that place. Make about thirteen miles today, cold and cloudy all day.

SATURDAY, MAY 21. Get a good start this morning. Weeks, Lyon and myself go a hunting today across the Little Blue, saw some wolves and one wild turkey. Drove about nine miles and camp for dinner. We came into camp at noon. Drive about nine miles more and look for camp. Have good wood, water and grass to-

171 A branch of the Little Blue, in western Jefferson county, Nebraska. Burton gives the distance from Rock creek to Big Sandy station as twenty-three miles.

172 The road now follows the valley of the Little Blue for about seventy miles, going to the north of Fairbury, Powell, Hebron, Oak and Ayr, Nebraska. This is the route of the Oregon Trail and of the stagecoach line.

night in the Little Blue. Make eighteen miles today, warm and pleasant.

SUNDAY, MAY 22. Being a beautiful morning we conclude to travel, and drive to Elm creek. Find plenty of wood and water for our stock. Country uneven, yet having a rich and fertile appearance. We still continue to hear all kind of news about the mines at Pike's Peak. Drive today fourteen miles and camp for night on a pleasant creek.

MONDAY, MAY 23 [1859]. Get an early start this morning and drive over a little more level country. After a drive of four miles we cross Thirty-two Mile creek.[173] Go on about six miles more and stop for dinner, in sight of a large Salt Lake train. After dinner Dickerson and myself go on in search of Emon Knudtson, which left the train at daylight, but not finding him we stop at the edge of the Platte bluffs and wait for teams, and as a storm was soon expected we camp without wood or water. O. Smith and I go to an adjoining camp and get some milk. Divide it among the crowd, drink it and go to bed.

TUESDAY, MAY 24. We arise this morning at three o'clock and make ready for a start to the river,[174] which we reach about eight o'clock, finding a wide shallow stream running swift and very muddy. As there was but little wood we have a hard time in getting breakfast, after which some of us leave teams and go to the fort,[175] which is about five miles. Here we meet Col. Leander,[176] the road engineer. He is a fine looking man. Get

[173] So named for its distance from Fort Kearny.

[174] The Platte river.

[175] Fort Kearny. For data on the fort, see this *Series*, IX, 140.

[176] Col. Frederick W. Lander (1821-1862), military man and civil engineer, who was employed by the federal government in western road making.

a letter from home, all well. Return to camp, four miles drive and pleasant. The storm blew over.

WEDNESDAY, MAY 25. Commenced arranging things for some to return and some to go ahead. Clouds up in the night and have heavy rain. Cold and rainy this morning, no wood. Some divide, we conclude to go on as we are and commence to sell off our surplus provisions, flour at three dollars, sugar at ten cents per pound, so as to lighten our loads as much as possible. Have little or no wood, and it is cold. Platte river water, which is bad as the river is rising fast.

THURSDAY, MAY 26. Some start to the fort in search of cart or wagon and return without any. New arrangements are made. We make an offer and are taken up in which Pike and Dickerson conclude to travel with us, putting in team with us. After changing our things we get supper and eat in our new family circle. It is a nice evening, and two wagons are going on, five in each wagon, and five or six are returning home. We sleep in our new homes.

FRIDAY, MAY 27. We arise this morning in good time and after breakfast we part with the boys that return and start on our way. Drive into the fort this morning in time to see the soldiers train, quite a sight for us. Go on about five miles and camp for dinner; water poor; pleasant and warm. Go on about five miles and camp on the banks of the river. Float wood is all. A nice evening, travel seventeen miles.

SATURDAY, MAY 28. Warm last night. Get a late start and drive nine miles and camp for dinner. Travel about five miles more.[177]

[177] The journal ends abruptly here. We are left to guess whether Pease continued on or turned back.

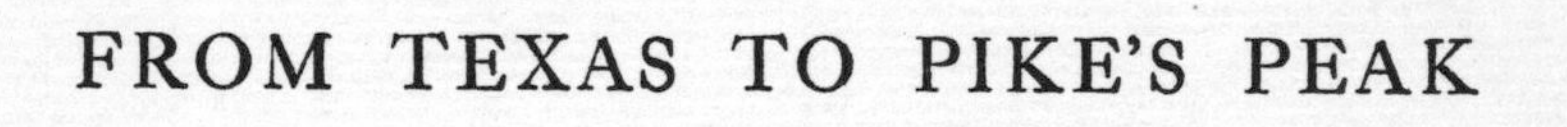
FROM TEXAS TO PIKE'S PEAK

FROM TEXAS TO PIKE'S PEAK

Diary of A. M. Gass
Editor's Introduction

This diary of a party of Texas gold seekers appeared in *The Standard* (Clarksville, Texas). Publication began on august 20, 1859, and was continued in the issues of august 27, and september 10, 1859. This interesting journal was found by Mr. Elmer R. Burkey while he was doing historical research work in 1937 for the State Historical Society of Colorado. We have found no biographical data on the diarist, Mr. Gass.

DIARY

LEFT BONHAM [178] on the 11th of april, 1859, and traveled west of north to Boggy depot, C. N.,[179] whence north of west to the Canadian [river], which we crossed at the mouth of Little river.[180] Thence to Shoto trading post,[181] and recrossed the Canadian to the south side; [182] then followed the divide [183] between the Washita and Canadian to the Antelope Butts.[184] On the twen-

178 Bonham, Fannin county, Texas, is on Highway U.S. 82, about sixty-five miles northeast of Dallas.

179 "Boggy Depot, Choctaw Nation," according to Grant Foreman, Oklahoma historian, "was a depot for the issue of rations to the emigrating Chickasaw Indians, established in 1839 on Boggy creek or river. It became a little inland village of considerable importance before the coming of the railroad." – Personal letter from Mr. Foreman in august, 1941.

It became a station on the Butterfield Overland Mail in 1858. See the map accompanying *The Overland Mail, 1849-1869,* by L. R. Hafen. Boggy Depot is some eight miles northwest of Caney, Oklahoma.

180 This would be about six miles southeast of present Holdenville, Oklahoma. "On the west side of Little river," says Grant Foreman, "was the trading settlement of James Edwards, where travelers almost invariably stopped to purchase supplies and have equipment repaired, etc. The place was known far and wide as 'Edwards'." Mr. Foreman has written much regarding it in his various historical books.

181 Chouteau's Trading Post, near present Lexington, Oklahoma, was established in 1835 by the well-known Southwest trader, A. P. Chouteau.

182 This crossing of the Canadian at the site of present Purcell, Oklahoma, was much used by the California emigrants. See Grant Foreman, *Marcy and the Gold Seekers.*

183 Along this divide went the route which was followed by Marcy and the California emigrants in 1849, by Lieutenant A. W. Whipple in 1853, and by other expeditions. Josiah Gregg also traveled this way.

184 Grant Foreman writes: "I am sure Antelope Buttes and Antelope Hills were names for the same group of elevations near the one hundredth meridian." They were on the south side of the Canadian and north of Crawford, Oklahoma.

tieth we first fell in with the buffalo. There are a great many in this part of the country. The entire company resolved itself into a committee of the whole, and made a general hunt of these ugly looking monsters of the plains. We killed eleven, the first evening. Since then they have ceased to be a wonder, and deer, turkeys and antelopes are so plenty, that the buffaloes are of no interest, except when we are hungry. The country this far (Antelope Butts), is one of the most beautiful farming countries, I have ever seen. There are fine running creeks in abundance; fish in inexhaustible quantities.

MAY 1st. Today we caught several large turtles – hard and soft shells, as large as fourteen inches across the back. Good eating I do assure you. The soil is a deep red color, and has great depth. The grass on the high divides is six feet high; last summer grass that has not been burnt off.

APRIL [May] 3rd. Today the company was startled by the appalling cry of Camanche, and truly they were coming like a small tornado. We called the company; it paraded in short order, and [was] drawn up in battle array to receive the savages in a proper manner. They continued to come, when within fifty yards they proved to be U.S. soldiers.

APRIL [May] 5th. Today we left the Washita river, and traveled up the divide to the Canadian. The face of the country is rather broken; yet in the valleys is the finest farming land. The valleys are wide, and well watered. Beautiful creeks and more or less timber on all of them – cottonwood, elm, hackberry and walnut, are the principal kinds.

APRIL [May] 6th. Today we are on top of the divide

between the two rivers before named, and a strange looking place it is. It looks like one vast potato patch – the round hills about one-fourth of a mile in circumference, and blood red; variegated now and then with veins of gypsum and ising glass [mica]. There are some awful looking canons ahead, with trees in them that you cannot see the tops of three hundred yards from them, and yet the trees are from sixty to one hundred and fifty feet high. Today is also a noted one in our travel, for we have killed a large black bear, weighing about 600 pounds.

APRIL [May] 7th. We came down the divide, to the Canadian, and camped, without any incident of interest.

APRIL [May] 8th. Today is rest day. We are camped in a very pretty place between the Canadian and Antelope hills.[185] We find a curious plant, with a very small top; but a root ten inches in diameter diminishing as it tends downward – about four feet in length, and in the middle tasting and smelling much like a yam potatoe; but very stringy outside.

APRIL [May] 9th. Today we are in prairie dog town, and have a fine time shooting them. Plenty of owls and rattlesnakes with them. Again startled by the cry "Camanches." Considerable excitement. False alarm.

MAY 13th. Today we crossed the Canadian, and shaped our course north thirty degrees west for Bent's Fort, and the Arkansaw.[186]

MAY 16th. We are now on a tributary of the Red

[185] See the preceding footnote.

[186] Inasmuch as they were at Antelope Hills on may 8 and do not leave the Canadian until the 13th, one would think they traveled some distance up the south side of the Canadian. But of this we are not sure. The direction taken upon leaving the river, and the fact that they reached the Arkansas at the lower Santa Fe crossing (see the entry below, of june 1st) would indicate that they left the Canadian shortly after passing Antelope Hills.

fork of Arkansaw.[187] Traveling is fine; water sufficient; grass good. There is an abundance of buffalo, alias curly mezquite, alias Bermuda grass, through this country. The soil is some lighter here than on the south side of the Canadian; the rocks are more flinty; timber is scarcer. We have, so far, had to cook with buffalo chips only one night; prairie dogs we are beginning to get familiar with, for we have been traveling through their towns for the last three days. The dog, itself, is indescribable – the only appearance of a dog about him, is his short, stumpy, *narrative,* the extreme end of which is tipped with black. Their yelp is similar to that of the fice from which resemblance, I presume they take their name.

MAY 17th. Today we left camp; and struck north twenty degrees west and arrived on the Red fork [188] of Arkansaw. The hills here, are mostly red soil, grass scant, timber tolerable, water plenty and good. The hills are covered with small boulders and pebbles of quartz and flint. This is the best prospect for gold, that I have seen during the trip. Yet in the valleys the sand is deep, and there are other inconveniences to overcome, to prospect successfully. We are camped on the north bank of Red river, for half a day, to rest. There have been some very heavy rains up here; yet we have not suffered any from them. They have fallen one or two days before us. So far as yet, we have not seen any hostile Indians, or any fresh sign of them. The boys are becoming braver each day, in the absence of danger. They even brag that they could kill an Indian every pop. I don't know how it would be.

187 This tributary was probably Wolf creek, a branch of the North Canadian river.

188 This must have been the North Canadian.

MAY 18th. Today we left the Red Fork, bearing north twelve degrees west. No buffalo sign since we crossed the Canadian. Deer and antelope plenty, yet they are like some of the young ladies, hard to come up with, and harder to bring down when you do get in reach. Prairie dogs, owls, rattlesnakes are the principal productions of this region. Speaking of snakes, the boys have only killed some sixty odd, today, as we traveled along. Today we have crossed another fine running stream.[189] The water is clear and cold, yet slightly impregnated with salt. I presume it is a tributary of Red Fork, but am not certain. We are camped on a high divide, and not a twig of timber in sight; but grass is good and water plenty (in our kegs,) which to some extent counterbalances the want of timber. Plenty of chips; so we are in no distress tonight.

MAY 19th. Nothing of interest has transpired today. We have traveled all day on a high divide,[190] camped without wood or water, except wood we hauled, and water standing in pools.

MAY 20th. Today we are still traveling over the divide – the country is becoming more broken. Today we captured young antelopes, which we have now alive. Tonight we are in sight of some water courses. I do not know what one it is. We are camped among the sand hills seven or eight miles from the stream. The face of the country here is covered with sand mounds from twenty to thirty feet. Weeds and grass are thinly scattered over them, yet there is fine grass between the mounds. Tonight we can get no wood – no buffalo chips to burn, yet we do better, if any difference, than if we

189 Probably the Cimarron.

190 They are crossing the eastern edge of the Cimarron desert.

could get the chips. We substitute the root of the wild sage, which grows here in abundance.

MAY 21st. Today we traveled north eight miles, then came in sight of Arkansas river, and Jerusalem, what a sight! Wagons – wagons – Pike's Peak wagons. Well! there were a few of them – I presume three hundred ox-wagons, in sight. I pressed forward to cross the river and have a talk with them. The river was muddy, and I thought was not deep; so bulged (never judge by outward appearances) and got half way across (two hundred yards) when the bottom dropped out, and I, and Big Dick – my horse – had to swim the rest of the way. I got over safe with a thorough wetting. I went up and spoke to the men; they told me sad news; said there is no gold at the Peak. Some that are going on, say that they have met three hundred wagons coming back, so convinced are they that there is no gold. One man came from the mines, and has some gold dust in a quill, and says there is no coarse gold there, a man cannot earn his provisions. We are going to see for ourselves. We struck the river one hundred and forty miles below Bent's Fort,[191] and three hundred miles from the Peak. We have to travel upon the south side of the river, for it is so high that we cannot cross it. There is a good road on this side, between the sand hills.

MAY 22nd. Today we are going up the river. We see a great many wagons on the other side; some turned back; some with their teams broken down; and some

[191] Gass does not indicate whether he means the *old* or the *new* fort. The original Bent's Fort, the more famous one, located some eight miles northeast of La Junta, Colorado, had been deserted since 1849. Bent's New Fort, across the river from present Prowers, Colorado, was operating in 1859. The distance from Bent's New Fort to the lower crossing of the Santa Fe Trail, at present Cimarron, Kansas, is approximately 140 miles, so Gass was apparently referring to Bent's New Fort.

resting their cattle. Today a rumor has reached us, that they have killed four men in the mines, for reporting false statements of gold – two hung, and three [sic] shot.[192]

MAY 23rd. Today our company has broken up. Some have become disheartened, and turned back for Fannin county. There are only three wagons out of seven still going on. Two of THEM have turned back, down the river. They are determined to cross, not wishing to go any higher, on this side. My wagon is still traveling up the south side of the river, and alone. There are four men of us, on this side; yet we do not apprehend any trouble. We intend to cross the river at Bent's Fort or Pueblo.

MAY 24th. Today we are still going up the south side of the river, and alone; we are getting along very finely. Today I can see twenty-eight wagons on the other side, going up. Two, are all I have seen coming back today. Hope, in me, is not yet extinguished.

MAY 25th. This morning the wind is whistling fiercely by; the heavens are concealed by lowering clouds; there is a drizzling rain descending; and to cap the climax it is so cold, that all our surplus clothing is very useful. Today we have only traveled six or eight miles; the rains has set in, very cold; and we are camped in a patch of small cottonwood bushes which will have to answer for fuel. The river is not so wide here as sixty miles below. The bottoms about here are from six to ten miles wide. The soil is sandy with flint and quartz pebbles scattered through bountifully. The soil is very good; the grass is tall and fine. The country is only tol-

[192] There were many such rumors, but all appear to have been false. See reports in the preceding volume (x).

erably well adapted to farming – not near so suitable as on the Canadian. I have seen no creeks putting in to the river. The main river itself is the only chance for water, and it is slightly brackish.

MAY 26th. Today the wind is blowing harder and colder than it did yesterday. The wind is from the north – in fact it is a severe norther, and very cold.

MAY 27th. Today our course has been upward and onward, still following the river. The valley has closed in so narrow, that the sand hills put in close to the river, and we have had to pull over them twice today. Timber is becoming more plentiful every day. The principal growth is cotton wood. Today we have found several beautiful fresh water springs. Musquitoes are a spontaneous production here. The soil and climate appear to agree with them. All kinds of game scarce – and plenty. Last night we had a very heavy frost, which killed most of the cotton wood leaves, and all the grape leaves.

MAY 28th. Today nothing of interest – monotonous traveling.

MAY 29th. Thus far (twelve o'clock, midday) nothing of interest, but much to annoy, if you would call quintillions of remorseless and bloodthirsty musquitoes any annoyance.

Night. We are camped on the bank of the river, with the advantage of wood, water and grass, and a fine place to fish. I caught a blue catfish twenty inches long, this evening.

MAY 30th. Today we are not traveling.

MAY 31st. Today we have traveled some sixteen or eighteen miles, and have, at last, got to Bent's new fort.[193] It is on the north side of the river, and is built of

[193] For description, see volume IX of this *Series*, pages 101, 178.

rock; is situated on a high bluff of sand stone, which terminates precipitously against the river. The river is up, and the ford is too [deep] to cross our wagon. A Chienne [Cheyenne] Indian came to us today: he lives at the fort, and can speak English. He says that there are but four men at the fort.

JUNE 1st. We are still going up the river, have crossed one very fine running creek. It is the first one we have seen since we first came to the river at the lower Santa Fe crossing.[194] The country is becoming more broken. We find large ledges of sand stone; abrupt terminating points of the high land as it approaches the river.

JUNE 2nd. Today, after traveling six or eight miles, we came to a tributary of the Arkansas river, known on the maps as Purgatory river.[195] It is a pretty stream, and is very heavily timbered with cotton wood, box elder and willow. We had to go up it two miles before we could find a crossing. The Arkansas backed it up and made it deeper than it would have been from its natural depth of water. After crossing, we found a curiosity to some of us. It was an Indian buried up a tree. There were poles laid on the branches of the tree, forming a level platform, over which the willows were bent very nicely, and secured with raw hide strings; the whole covered with buffalo skins, a skin also living [lining?] the curiously constructed tomb. Inside of this is the corpse rolled up in blankets. The first blanket is rolled around the body, then tied on securely with a tug. The

---

194 This indirect reference is the first definite statement given as to where they reached the Arkansas river.

195 It enters the Arkansas just east of Las Animas, Colorado. Regarding this stream, see A. W. McHendrie, "Origin of the Name of the Purgatoire River," in the *Colorado Magazine*, v, 18-22.

same plan is followed until three blankets are around the body, when the bows, arrows, spoons, cooking utensils, and other valuables are placed around the corpse, when comes another envelope of blankets. Then a buffalo robe is securely fastened around all, and the body is then placed in its aerial vault.[196] One of our men climbed up to it, and as soon as he was convinced that it was a half rotten Indian, he came down fast, and as pale as a sheet.

Above the Purgatory river I find a vein of excellent stone coal. What amount there is, I cannot say positively, but I believe it is inexhaustible. The country is well adapted to agricultural purposes.

JUNE 3rd. We are still going up the Arkansas. We passed Bent's old Fort,[197] this afternoon. Here we find some blue limestone with veins of satin spar traversing it northeast and southwest. Timber, water and grass plenty and good.

This evening the clouds came up thick and fast, the wind blew, the lightning flashed, the thunder roared, and the rain descended in torrents. We camped and pitched our camp in short order.

JUNE 4th. Today we have passed some of the best land I have seen on this river. It is a very black sandy soil. The bottoms, here, are on an average four miles wide. The ground is covered with an luxuriant growth of wild sage from one to ten feet high. Today we saw some very fine veins of stone coal, where it cropped out of the creek banks. The coal is of an excellent quality, and there is plenty of it.

JUNE 5th. Today we have seen nothing unusual, ex-

[196] The Cheyennes, Sioux and some other plains tribes buried their dead in this manner.

[197] See volume IX of this *Series*, page 101.

cept the snow covered mountains, which we are at last in sight of. At least some of the high points are very white, and we presume it is snow. Today we have passed over some very fine land, good soil, and in large bodies.

JUNE 6th. Today we came to Auteby's ranch, situated on the west side of Huerfano river.[198] The ranch consists of some four or five square cabins, built of round cotton wood logs, and covered with poles and mud-flat roofs. The owner, himself, is an old French trapper; his wife is Mexican. They are farming on a small scale. Corn is three or four inches high. The snow clad peaks I spoke of yesterday, are Pike's Peak and its associates, and they are about one hundred miles off. The Huerfano river comes from these white peaks and is as cold as snow.[199] Huerfano is the Mexican term for orphan. In attempting to cross the Huerfano, we were a little unlucky. It is very swift and the banks are steep. In driving our wagon in, one side of the bank being higher than the other, the wagon capsized in the water, which is five feet deep. After considerable discussion of the difficulty, which I am sorry to say was not done in pius terms, we got out, and unloaded to dry: and this ended this day's progress.

JUNE 7th. Today at twelve noon, we find everything dry, and not much damaged. We backed up and started down to the Arkansaw, to cross, there being a small boat near by. Before getting to the river, we got into a bog, and had to unload before we got out of it, carrying all our load forty or fifty yards through water and mud three feet deep. Oh, I know you envy our happiness. But we are now out of the slough of Despond, and are

198 For a note on Charlie Autobee and the Huerfano river, see volume IX, 102-103.

199 The Huerfano rises near the Spanish Peaks, instead of at Pike's Peak.

comfortably camped on the bank of the river, wet to the waist, and ready to enjoy life. There are, I presume, some fifty persons here, at Auteby's. They are farming by irrigation. They raise fine corn and pumpkins, and very fine garden vegetables. They sell their corn for five dollars a bushel. Flour is worth fifteen dollars per hundred pounds, bacon, fifty cents per pound, coffee, forty cents, sugar – none in the country. The people here say that the Indians would eat the world up, regardless of price, if it were made of sugar.

JUNE 8th. Today we unloaded our wagon, took it to pieces, and have crossed the Arkansaw, in what may truly be called a 'dug-out.' We left the crossing, and have come eight miles up the river. There are five or six log shanties put up along in that distance, occupied by whisky sellers. The land is not good, judging from the color, grey sandy.

JUNE 9th. Today we have traveled up the north side of the Arkansaw, until noon, when we got to Fountain city,[200] which consists of forty or fifty log and mud cabins, inhabited by Americans and Mexicans; or rather WERE; for most of them have gone to the diggings. We are now following up a small stream known by the name of Fountain Chabougha [Fontaine qui Bouille], or boiling springs. It heads near Pike's Peak, of which we are now in full view – can see the snow up there, which, looks so nice and cool, while it is as hot as blazes where we are. We are daily hearing better and better news of the gold mines.

JUNE 10th. Still going up Fountain Chabougha. Land good in the valley – grass scarce.

JUNE 11th. Two months out from home today; and

[200] Part of present Pueblo, Colorado.

as I raise my eyes Pike's Peak appears about two miles from me; yet it is fifteen miles away. The gold diggings are some sixty or more miles further on. The Peak is a grand sight; is said to be twelve thousand feet high.[201] One-third of the top is covered with snow. There is some, as fine farming prairie around the base of the Peak, as I have seen anywhere. Plenty of timber on the mountains and creeks. We nooned, today, at a spring of the coldest and best water that I have seen on the route. It is known as Jimmy's spring,[202] or Alexander's grave; a Missouri man, by the latter name, having been buried here on the twelfth of april, 1857.[203] Tonight, we are camped by a beautiful spring, beside a pinery, pine timber is the only kind in sight. It is from one to two and a half feet in diameter, twenty to forty feet without limbs. The grass here is good. This region, I think, is well adapted to the growth of corn.

JUNE 12th. Today we are traveling through an extensive Pinery,[204] twelve miles across. Five miles from the edge of the pine, there is a branch of clear, cold running water. On this creek are three graves, two of them made this spring; the other in '58. From these, six miles, we get to Fagan's grave [205] which is also on a beautiful branch. The land passed over today is very indifferent; fit only to grow pine and strawberries. There is an abundance of the vines, which are just in bloom; berries, not formed.

---

[201] The altitude is 14,109 feet above sea level.

[202] For data on Jimmy's Camp, see volume IX, 104. Frank Hall, in his *History of the State of Colorado,* III, 341-342, says that Jimmy Hayes established his trading post at this point in 1833, and that he was killed here by Mexicans.

[203] We have found no further data regarding this.

[204] From this pinery Denver received most of its lumber during the early years.

[205] See volume IX, 105, for information on Fagan.

JUNE 13th. Today we are traveling over a high divide. Tonight we are camped on the far famed Cherry creek. Very little gold has been as yet discovered on this creek. I saw a man wash a pan of the surface dirt. He got about one cent of very fine scale gold. Under the surface there is no gold, as they have not been able to find a bed stone. There has been much work done here prospecting. Several cabins have been built, and forty or fifty more commenced and left unfinished;[206] and nearly all have left here and gone to Clear creek diggings, west of the Platte river. The gold here is of fine quality, but not in sufficient quantity to pay. The most that I can hear has been made here in a day, was one dollar and fifty cents. There is a steam saw mill here, on the head of the creek, and it is making a vast amount of timber; yet can hardly supply the demand, at eight dollars per hundred, at the mill; which increases to thirty dollars, in the mines, sixty miles from here. Denver city is thirty miles from the head of this creek. We have to go there to cross the Platte; ferriage eight dollars.

---

[206] This was Russellville. See map accompanying volume x.

LEAVENWORTH AND PIKE'S PEAK EXPRESS ROUTE

LEAVENWORTH AND PIKE'S PEAK EXPRESS ROUTE

Diary of Albert D. Richardson

Editor's Introduction

A new and shorter route than previously traveled was explored and marked early in 1859 by the Leavenworth and Pike's Peak Express. This company, the organization of which is described in the preceding volume of this *Southwest Historical Series* (pp. 288-289), was formed in early february, 1859, by W. H. Russell and John S. Jones. They decided to establish a line of stagecoaches from Leavenworth City to Denver and were anxious to select the shortest practicable route. Accordingly, they dispatched a party to make a reconnoissance of the line. Of this preliminary survey we find the following account in the *Leavenworth Times* of april 30, 1859:

"THURSDAY AFTERNOON [april 28, 1859], Messrs. Ewbank and Downing, two experienced mountaineers and old Californians, returned from the *reconnoissance,* upon which they with others had been dispatched by Messrs. Jones and Russell, of the Overland Express. Their statements are clear and explicit and must effectually put an end to all idle cavilling, as to the wisdom and foresight of the company in adopting a route which they pronounce unequalled for the requirements of travel, and of which the maximum distance is not to exceed five hundred miles from Leavenworth to Denver city.

"The locating party left this city on the fifteenth of march, were several days in Denver city, were obliged to halt at least three days to refresh their animals, and at no time traveled after dark, and yet they have performed the round trip in forty-four days, taking into account all detention which they met with, and the time necessarily consumed in the performance of their duties. They left Denver city on the ninth of april, and were thus only nineteen days on the return journey, two and a half days being lost by necessary stoppages on the road to recruit their animals. Here is their description of the route.

"After leaving Junction city our party struck out on the divide between the Republican and Solomon's forks, bearing mostly towards the latter stream; thence the route passes over the tributaries of the Republican Fork, up that stream until the divide between the Arkansas and South Platte is reached, through extensive pineries, thence to the headwaters of Cherry creek and along that stream to Denver city. On this route there is no poisonous or alkaline water, nor sage brush, two peculiarities and disadvantages of the Santa Fe route; there is no sand except in one body of forty miles in extent, and this is along the Republican, with plenty of water, timber and grass close at hand. They further say that the region over which they just traveled, is the best grass country in the West, that there is an abundance of water and timber for emigrants and that in these essential respects, it is far superior to the Platte route.

"The company have in all, twenty-seven stations, seventeen of which were erected and in full operation when this party returned, and the rest were going up, and are undoubtedly ere this completed. They passed the stages which left Leavenworth on the eighteenth, near the head waters of Solomon's fork, and are fully convinced, according to the progress which the coaches had made, that they reached Denver city on the 28th instant, and since they themselves returned a greater distance, and far more leisurely than the coaches traveled, the conclusion is perfectly just. The road from Junction city is far better than that from this city to Fort Riley. It is smoother in surface, and there are no streams of any magnitude to pass, nor in fact any that may not be readily forded at all times. The Government had located the site for a substantial bridge over the Blue, where there is now an excellent ferry; in short, there have been no representations made of the route, which are not more than sustained by the statements of these gentlemen. . .[207]

"Messrs. Ewbanks and Downing estimate the number of people in and about Denver at about one thousand.

"The emigrants were beginning to arrive, and a hand cart company reached Denver about the time our informants departed. They passed a continuous line of wagons and people on their way, all following the express route, and getting along well. A simple instance of the advantage of this route in speed over the Platte road is given. Mr. Smith, who carried out an express via the northern route, and left the Missouri several days previous to the departure of these parties, reached Denver as they were about returning. Mr. Smith very

207 There follows a description of Denver and of mining prospects in the region.

naturally concluded to return by the route, which, we opine, will very soon absorb the entire travel to the mines."

On april eighteenth the first stages – a pair of Concords – set out from Leavenworth.[208] B. D. Williams and John M. Fox, officials of the company, were aboard. The party reached Denver on may 7.[209] Of the trip and the route Williams writes as follows:

"Denver City, K.T. May 9, 1859

"Mr. J. S. Jones, Leavenworth City, K.T.:

"DEAR SIR: – The road which we have just laid out between the thirty-ninth and fortieth parallel of latitude from Leavenworth city to Denver city, is 689 miles in length by the roadometer, which will be reduced to five hundred when properly straightened out, passing over the most beautiful and fertile country in the Territory. After leaving Junction city our course was along the tributaries of the Solomon, about ten miles from its north bank, crossing beautiful streams of never failing water every six to ten miles. Leaving the waters of the Solomon, we struck over to those of the Republican, and struck Prairie Dog, Sappa, and Cranmer's creek, near their head, then traveling a long divide of twenty-six miles we reached the main Republican, just above the mouth of Rock creek, and made station No. eighteen, in a beautiful grove of cottonwoods.[210] Up to this point, wood and water is in abundance; also, grass in the proper seasons. After leaving No. eighteen, we kept up on the southern side of the

208 See the preceding volume, pages 299 and 315.

209 *Rocky Mountain News,* extra, may 9, 1859. The returning coaches reached Leavenworth on may 20.

210 The route will be traced and discussed in connection with the Richardson diary, below.

Republican to near its head, when we crossed the main prong to the middle prong, which we followed to its head. Along this portion of our route, wood is scarce and hard to get; grass and water plenty. We then kept our course, and struck what we think is the most southern branch of the Republican, on which we established station No. twenty-four, where another road comes in from the southeast. We traveled up this road about fifteen miles, when it bore off to the south. We continued our course due west, and struck Bear creek, with wood and water, and made station No. twenty-five. Continued west, and in ten miles reached the pine forest. Continuing our course through high prairie, we passed a large forest of pine, crossing the Bryou [Bijou] and two Kioways, and reached Cherry creek twenty-two miles above its mouth, and then traveled down one of the most beautiful vallies I ever saw, and very fertile, until we reached Denver city, when the people all flocked together to look at the stages, etc. . . [Discussion of the mining prospect follows.] Yours truly,

B. D. WILLIAMS, Agent, L. C. & P.P.E.C." [211]

The most satisfactory accounts of journeys over the Express company route are those of the journalists, Horace Greeley, Albert D. Richardson and Henry Villard. Inasmuch as Richardson's journal is the most complete and specific, it is presented here. Supplemental data from Greeley, Villard and others will be supplied in the notes.

[211] *Leavenworth Weekly Times,* may 28, 1859. In the same issue of this paper appeared a letter written from Denver by J. M. Fox on may 8, 1859. This letter was published in the preceding volume of this *Series,* pages 344-347.

DIARY[212]

MAY 25 [1859]. I left Leavenworth by the overland mail carriage built in Concord, New Hampshire, known as the Concord wagon.[213] In a dozen localities its manufacture is imitated with more or less success but never equaled. . .

Two coaches, each drawn by four mules, leave Leavenworth daily and make the entire trip together, for protection in case of danger from Indians. A crowd gathered in front of the Planters' House to see our equipages start. Amid confused ejaculations of "Good-by, old boy." "Write as soon as you get there." "Better have your hair cut, so that the Arapahoes can't scalp you." "Tell John to send me an ounce of dust." "Do write the facts about the gold," the whips cracked and the two stages rolled merrily away.

Beyond Easton [214] and Hickory Point we passed hundreds of freight and emigrant wagons stalled in the mud. William H. Russell the chief freighter of the plains, owns many of them. Last year he employed twenty-five thousand oxen and two thousand wagons, chiefly in transporting supplies for our army in Utah.

---

212 Taken from Albert D. Richardson, *Beyond the Mississippi* (1867), 159-177. For biographical data on Mr. Richardson, see volume x of this *Series*, page 42.

213 For a description of the Concord stagecoach, consult L. R. Hafen, *The Overland Mail*, 306, 309. See also E. G. Burgum, "The Concord Coach," in the *Colorado Magazine*, XVI, 173-180.

214 Easton, on Stranger river, about ten miles west of Leavenworth City, was named for L. J. Eastin, pioneer Kansas newspaperman. For data on Mr. Eastin, see volume IX of this *Series*, page 229.

ALBERT D. RICHARDSON
From a photograph, about 1880

He stipulates that any one of his teamsters who whips cattle unmercifully or utters an oath, shall forfeit his wages. Of course the precaution proves ineffective, for there is a logical connection between mud-holes and profanity.[215]

Before night we entered the Pottawatomie Indian reservation,[216] where prairie wolves, prairie hens and rabbits abound. Spent the night at Silver Lake (Station four),[217] with a half-breed family. Playing upon the floor were two dusky children both, as we were informed, born like Richard with teeth; and in the mother's arms reposed an infant three months old, whose jaws already displayed similar ornaments.

At midnight arrived two return coaches from the mines. The passengers encountered the Missourian, with whose horrible story we were already familiar.[218] He showed them the severed head of his brother, and declared that he found the brains a delicious morsel. Day's travel sixty-eight miles.

MAY 26. This morning rode in a driving rain over the prairies. Passed St. Mary's Catholic Mission [219] – a pleasant, home-like group of log-houses, and a little frame church, bearing aloft the cross – among shade

[215] Russell, Majors and Waddell was the great freighting firm of the day. Alexander Majors was the religious one in the partnership, and was responsible for the rules regarding profanity, etc. See his *Seventy Years on the Frontier.*

[216] The reservation was in Pottawatomie and Calhoun (now Jackson) counties. See the map of Kansas and Nebraska published by J. H. Colton in 1859.

[217] This was at the present town of Silver Lake. Mr. George Root, of the Kansas State Historical Society, from his study of the stage route, concludes that the first three stations were: Leavenworth City, Easton and Ozawkee.

[218] We shall present data on this famous tragedy in the section on the Smoky Hill Trail.

[219] St. Marys is at the junction of the present highways, U.S. 40 and number 63.

and fruit trees, in a picturesque valley. The mission has been in operation twelve years. In the school-room we saw sixty Indian boys at their lessons.

Rock creek was swollen to a torrent, which compelled us to spend the afternoon and night at the city of Louisville – a city of three houses.[220] Its hotel affords the inevitable fat pork, hot biscuits and muddy coffee. The land lady is a half-breed; and her two daughters with oval faces, olive complexions and bright black eyes the only pretty Indian girls I have ever seen.

Scores of emigrants are encamping along the stream. One having caught a turtle as large as a peck measure, invited us to partake of a savory soup, which we imbibed from tin cups, sitting on a log.

Two returning coaches filled with passengers were detained on the opposite side of the stream through the night. One enterprising traveler attempted to reach our side in a skiff; but was overturned, and gained the bank by swimming. Day's travel twenty-eight miles.

MAY 27. At daylight the creek had fallen so that our mules crossed without swimming. Some of the countless emigrants on the road have cows yoked with oxen, serving as motive power by day and giving milk at night. We passed one two-wheeled cart drawn by a horse in the shafts, with a yoke of oxen before him. Beyond the three houses which compose the town of Pittsburg, we crossed the Big Blue and reached Manhattan – a flourishing Yankee settlement of two or three hundred people in a smooth and beautiful valley.[221] It is overlooked by a conical mound two hundred and fifty feet high,

[220] Louisville, on Rock creek, is about three miles north of Wamego (on U.S. highway 40).

[221] At the junction of the Big Blue and the Kansas rivers. The population of Manhattan in 1940 was 11,659.

commanding a fine view of the rich, well timbered soil along the Kansas and the Blue.

Thus far I had been the solitary passenger. But at Manhattan Horace Greeley after a tour through the interior to gratify the clamorous settlers with speeches, joined me for the rest of the journey.[222] His overland trip attracted much attention. A farmer asked me if Horace Greeley had failed in business, and was going to Pike's Peak to dig for gold! Another inquired if he was about to start a newspaper in Manhattan. And as we were leaving one station an Indian girl said to a new-comer: "Horace Greeley in his old white coat is sitting in that coach!"

Twenty miles beyond, after passing three large farms based on "a horizontal rather than a perpendicular agriculture," we reached Fort Riley, one of our most beautiful military posts, and in the geographical center of our national possessions. All the buildings are two stories high, of light limestone resembling marble.[223]

Just beyond, we crossed the Republican river,[224]

---

222 Greeley's account of the trip was published in his *New York Tribune* and subsequently in *An Overland Journey from New York to San Francisco in the summer of 1859* (1860).

223 Henry Villard went with the second pair of stagecoaches over the Express route to Denver. He was at Fort Riley about three weeks ahead of Richardson and Greeley. Of the post Villard writes: "Fort Riley is the best military post I have seen upon my extensive travels through the West. Officers' quarters, sutlers' establishments, stables, etc., all have an appearance of solidity and cleanliness which differ greatly, and pleasingly to the eye, from the rudely constructed cabins of which the towns we had passed consisted."

This is taken from a letter written by Villard at Denver on may 17, 1859, and published in the *Cincinnati Daily Commercial,* june 3, 1859. Villard was a special correspondent for this paper.

224 Greeley (*An Overland Journey,* etc., 72) reports that they crossed the Republican by a rope ferry. He says: "All day, as on preceding days, we had been meeting ox-wagons loaded with disheartened Pike's Peakers, returning to their homes, but some of them going down into southern Kansas in search of 'claims'."

which rising near the Rocky mountains, winds eastward for six hundred miles and here unites with the Smoky Hill fork to form the Kansas. The dim, conical, smoky hills from which the chief tributary is named are visible on the horizon though a hundred miles distant. Timber abounds near the fort; a cottonwood tree nine feet in diameter, was recently cut here. We stopped for the night at Junction city (Station seven), the frontier post-office and settlement of Kansas.[225] The editor of its weekly newspaper, an old Californian, spoke with great enthusiasm of the Golden State. Mr. Greeley replied:

"I have heard some hundreds of returned Californians use the same expressions; but one thing I cannot understand. If you liked California so well why didn't you stay there?"

"Because I was a d—d fool!" replied the roving journalist.

In the evening by invitation of the citizens, Mr. Greeley addressed an attentive audience in the unfinished stone church. Theme, "Republicanism." Day's travel forty miles.

MAY 28. At a creek-crossing, a little tent beside our road is labeled "grocery" in enormous letters. With keen appetites we awake the melancholy merchant who

[225] George Root says that St. Marys was station five, and Manhattan was station six. Of the route to Junction City, Villard says *(op cit.):*

"From Leavenworth to Junction City the route of the Express company follows the old military road to Fort Riley. It leads over undulating prairies that occasionally change into hilly elevations; are traversed by streams of water, and combinedly form landscapes whose claims to beauty are as well founded as that of any other section of the West. Many towns are springing up on the banks of the various creeks that course across the country toward the Kaw river, among which Easton on the Stranger, Ozawkee, and Manhattan on the Big Blue, and Junction City, a short distance from the Republican, are the most prominent."

in green spectacles is sleeping soundly between two whisky barrels.

"Have you any crackers?"

"Nary cracker."

"Any bread?"

"Any what?"

"Bread."

"No Sir," (indignantly,) "I don't keep a bakery."

"Any ham?"

"No."

"Any figs?"

"No."

"Well what have you?"

"Why I have sardines, pickled oysters, smoking tobacco, and stranger, I have got some of the best whisky you ever seen since you was born!"

The narrow valleys of the streams are still rich; but the upland soil grows thin and sandy. At one fertile valley-farm we saw herds of fat cattle and a corn-field of a hundred acres, in addition to the common frontier spectacle of a tow-headed mother, with nine tow-headed children.

Left behind were the last outposts of civilization; now

> Away, away, from the dwellings of men
> To the wild deer's haunt, and the buffalo's glen.

Dined at Chapman's creek,[226] in a station of poles covered with sail cloth, but where the host, superior to

[226] This according to Greeley (*An Overland Journey*, 75), was station eight, twenty-three miles from Junction City. They were now following the new road of the Express company. From Junction City it led northwest, along the divide between the Republican and the Solomon forks of the Kansas river. It crossed Chapman's creek about fourteen miles from Junction City and thence followed the west side of the creek to Station 8.

daily drenchings, gave us an admirable meal upon a snowy table-cloth.

Timber disappearing; only straggling fringes remain along the creek, with an occasional solitary tree on the prairie indicating the whereabouts of water.

Began journeying now among the buffalo grass, two inches high, thick, wiry, nutritious and little injured by frost or drowth. Prairies spangled with wild onions, and antelopes bounding over the slopes.

Met thirty Cheyenne Indians on a begging and stealing expedition, who asked for whisky and tobacco. Nearly all bore certificates of good character from white men; but one solemn old brave complacently presented me the following testimonial which some wag had given him:

"This Indian is a drunkard, a liar and a notorious old thief; look out for him!"

Stopped for the night at Station nine,[227] consisting of two tents. In the evening wrote newspaper letters in the coach by a lantern. As the air was damp and chill with rain and the vehicle shaken with wind, I fancy the *Tribune* printers will find Mr. Greeley's manuscript even less legible than usual. At ten o'clock composed ourselves to sleep in the carriage to the music of howling wolves and heavy thunder. Day's travel sixty-eight miles.[228]

MAY 29. Wild roses, wormwood of various species, thistles, narrow-leafed dock and many other new plants

227 This station, according to Greeley (p. 80) was on Pipe creek, a tributary of the Solomon. The station appears to have been at a point where the settlement of Pipe creek was later founded (shown on the General Land Office Map of Kansas of 1879). This was about three miles northwest of present Lamar, in Ottawa county.

228 Greeley reports the distance as fifty-eight miles, which appears to be more accurate.

and flowers, some of rare beauty, appear along our road.[229] Crossed Hurricane creek, named from a furious tornado two weeks ago, which overturned heavy freight wagons, blew a light buggy into fragments, tore open boxes and scattered dry-goods for several miles, and rolled cooking-stoves forty or fifty yards.

The distant slopes are dotted with the antelope, the best living illustration of the poetry of motion. Miles away, when his earth-colored body is quite indistinguishable, one sees his white tail fluttering in the breeze like a shred of linen – a perpetual flag of truce to human enemies. Here he ventures near us, but on the older roads, rifles and shot-guns have made him shy and difficult to approach. Old hunters are wont to stick a ramrod in the earth with a handkerchief flying from it, and then conceal themselves among the grass or sand-hills. The antelope, lured by a curiosity fatal as mother Eve's, circles nearer and nearer, until he falls by the cruel bullet. From a close view his liquid eyes suggest infinite pathos and more than human tenderness. He is easily domesticated, and naturally tame.

The antelope and the buffalo are antipodes. One is incarnate grace; the other clumsiness itself. The antelope gallops airily over the hills, with an elasticity surpassing the fleetest racehorse. The buffalo is heavy and awkward; and the male, with huge head and enormous shaggy neck from which the hair hangs to the ground, canters lumberingly along like a mastodon suddenly awakened and uncertain of his native element.

Dined at Station ten [230] sitting upon billets of wood,

---

229 Greeley says the route was parallel to the Solomon fork, two to six miles from the stream.

230 If this station was halfway between numbers nine and eleven, it was probably a few miles northeast of Beloit, in the northeast corner of Mitchell county.

carpet-sacks, and nail-kegs, while the meal was served upon a box. It consisted of fresh buffalo meat, which tastes like ordinary beef though of coarser fiber, and sometimes with a strong unpleasant flavor. When cut from calves or young cows it is tender and toothsome.

Hundreds of deep buffalo trails cross our road; and through the whole afternoon the prairies for miles and miles away, quite black with the huge animals, look like bushes covered with ripe whortleberries, or like woodland afar off. The cows are about the size of our domestic cattle. The bulls are twice as large, and roll in the sand and wallow in mud-holes like hogs. While great droves are feeding in the valleys they keep sentinels on the ridges, ready to give notice of the approach of danger. Running herds produce clouds of dust, and shake the earth like thunder. The calves are kept in the center of the drove for protection against men and wolves.

A huge tree beside our road is completely covered with names of emigrants and dates and messages for their friends behind; an ingenious and very public post-office.

Six weeks ago not a track had been made upon this route. Now it resembles a long-used turnpike. We meet many returning emigrants, who declare the mines a humbug; but pass hundreds of undismayed gold-seekers still pressing on.

One Ohio wagon bears the inscription, "Root Hog or die." A returning passenger states that further on he encountered a philosophical emigrant whose wagon was labeled, "Pike's Peak or Bust." One after another the traveler's cattle died, till only one cow and an ox were left. During a luckless night these either strayed away or were stolen by Indians. The next day my informant found this prairie Micawber sitting upon his wagon-tongue smoking his pipe and waiting for something to turn up. But under the first inscription he had penciled with charcoal: "Busted, by thunder!"

Spent the night at Station eleven,[231] occupied by two men who gave us bread and buffalo meat like granite. Day's travel, fifty-six miles.

MAY 30. Large gray wolves abound near our road. They often kill old or wounded buffaloes, and sometimes open graves and devour human bodies. Upon this newly-opened thoroughfare through the heart of the buffalo country the animals are very tame. Tens of thousands are feeding beside the track, and they often cross it five or six yards before us, compelling the driver to stop, lest they should stampede the mules. The mule

[231] Station eleven was at the junction of the Leavenworth and Pike's Peak Express route and the "Parallel Road" leading due west from Atchison, Kansas. From this junction to Denver the two routes were identical. A detailed log of the Parallel Road, from the notes of E. D. Boyd, was published in the Atchison *Weekly Champion,* june 25, 1859, and are republished in this volume as Appendix A. Boyd says that Station eleven was 172 miles west of Atchison, 31 miles west of the Republican, and ten miles north of the First Standard Parallel south of the Base Line. He gives the location at latitude 39° 42′, longitude 98° 12′. The First Parallel runs through Atchison and forms the southern boundary of Jewell and most of the other northernmost tier of Kansas counties.

According to Boyd's mileages, the location of Station eleven would be about three miles north of present Ionia, in southern Jewell county. His longitude reading would place it a few miles east and north of Ionia.

Greeley (p. 80) says Station eleven was on a stream which he calls Clear creek, and he says that the road from Stations nine to eleven was from two to six miles north of the Solomon. Richardson says Station eleven was fifty-six miles from Station nine. Greeley's Clear creek is probably the stream shown as Limestone creek on the General Land Office Map of Kansas of 1879. Greeley would appear to place the station not more than six miles north of the Solomon, and thus a little south of Ionia. A compromise between the Boyd and Greeley distances would give us a location for Station eleven at about the site of present Ionia.

never becomes reconciled to buffalo or Indian, and if stampeded, the most rheumatic animal will dash off at incredible speed. In some instances they have run fifty miles before they could be stopped.

One serene old bull approaches within twenty rods of us and the driver waits while I fire at him again and again with Sharpe's rifle. He continues to approach, only greeting each ball that strikes him with a nervous movement and switch of the tail, as a sensitive horse would respond to a fly. As he is facing me I am unable to hit him back of the fore-leg; and forward of that, the buffalo is not vulnerable. After I have fired four or five times he turns and limps slowly away into a ravine. Afterward I fire at several others with the same brilliant success. Mr. G. [Greeley] urges me to continue, on the ground that it amuses me and does not hurt the buffalo; but is quite too uncertain of his own marksmanship to try the rifle. . . .

At Station twelve [232] where we dined, the carcasses of seven buffaloes were half submerged in the creek. Yesterday a herd of three thousand crossed the stream, leaping down the steep banks. A few broke their necks by the fall; others were trampled to death by those pressing on from behind.

This afternoon our coach was stopped at a creek-crossing by a mired wagon which blocked the road. Several Ohio emigrants with their weary cattle were endeavoring to extricate it. . . .

After being mired in the same creek for two hours, our own vehicle was drawn out by the oxen of friendly emigrants. Spent the night at Station thirteen.[233] Day's

[232] Boyd (see Appendix A, at the end of this volume) locates Station twelve on a creek 32½ miles from Station eleven. The station was probably about six miles north of Gaylord, Smith county.

[233] Greeley (p. 86) places Station thirteen on a stream he calls Reisinger's

travel, fifty-six miles, buffaloes the whole distance.

MAY 31. Though still plentiful, the buffaloes are diminishing. Mr. G. believes them nearly identical with the buffaloes he has seen on the Campania, in Italy, though considerably larger. But the authorities call the American animal the bison, to distinguish him from the Asiatic buffalo. The former was never seen by Europeans till Cortez and his followers found two or three in the zoological gardens of Montezuma.

When Lewis and Clark ascended the Missouri, half a century ago, a herd of these animals crossing at one point choked the stream for a mile, compelling the explorers to wait till they had passed. Their report hesitatingly asserts that they thought they saw twenty thousand at once; but I am confident we looked upon forty thousand from one stand-point, and that in all we have seen half a million. For several days we have never been out of sight of them except when our coach was in some deep ravine.

To-day we have been among prairie-dog towns, passing one more than a mile long. Some of their settlements are said to be twenty miles in length, containing a larger population than any metropolis on the globe. The little animal is a trifle larger than the gray squirrel, subsists on grass and has none of the characteristics of the dog but his yelp, which is like that of a young puppy. Small owls perch upon the mound beside his hole; but there are no signs of the traditional rattlesnake said to be an unwelcome joint occupant of his subterranean city, whose labyrinthine passages honeycomb the ground. The hillock of earth extracted from each hole, is ten or twelve inches high and two feet in

creek. Station thirteen appears to have been about six miles east of Phillipsburg, in Phillips county.

width. Upon this stands the prairie-dog, erect on his hind legs. His house is his castle. His own picket and scout, he maintains a sharp lookout for his foreign enemy the wolf, and has an occasional domestic feud with his persistent co-tenants, the rattlesnake and the owl. . . .

We spend the night at Station fifteen,[234] kept by an ex-Cincinnati lawyer, who with his wife, formerly an actress at the Bowery Theater, is now cooking meals and making beds for stage passengers on the great desert three hundred miles beyond civilization. The mimic stage presents few sharper contrasts. Our road, following the valley of the Republican river, is here two thousand three hundred feet above sea-level. At midnight arrives a return coach bringing a fair delicate Indiana boy who ran away last spring, froze his feet en route for the mines, and after many hardships is now glad to return to home and school. Day's travel, fifty-six miles.

JUNE 1. Like Dombey and Son the Indiana boy proved "a daughter after all!" She was dressed in male costume with a slouching hat which she wore at table to conceal her features. She talked little, but in walking from the tent to the coach her gait betrayed her. She is twenty years old; appears intelligent and well educated; professes to be returning to her parents in Indiana after spending three months in the mines; but gives

---

234 Richardson does not mention Station fourteen. According to Boyd, it was on the Solomon river drainage and 27½ miles from Station thirteen. This would place it at the eastern edge of Norton county.

Greeley (p. 91) locates Station fifteen on Prairie Dog creek, a branch of the Republican. Boyd says the road crosses the divide between the Solomon and the Republican drainages twelve miles west of Station fourteen, and that the road reaches Prairie Dog creek three miles beyond the divide and follows the creek 10½ miles to Station fifteen. This would place Station fifteen in west central Norton county, Kansas.

no reason for her dangerous and unwomanly freak.

Dined at Station sixteen,[235] kept by a Vermont boy who has roamed over twenty-seven States of the Union. Near it was encamped a party of Arapahoes, with thirty or forty children playing upon the grass. Those under four or five years were entirely naked. The older boys wore breech-clouts of buffalo skin, and the girls were wrapped in robes or blankets. All were muscular and well developed. Old trappers assert that they never saw an Indian idiotic or naturally deformed. Only in the centers of civilization, the bee-hives of the human race, are the helpless little ones thus smitten. Herbert Spencer describes the British laws as "those twenty thousand statutes which every Englishman is supposed to know and which no Englishman does know." Relentless nature is like the State. She presumes every man to know her laws; she pardons none for his ignorance; she inflexibly punishes every disobedience. Nay, severer still, she visits the sins of the fathers upon the children to the third and fourth generation.

Indian women, accustomed to hard labor in the open air, never compel a traveling party to stop more than three or four hours on the birth of a child. If left behind they overtake the expedition the same evening or the next day, with the little new-comer strapped on the maternal back. They ride astride like men.

The boys of this company were very expert with the bow, easily hitting a silver half-dollar at sixty or seventy yards. All were inveterate beggars, asking by signs for food and drink. Their camp consisted of twenty

[235] This station, according to Boyd, was near Sappa creek. At a point ten miles beyond Station fifteen and twenty-one miles east of Station sixteen, Boyd took an astronomical observation and recorded the latitude as 39 degrees, 52 minutes; longitude 100 degrees, 7 minutes. This point, if his readings were correct, would be near present Reager, in Norton county.

conical lodges twelve or fifteen feet high – buffalo robes with the fur inside, stretched around a circle of poles. These dwellings ten or twelve feet in diameter, with a hole at the top for the escape of smoke, are warm in winter and cool in summer. The Sibley tent used in our army is modeled upon them.

In front of each the shield and quiver of the brave rested upon a pole or tripod. The shields, worn upon the left arm, are covered with antelope skin or buffalo hide stuffed with hair, and will usually ward off any rifle ball which does not strike them perpendicularly. The bows have great force, sometimes throwing an arrow quite through the body of a buffalo.

Several squaws who were making moccasins fringed with beads offered me a pair for a cup of "sooker" [sugar]. Others were eating soup with their fingers from a kettle, while naked children on the ground were gnawing tough buffalo meat. A dozen muscular half-naked braves lying in the sun shook hands with me, declaring themselves "Good Indians." But only yesterday they threatened to kill and scalp a station-keeper unless he should leave their country.

Descending an abrupt hill, our mules, terrified by meeting three savages, broke a line, ran down a precipitous bank, upsetting the coach which was hurled upon the ground with a tremendous crash, and galloped away with the fore-wheels. I sprang out in time to escape being overturned. From a mass of cushions, carpet-sacks and blankets soon emerged my companion, his head rising above the side of the vehicle like that of an advertising boy from his frame of pasteboard. Blood was flowing profusely from cuts in his cheek, arm and leg; but his face was serene and benignant as a may morning.

He was soon rescued from his cage, and taken to Station seventeen,[236] a few yards beyond, where the good woman dressed his galling wounds.[237]

From their village near by many Cheyennes pressed around our baggage which was scattered upon the ground. They are instinctive thieves, and we watched them with drawn revolvers until it was carried to the station. There were three chiefs in the party: "Little Bear," "Antelope," and "Black Wolf." Two had cut-throat faces; their features, as often occurs among savages of every race, reminding one strongly of wild beasts. But Black Wolf looked good-humored and honest. Complacently joining me in a cigar he assured me by signs and the few English words in his vocabulary, that he was going to shoot "heap of buffaloes." Then pointing toward the west and digging in the ground with his fingers he ejaculated: "Money! money!" to indicate his knowledge of the gold discoveries. An old brave of at least ninety now hobbled up, telling me in dumb show that he was aged, almost blind and should soon sleep in the ground, and – would I give him a little tobacco?

In the evening Black Wolf took me through his village. The warriors wore long hair dressed in cues, and lengthened by a strand of buffalo hair until it reached the ground. Ornaments of tin and silver jingled from their ears. The cheeks and foreheads of squaws were painted bright vermillion. At nightfall the women

236 Station seventeen, according to Greeley (p. 98) was on Gouler creek. Boyd records: "Station 17 – on N. [north] bank [branch?] of Sappa creek." The station was probably on what is now Beaver creek, which is the north branch of Sappa. The distances given eastward to Station sixteen and westward to eighteen substantiate the identification of Station seventeen on Beaver creek. It was probably near present Ludell, Kansas.

237 Greeley tells, on page 106, of the upsetting of the coach.

brought in the ponies and picketed them among the lodges, that they might not be unprepared for a midnight alarm. In profoundest peace, the Indians maintain all the system and precaution of an army in time of war. As usual we sleep in the coach which, vibrating in the strong prairie wind, rocks like a cradle. Day's travel forty-nine miles.

JUNE 2 [1859]. Mr. Greeley awoke so stiff and sore that he could not move a muscle without suffering; but we continued on by the sandy valley of the Republican, destitute of tree and shrub and barren as Sahara.[238] Spent the night at Station nineteen.[239] Day's travel, sixty-four miles.

---

238 They had passed Station eighteen and presumably had made the noon stop there. At this point Greeley writes (p. 100): "I would match this station and its surroundings against any other scene on our continent for desolation." The station was on the south bank of the Republican river.

Mr. E. S. Sutton, of Benkelman, Nebraska, has determined the route through Nebraska. In the field notes of the base line survey (fortieth parallel of north latitude, and boundary between Kansas and Nebraska) made in august, 1859, by C. A. Manners, Mr. Sutton found the exact point where the road left Nebraska. This was on the South Fork of the Republican. He contacted Mr. Arthur Carmody of Hitchcock county, Nebraska, who found in the field notes this description of where the road entered Nebraska: "Jones-Russell Express Road to Denver City bears N.W. 76.25 ch west of S.E. one-quarter sec. 35 town 1 range 34 W." This is about two miles west of where present Highway 25 (between Atwood, Kansas, and Trenton, Nebraska) crosses the state line.

County divisions and the range lines in this section of Nebraska were run in 1869 and subdivisions in 1872. The field notes of these surveys show the location of the road. From these various notes and from examination of the terrain, Messrs. Sutton and Carmody determined the route of the old road. They locate Station 18 in section 29, township 2 north, range 35 west. This is about four miles west of Stratton, Nebraska.

239 The road, following the south fork of the Republican, had re-entered Kansas. Mr. E. S. Sutton has found the remains of an earth enclosure that appears to be the ruins of Station nineteen. This is in section 34, township 1 south, range 39 west. It is the proper distance (26 miles) from Station eighteen. The location is about twelve miles northeast of St. Francis, in Cheyenne county, Kansas.

JUNE 3. Encountered several Indian villages moving; their ponies drawing the lodge-poles, beside carrying heavy loads upon their backs. The life of these Indians is simply a bivouac, never a settlement....

As usual passed hundreds of emigrants. The latest coach from Denver brings fine specimens of gold dust, and reports new rich discoveries, to the great elation of all the pilgrims. At Station twenty-one [240] where we spent the night, we first encountered fresh fish upon our table. Here the enormous cat-fish of Missouri and Kansas has dwindled to the little horned-pout of New England, lost its strong taste and regained its legitimate flavor. Day's travel, fifty-nine miles.

JUNE 4. We still follow the Republican which at one point, sinks abruptly into the earth, running under ground for twenty miles and then gushing up again. We saw one thirsty emigrant digging in the dry bed for water. At the depth of four or five feet he found it; but it argues a lively imagination to speak of such a sand plain as a river. These subterranean passages are as common among the streams of our deserts as in the far Orient.

After riding twenty-five miles without seeing a drop

240 Boyd says that Station twenty was on the Republican, twenty-three miles beyond Station nineteen. Number twenty was a little east of the Kansas-Colorado line, in southwestern Cheyenne county.

Station twenty-one, according to Boyd, was at latitude 39 degrees 33.5 minutes; longitude 102 degrees, 26 minutes. Dr. Margaret Long, in her article, "The Route of the Leavenworth and Pike's Peak Express," in the *Colorado Magazine,* XII, 187, locates the station in "Sec. 4, T. 6 S., R. 45 W., in Kit Carson county, Colorado. At Station twenty-one Greeley wrote (p. 103) that he had traveled ninety miles up the south branch of the Republican" (which forks a few miles above Station 18). Greeley and Boyd both say that the water in the river disappeared six miles above the station. This dry river bed began at the mouth of Spring creek and continued to Station twenty-two, twenty-three miles above.

of water, at Station twenty-two [241] we crossed the Smoky Hill route which from a point far south of ours, abruptly turns northward across the Republican to the Platte.[242] Emigrants who have come by the Smoky Hill tell us they have suffered intensely, one traveling seventy-five miles without water. Some burned their wagons, killed their famishing cattle and continued on foot.

We are still on the desert with its soil white with alkali, its stunted shrubs, withered grass, and brackish waters often poisonous to both cattle and men. Day's travel, forty-eight miles.[243]

JUNE 5. At daylight [244] Pike's Peak more than a hundred miles away, appeared dim and hazy on the horizon and we began to feel the inspiring breath of the

---

241 Five and one-half miles below this station Boyd made the following readings: latitude 39 degrees, 23 minutes; longitude 102 degrees, 49 minutes. The station appears to have been located at the junction of the South Fork of the Republican and its Sandy fork, about four miles north of present Seibert, in western Kit Carson county, Colorado.

242 Greeley writes (p. 108): "From this point [Station twenty-two] westward, the original Smokey Hill route is abandoned for that we had been traveling, which follows the Republican some twenty-five miles further."

243 This brought them presumably to Station twenty-three. Boyd does not give the exact location of this station, but places it between mileage points 346 and 350½. Station twenty-one, of the previous night, was at mileage point 300½.

244 Apparently some night driving was done here, and no stop made at Station twenty-four, which was on the Big Sandy. Upon leaving the Republican, Greeley writes (p. 109): "A ride over a rolling 'divide' of some twenty miles, brought us to the 'Big Sandy,' running southwest to become a tributary (when it has anything to contribute) to the Arkansas." Boyd makes the distance fourteen miles from the head of the Republican to the Big Sandy (which he describes correctly but which he calls the South Fork of the Republican).

Station twenty-four, where the road struck the Big Sandy, must have been about seven miles northwest of Hugo. This location is arrived at by the measurement from this station to the point where the road leaves the Big Sandy, at its abrupt bend, a little west of present Riverbend. Boyd gives this distance as seventeen and one-half miles. Boyd's astronomical readings at mileage point 358 (see Appendix to this volume) are apparently right as to longitude, but are certainly wrong as to latitude (being about fifteen miles too far south).

mountains. Most emigrants were encamping out of respect for the Sabbath, and the sore feet of their cattle, which they carefully bandaged.

At our dining Station, twenty-five,[245] I met several old Kansas acquaintances, so dust-covered and sunburnt that for several minutes I did not know them. That would be a keen-eyed mother who could recognize her own son at a glance under the dirt and disguise of plains-travel. Toward evening, Pike's Peak loomed up grandly in the southwest, wrapt in its ghostly mantle of snow and streaked by deep-cut gorges shining in the rays of a blazing sunset –

> The seal of God
> Upon the close of day.

In the northwest Long's Peak was sharply defined against a mass of ominous black clouds which rising slowly left behind them a scattered trail, dark and wild as the locks of the storm-god. . . .

Supping at Station twenty-six[246] we made a comfortable bed in the coach, and rolling on at the rate of seven miles an hour, slept quietly through the night.

JUNE 6. Woke at five, still in motion, and obtained a glorious view of the mountains, their hoary peaks covered with snow and their base, thirty miles across the valley into which we were descending, seeming not more than two miles away.

At last we struck the old trail from Santa Fe to Salt

245 Boyd locates this station ten miles beyond the abrupt bend of the Big Sandy and on a dry creek that runs north to the South Platte river. This creek is doubtless the east fork of the Bijou.

246 Boyd places this station on Kiowa creek, at the following location: latitude 39 degrees, 29 minutes; longitude 104 degrees, 29 minutes. At the Horse Shoe Ranche, near this location, in Section 32, Township 6 south, Range 62 west, Dr. Margaret Long found traces of the old trail. See her article in the *Colorado Magazine,* XII, 193. Station twenty-six was about ten miles north of the present town of Kiowa.

Lake,[247] rode a mile along the dry bed of Cherry creek,[248] and at eight this eleventh morning reached Denver city. Day-and-night's travel, one hundred and thirty miles. During our journey from Leavenworth we have doubtless passed ten thousand emigrants.[249]

---

[247] This trail came over the divide between the Arkansas and South Platte drainages and descend Cherry creek. See the map in volume x of this *Southwest Historical Series* for the route in this area.

[248] The Leavenworth and Pike's Peak Express road struck Cherry creek fifteen miles from its mouth, according to Boyd. Greeley says that the stage in which he and Richardson were riding, stopped at sunrise to change mules on Cherry creek, twelve miles from Denver (at the mouth of Cherry creek). For recollections of this station see James Harvey, "The Twelve Mile House," in the *Colorado Magazine,* XII, 173-178.

[249] If this figure is correct it indicates a large emigration to the gold fields, for the Platte river and the Arkansas routes were traveled by many more gold seekers than traversed the Leavenworth and Pike's Peak Express road.

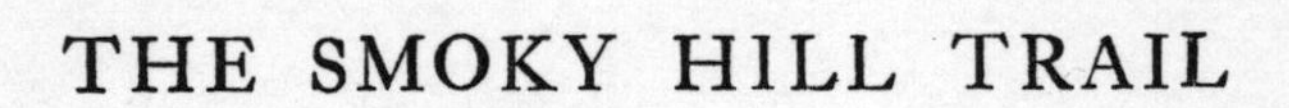

THE SMOKY HILL TRAIL

THE SMOKY HILL TRAIL

Introduction

The Smoky Hill trail followed the Kansas river and its Smoky Hill branch to the source of this affluent, and thence went over dry stretches of the high plains to the upper waters of Cherry creek and down this stream to Denver.[250] It was a short route to the gold region, but one that for long stretches was inadequately supplied with water and grass. Of the emigrants who took this course in the spring of 1859, all endured great hardships and a number perished. The trail was generally condemned by the early gold seekers. The following expression in a Denver newspaper was typical: "Three roads will be traveled next summer. The Arkansas, by those from the South and Southwest, the Smoky Hill by the foolhardy and insane, and the Platte by the great mass of the emigration.[251]

Despite misfortunes suffered on the Smoky Hill trail in 1859, its directness continued to recommend it. Especially was Leavenworth city interested in its use and especially in the establishment of Leavenworth as the eastern terminus and outfitting point. Early in 1860 this ambitious city raised funds and sent out an expedition to locate a practicable route. The *Leavenworth Times* of march 30, 1860, reported the employment of William

[250] For the western section of the trail see the articles of Dr. Margaret Long in the *Colorado Magazine,* IX, 218-231; XI, 70-78.

[251] *Rocky Mountain News,* april 11, 1860.

Green Russell, pioneer Colorado prospector, to explore such a course. His report is published below.

No satisfactory diary covering the Smoky Hill Trail in 1859 has been found. In lieu of such, we present a number of contemporary reports concerning this route and travel upon it.

PERILS OF SMOKY HILL ROUTE [252]

We were called upon yesterday by James W. Hamilton, of Palestine, Crawford county, Illinois, just returned from Pike's Peak, who gave us the following narrative. We will state that Mr. Hamilton represents himself to be a farmer, in good circumstances, living on the Wabash, and for the truth of this statement, he can be addressed by letter either at Palestine, Illinois, or Merom, Indiana.

He left home on the first of march and arrived at St. Louis the next day. At St. Louis he was met by an agent, or one who represented himself as such, of Jones and Russell's Leavenworth and Pike's Peak Express, who informed him that by going to Leavenworth he could take the Express stages, which left every morning, and go through to the mines in ten days, for fifty dollars. He accordingly shipped for that city, and on his arrival went to the Express office to engage passage for himself and a young man he was taking with him. He was there informed that "the stages would not start before the first of april." Here he was informed that the route to go was by the Smoky Hill, as it was well supplied with wood, water and camping places, throughout its whole extent, and was two hundred and fifty miles nearer than any other.

[252] Printed in the Kansas City *Journal of Commerce,* may 25, 1859.

He accordingly took the mail stage to Fort Riley and Junction city, arriving there on the sixteenth of march. He then bought two mules on Saline creek, and fitted himself with blankets, robes and provisions for the journey – sufficient to have taken them through with comfort, had the route been anything like what it was represented to be. The company at this time numbered nineteen men, two mules, and seven ponies. After leaving the settlements beyond Junction city, every vestige of a road vanished, and for about one hundred and twenty-five miles they found the country cut up by deep ravines and difficult streams, but wood and water sufficient for all necessary purposes, although the water was very brackish in many places, and it was with great difficulty they could use it.

They were guided by directions on printed cards, which had been furnished them by the agent at St. Louis and at Leavenworth; but after leaving Junction city these became perfectly worthless, being false in everything they pretended to give.

For several days they kept on over a barren plain, destitute of everything to support life, and seeing nothing on all sides but sand, they turned northward and traveled for three days without discovering any traces of timber. They followed for two days what they supposed to be a wagon track, but on coming to a sandy creek it was discovered they had been tracing the trail of Indian lodge poles, which our frontier readers so well understand. Their provisions giving out they in despair abandoned the effort and turned their faces southward, and after four days hard travel reached the Arkansas river, about forty miles above Bent's Fort.

It needs no other evidence than the appearance of

Mr. H. to believe in the suffering he has undergone. For nine days the party had nothing to eat but prickly pear and wild onions, and were three days and nights without a drop of water. The only flesh they had during two weeks was a rattlesnake they killed and ate the day before they reached the Arkansas. So emaciated had they become, that when they reached provisions, they had to be watched through the first night and fed a moiety at a time. Our informant describes the suffering for want of water, as the most horrible to be conceived. He could have consented to have died, and died with resignation, of hunger, but the want of water was maddening.

Mr. H. states that his party left a company of five Frenchmen, about two days before they reached relief, who had given up, and refused to go farther. He has never heard from them since.

He states that there is not the slightest sign of a road anywhere on the route he was sent over; and that not a word of truth was told him from the time he landed at St. Louis until he left Junction city. He was told at Fort Riley by a soldier not to undertake the trip, but the "agents" told him he was only a common soldier and knew nothing of what he was talking about. Mr. H. speaking of his return says:

"I returned by the Arkansas and Santa Fe roads. It is the best road I ever traveled of anything like its length. I was two days at Bent's Fort. From Pawnee fork to the mines I have never seen a road in the States that can compare with it, except a plank road. I met wagons that started from Kansas City with from two to four yoke of oxen, that were going along easily with but one yoke, the others being loose, and grazing along the road; one yoke being driven part of the day and then another. So easy and solid is the track. I saw others with mules, which had only one span attached to the wagons, the others having been taken out of harness, to ride. I met not a solitary case of suffering – the stock all looked well, the men cheerful and in fine spirits – the only complaint being that in some instances the Indians had stolen cattle."

A LEAVENWORTH COMPANY'S TRIP TO THE MINES
Special Correspondence from Denver City [253]

We are finally here, but such a trip! It is dreadful to contemplate. Let me briefly review.

We left Leavenworth full of confidence in what is known as the Smoky Hill route. On reaching the Saline – two hundred and sixty miles – we lost all track of a route, and were forced to make our own track. We found water and timber in plenty on the Smoky Hill, but scarce a vestige of grass. After traveling four hundred miles, two yoke of our cattle were spirited away by the Indians. Leaving our wagons we traveled with the other yoke until our feed gave out. Then, packing up provisions enough to last for twelve days, and taking our mining tools, we pushed ahead on foot.

After following the Smoky Hill to its head, we struck across for the head of Cherry creek, which we considered to be about sixty miles distant. We traveled over two hundred miles before we discovered the peaks, and our provisions were entirely gone. We found Col. Carpenter's wagon, which had preceded us a few days, and which he had abandoned with his horses. We descended into the valley country, striking a stream running north-

[253] Published in the *Leavenworth Times*, may 28, 1859.

west, which brought us to the Little Vermillion. We pushed for its mouth; killed a horse to keep us from starving. Finally we made the Platte, sixty miles above St. Vrain's Fort, and one hundred and twenty miles from Cherry creek, where we arrived safely.[254]

Col. Carpenter beat us in a few days. Some eight or ten emigrants were starved to death who attempted to pack through ahead of us, and one man died after reaching here, having been so long without food that nothing would remain upon his stomach. We traveled over eight hundred miles, and were glad enough to reach here alive. It is yet too early to mine to any advantage. [There follows a description of mining prospects.]

THE BLUE BROTHERS

Denver City, May 8, 1859[255]

I arrived here last night after a long and tedious trip. There has been a great deal of suffering on the route by people taking the Smoky Hill road. They have got lost, run out of provisions, and actually starved to death. On wednesday evening, the fourth of may, we camped on Beaver creek, some sixty miles east of Denver. While there a man was brought into camp by an Arapahoe Indian almost dead for want of food. He had eaten up two of his brothers.

The circumstances are as follows:

Eight emigrants left Kansas City on the fifth of march. They bought a pony and packed two hundred pounds of flour on him. The rest of provisions they packed themselves. They took the Smoky Hill route, had their pony stolen, and were forced to pack what they could – lost their way, ran out of provisions and

[254] These distances and locations are contradictory.

[255] Letter published in *Leavenworth Weekly Times*, may 28, 1859.

starved to death. One of them died. They left him on the plains. The next that gave out was one of three brothers. Two of the party went on and the three brothers remained together. They were from Whiteside county, Illinois. Their names were Alexander, Charles, and Daniel Blue. The oldest brother died first. He requested his brothers to eat him, that they might save their lives, and when they returned, take care of his wife and children.

They did so, and traveled for some distance. At last, worn out with fatigue and hunger, the youngest one gave out and died. This was within four miles of our camp. The remaining brother laid there four or five days, living on his brother, and unable to move even to get a drink of water, which was close at hand.

He was found by an Indian, who took him to their camp and treated him well. They gave him some corn meal gruel, which he said was the best thing he ever ate. The next day the Indian brought him on horseback to our camp. He was treated kindly by Mr. Williams, Superintendent of Jones and Russell's Express line, who gave him a passage in the coach to Denver. The next morning Mr. Williams, accompanied by the Indian, rode up the creek and found the remains just as they had been left, with all the flesh gnawed from the bones, and the skull split open and the brains taken out.

The poor sufferer was almost a skeleton. His cheeks sunken and his eyes protruded from their sockets. He looked wild and had almost lost his sight. At times his mind would wander, and he seemed to be very much affected. Mr. Williams gathered the remains and had them buried. Yours, J. HEYWOOD [256]

[256] Mr. Heywood of Sacramento, California, was a passenger on the first stagecoach to reach Denver.

FROM THE GOLD REGIONS [257]

Denver City, May 20, 1859

. . . At the latter point [Station twenty-two on the Leavenworth and Pike's Peak Express route] a branch of the Smoky Hill route crosses the Express route, and I found a whole city of canvass, inhabited by weary emigrants who wanted to give themselves and stock a few day's rest, at and about the junction of the two roads. I conversed freely with such as had come via the Smoky Hill route, and they were all unanimous in their denunciations of the same. The Indians had burned off all the early grass, and were themselves congregated in large numbers along the road and very overbearing and troublesome.

The travelers had an absolute desert of one hundred and fifty miles to cross. A number of bodies of starved emigrants were found by the different trains at various points on that route – a circumstance which is amply verified by the experience of the company of footmen under the command of John Gibbs, formerly of your city. When they left Junction city they numbered seventeen, of whom but three reached the settlements along the Rocky mountains alive! Mr. Gibbs buried three members of the company that had died of fatigue and want of food, with his own hands, and lived himself on such roots as he could find on the prairies, before he was picked up by some parties in the neighborhood of Russelville, forty miles south of this locality. Of the truly horrifying fate of the Blue brothers, who were also members of Mr. Gibbs's company, had journeyed

[257] This is an extract from special correspondence to the *Missouri Republican* and published in that St. Louis newspaper on june 7, 1859. The letter is unsigned, but circumstantial evidence indicates that it was written by Henry Villard.

northward upon the breaking up of the same, and finally devoured each other's bodies in their hungry madness, our readers will doubtless have seen the authenticated statement before this reaches you.

And such suffering, unfortunately, is not likely to be the only one on record. I found every one of the western stations of the Express company beset by gangs of half-starved men – mostly of the hand-cart and walking gentry – that had consumed their last, days ago, and were now driven to appeal to the feelings of compassion of the employes of the Express company. And heartily and humanely was this appeal responded to in most cases. Otherwise, the road would be covered with the bleaching bones of such as had breathed their last in the merciless wilderness, for want of the means of physical subsistence.

DANIEL BLUE ON THE SMOKY HILL TRAIL [258]

Statement of Daniel Blue, late of Clyde township, Whiteside county, Ill., made the twelfth day of may, 1859, at the office of the Leavenworth and Pike's Peak Express company, in the city of Denver.

"On the twenty-second day of february last I left my home in company with my two brothers, Alexander Blue and Charles Blue, two other residents of the same county, John Campbell and Thomas Stevenson, for the Pike's Peak gold regions. We arrived at and left Kansas City on the sixth of march, taking the Smoky Hill route. In the neighborhood of Topeka we fell in with nine others, also bound for western Kansas. The company

[258] This appeared in the correspondence of Henry Villard, written at Denver on may 17, 1859, and published in the Cincinnati *Daily Commercial* of june 3, 1859. Following Mr. Blue's statement, Villard added: "Mr. Blue came up to this place on the same coaches that I did. He looked like a skeleton, and could hardly use his limbs, and his sight was impaired."

had one horse, which belonged to the original Blue party, and was to carry their provisions. The rest were footmen, carrying their provisions on their backs. We journeyed together for sixteen or seventeen days on said Smoky Hill route. Myself and eight others then continued our journey, while the rest remained behind for the purpose of hunting buffalo.

Three or four days elapsed after the separation, when we lost our packhorse. Our stock of provisions was then very much reduced, and we packed whatever we had left and pushed onward. After having traveled eight more days, two other members of the company left us. Upon their leaving, our provisions became exhausted, and for ten days we laid still, endeavoring to kill a sufficient amount of game for our subsistence. A few hares, ravens and other small game was, however, all that came within our reach. Our only firearms was a shotgun, all other arms having been thrown away in consequence of the weakness of their owners.

At about the same time three others parted with us, with the intention of making for the nearest settlement for the purpose of securing relief to the remaining ones – leaving but the three brothers Blue and one man by the name of Soleg, from Cleveland, Ohio – all of the party being very weak and nearly exhausted. After a short effort to continue our journey we were again compelled to lay up, and the next day Soleg died from exhaustion and want of food. Before he breathed his last, he authorized and requested us to make use of his mortal remains in the way of nourishment. We, from necessity, did so, although it went very hard against our feelings. We lived on his body for about eight days.

We then were, as I afterwards learned, on Beaver creek, which empties into the Bijou, one of the tributaries of the South Platte, and about seventy-five miles east of Denver city. After the consumption of Soleg's body, Alexander, my eldest brother, died, and at his own last request, we used a portion of his body as food on the spot, and with the balance resumed our journey.

We succeeded in traveling but ten miles, when my youngest brother, Charles, gave out, and we were obliged to stop. For ten days we subsisted on what remained of our brother's body, when Charles expired from the same causes as the others. I also consumed the greater portion of his remains, when I was found by an Arapahoe Indian, and carried to his lodge, treated with great kindness, and a day and a half thereafter (that is, on wednesday, the fourth day of may) brought to the encampment of the Leavenworth and Pike's Peak Express company's train, en route for Denver city, under the charge of Mr. Superintendent B. D. Williams, where I was received and taken care of, and left at station twenty-five to recover sufficient strength for the continuation of my journey. By direction of Mr. Williams, the second coaches that came along took me up and brought me safely to this point free of charge.

The above statement I make freely, voluntarily, and without compulsion. Knowing that it will reach the eye of the public at large, I wish to give expression to the sincere gratitude I entertain towards the employees of the L. and P. P. Express company in general, and Mr. Williams in special, for their humane treatment of us.

DANIEL BLUE."

Denver city, may 12, 1859. Subscribed in the presence of
J. Heywood, Sacramento, Cal.
Wm. T. Carlyle, Saline County, Mo.
M. K. Lane, Leavenworth City, K. T.
Jo. M. Fox, Gen'l Agent L. & P. P. Ex. Co.

THE EXPERIENCE OF A PIKE'S PEAKER [260]

The following is the copy of a genuine letter from Pike's Peak. It was addressed by a young man to his father, a resident of this county, a gentleman of property, and one of our old citizens. The writer joined the throng of adventurers, who had been deluded into the belief that a fortune could be made by gold hunting at "Pike's Peak." It is dated at Denver city, the eighth, and in simple terms tells the story of one of the unfortunate as well as, probably, that of all who struggled through to the journey's end:

DEAR FATHER: I arrived here today in good health, but suffered much on the journey. Our party took the Smoky Hill fork route, and were sorry for it. About a hundred miles from our journey's end our team gave out, and we had to pack through the balance of the way. We soon got out of all our provisions, save a few crackers. On these we subsisted for six days, our daily allowance being two crackers each, except now and then we could buy a little of those we overtook, paying dearly enough for it. The suffering on this route has been terrible. Out of one party of seventeen, all but one starved to death. There were three brothers, two of whom died, while the third actually devoured their remains.

Times here are hard and dull. There is no gold at Pike's Peak. No man can make ten cents a month. I am out of money, and without a chance to make any. Therefore, dear father, send me one hundred and twenty-five dollars to take me back home, where I know I can make something. Tell Sam'l F—— to send S—— some money to get back again, for I had to pay his way.

[260] From the *Daily Missouri Republican*, may 29, 1859.

If you don't send me some money I will starve to death. Send it in haste. F. ST. C——.

Auraria, K. T., May 2, 1859 [261]

MR. EDITOR: Permit me, for one, to render tribute to some of those (whose names should be handed down for ages) who left their business and invested their means, without hope of reward, to relieve the many hundred pioneers who went on the Smoky Hill route to this place, and who must have perished, if no assistance had been rendered. Some of them I shall never forget, among the few God-like, were Mr. J. H. Bliss of New York, Dr. E. H. Boyd of Springfield, Missouri, and Messrs. Russell, Waddel & co. Missourians should always keep in grateful remembrance their names, and I, for one, who was one of the sufferers, and was relieved and cared for by Dr. E. H. Boyd and Mr. Bliss, when in a starving state. I crave of you the favor of giving this a place in your valuable paper. Yours truly,

JAMES L. SIMPSON.

GREEN RUSSELL'S REPORT ON SMOKY HILL TRAIL, 1860 [262]

We have been furnished by Russell Green [Green Russell], Esq., with the following digest of a report of the road from Leavenworth to Denver, the survey of which he has just completed, and which will be interesting to our readers. It will be seen that the report of the Indians having attacked the party is entirely fabulous, and they may say that the Indians were perfectly peaceable. The party consisted of thirty-six, all in good

---

261 *Ibid.*

262 Published in the *Rocky Mountain Herald* (Denver), may 5, 1860. As indicated in the preceding introduction, Russell was employed by Leavenworth City to locate a practicable route along the Smoky Hill.

health and spirits, and many of them are old friends of last season, to whom we gave a cordial greeting on their return. We may expect some prospecting from this party in the mountains, which may help to develop their richness. Men of the practical mining experience of Green Russell and company must be considered an influential addition to our company.

"Denver, May 4th, 1860.

"DEAR SIR: – Thinking that perhaps a brief report of our travels from Leavenworth to Denver, by way of Smoky Hill, might not be uninteresting to yourself and readers, I shall give you a short account of the road and country as we found it.

"The road from Leavenworth to Salina is too well known to require a description. From Salina we started out over the old emigrant trail across the big bend to Smoky Hill, a distance of fifty-two miles.[263] On this road we found plenty of wood, water and grass, and with the exception of a few hills and the fording of two creeks, it is a good road.

"On striking the Smoky Hill the road turns up it, running sometimes close to the river and again a distance of several miles, until it crosses the mouth of Big creek, a distance of thirty-four and three-fourths miles.[264] Here the old road crosses the Smoky Hill, after making a bend down Big creek. At this point we left the old road, crossing the mouth of Big creek, instead of Smoky Hill, and striking over a level plain, leaving the river about ten miles to the left, and striking it again fifteen miles from the mouth of Big creek. We then

[263] This road must have run north of Highway U.S. 40 S., and have struck the Smoky Hill river some ten miles northwest of Ellsworth.

[264] Big creek enters the Smoky Hill about six miles southwest of the town of Russell.

kept up the river until we struck the old road again, forty-two and one-half miles from the mouth of Big creek. For this cutoff we found plenty of wood, water and grass, and made a very good road.

"We kept the old road after striking it until it turned up the North fork [265] of Smoky Hill, with the exception of one place where we left it for a short distance to avoid crossing the river. There is plenty of wood and water on the road, with the exception of fifteen miles after leaving North creek.

"We left the old road about two miles above the mouth of the North fork of the Smoky Hill, and struck the South fork about eight miles above the junction. We kept up the South fork to Willow creek,[266] up Willow creek three miles, crossed it and struck the South fork at a big grove of cottonwood, about five miles above the mouth of Willow creek. Up to this point we had plenty of wood, water and grass. Leaving the South fork at Big Grove,[267] we kept nearly a due west course until we struck the old Express road,[268] at its most southern point, a distance of seventy-five miles from Big Grove.[269] There is no wood on this road. We found plenty of water in pools and sandy ravines by digging, though the

[265] The Smoky Hill forks about five miles west of Russell Springs.

[266] This is presumably the same as Willow Springs, which, according to Root and Connelley, *The Overland Stage to California,* 398, was fourteen miles west of Pond creek (later the site of Fort Wallace). Bayard Taylor, *Colorado: A Summer Trip,* 31, gives the distance between Pond creek and Willow creek as eighteen miles.

[267] This was probably at the mouth of present Big Timber creek, about seventeen miles east of present Cheyenne Wells and near the Colorado line of today. This distance agrees with the table given by Root and Connelley.

[268] The road of the Leavenworth and Pike's Peak Express.

[269] There were several variations of route in this region. The distance given would indicate that Russell's trail reached the Big Sandy in the vicinity of present Hugo. Dr. Long, in the *Colorado Magazine,* XI, 72, calls this the "Smoky Hill North."

probability is that the dry season water will be very scarce. We crossed several large sandy ravines running northward, in one of which we found a large pool of water. After striking the Express road we followed it all the way to Denver, with two exceptions – once to avoid some hills, and once to make a cut-off. We found the Express road a very good one, though very crooked, with plenty of wood, water and grass; – the distance from Leavenworth to Denver six hundred and ten miles, measuring every turn of the wheel.

"We saw two small parties of Indians on the Smoky Hill – a party of about fifty Cheyennes and a party of about twenty Comanches. Buffalo and antelopes are abundant on the road.

"Time will not admit of a more explicit report at the present.

W. G. RUSSELL."

Stations on the Smoky Hill Stage Route, 1866 [270]

FROM ATCHISON AND LEAVENWORTH TO—

	Miles		*Miles*
Fort Riley	116	Eaton*	12
Junction City* . . .	3	Henshaw Creek . .	13
Chapman's Creek . .	12	Pond Creek* . . .	11
Abilene*	12	Willow Creek . . .	14
Solomon River . .	10	Blue Mound . . .	9
Salina*	13	Cheyenne Wells* . .	13
Spring Creek	15	Dubois*	24
Ellsworth*	14	Grady's	11
Buffalo Creek	12	Connell Creek* . .	13
Hick's Station* . .	15	Coon Creek	12
Fossil Creek	15	Hogan	11
Forsythe's Creek . .	11	Hedinger's Lake* .	9
Big Creek*	11	Big Bend of Sandy .	13
Louisa Springs . .	12	Reed's Springs* . .	13
Bluffton	14	Bijou Creek . . .	12
Downer*	13	Kiowa Creek . . .	9
Castle Rock Creek .	9	Ruthton*	9
Grannell Spring . .	11	Cherry Valley . . .	16
Chalk Bluffs	12	Denver*	14
Monument*	13		——
Smoky Hill Spring .	11	Total distance . .	592

*home or eating stations.

[270] Taken from Root and Connelley, *The Overland Stage to California*, 398. These were the stations on the stage line of the Butterfield Overland Despatch. For a good description of a trip over this line in 1866, see Bayard Taylor, *Colorado: A Summer Trip*, 16-36.

APPENDICES

APPENDIX A

[*Boyd's Notes on the First Parallel Road*][271]

The Great Central Route to the Gold Mines of Western Kansas—Notes of Travel

Interesting Particulars of the Journey by the Atchison Company

To the politeness of Judge F. G. Adams, the president of the Atchison and Cherry Creek Bridge and Ferry company, we are indebted for the following very interesting particulars in regard to the Great Central route along the first standard parallel, to western Kansas and the gold regions of the Rocky mountains. We published last week the letter of Mr. E. D. Boyd, the civil engineer of the company, giving some interesting facts in regard to the mines. The following table of distances were compiled by the same gentleman, who is now at Denver city, from actual survey and personal observation. It is the most interesting as well as the fullest description of the vast plains lying west of us, that has ever been published, and we give it to our readers feeling confident that it will be as interesting to them as it has been to us.

As the prospect now is that there will yet be a large emigration to the gold regions of Pike's Peak, all facts

271 From the Atchison *Weekly Champion*, june 25, 1859. A photostat of this was kindly supplied by the State Historical Society of Kansas.

in relation to the road opened by the Cherry Creek Bridge and Ferry company, will be of service to the public. The road passes nearly due west from Atchison to a point on the road established by Jones and Russell's Express company; 172 miles from here, and 10 miles north of the 1st Standard Parallel, and thence follows the Express company's road to Denver city. The route has been carefully selected from this point to the intersection, and ferrys will in a very few days be completed across the Blue and Republican rivers, when the road will be opened. The distance gained over the road as traveled by the Express company, from Leavenworth by the way of Riley is 65 miles, and the road will be much better as it avoids most of the streams falling into the Kansas river this side of Fort Riley. The total distance from Leavenworth is 706 miles, while from Atchison by the Parallel Route it is but 641.

The road crosses the Grasshopper at Muscotah and passing along the Parallel to Clear creek, a branch of Red Vermillion, it bears north of west, crossing the Black Vermillion near Barrett's mills and the Big Blue at the mouth of Elm creek, 7 miles north of the Parallel. Then following up the Blue and Little Blue, passing Marble Falls near the mouth of the latter, the road passes along a divide between the Little Blue and the branches of the Republican which run south, crossing the Republican 10 miles north of the Parallel and passing due west intersects the Express Company's road at station No. 11.

The surface of the country, soil and timber, do not vary materially until station No. 11. There is no interval of ten miles on the road without wood, and water is still more frequent. The soil is rich and grass luxuriant till we cross the Republican, where it becomes shorter though still thick and nutritious.

With this explanation the following notes of distances, etc., will be understood. They have been furnished principally by Mr. E. D. Boyd:

FROM ATCHISON TO

	Miles
Muscotah, crossing of the east fork of Grasshopper	20
Main Grasshopper, immediately below mouth of Walnut, near line of the Kickapoo Reserve	21½
Crossing of Spring creek, at Eureka, on west line of Kickapoo Reserve	32
Elk creek	40
Soldier creek	45
America, on main branch of Red Vermillion	50
Coal creek	54
Clear creek – the last two are branches of Red Vermillion, and all the streams thus far flow southerly into the Kansas river	59
Clear Fork, a branch of Black Vermillion flowing northwest	63
Branch of above	64½
Barrett's Mills, at crossing of Black Vermillion	73
Blue, at mouth of Elm creek	82
Marble Falls, on Little Blue, one mile above mouth. Here is a fine water power and an extensive bed of Gypsum. This place is eight miles north of the Parallel; from here the road passes up the Little Blue to	86
Crossing of mouth of Kuhn creek	90
Branch of above	95

FROM ATCHISON TO *Miles*

Mormon trail. The road now follows this trail in a direction a little north of west, crossing two or three small branches of Mill creek, which is a branch of Little Blue for eight miles . . 101

To where the Mormon trail turns northerly to cross Mill creek. Here we are about the centre of Washington county, and in the divide between the branches of Republican and Little Blue, and fifteen miles north of the Parallel 109

Bearing westerly we cross the head of Parson's creek, which, with the two following fall into the Republican 116

Uphill creek 122

Knob creek 127

West branch of Knob 132

Dry creek 137

Republican, 470 ft. wide, shallow and sandy, 10 miles north of the parallel 141

FROM THE CROSSING OF THE REPUBLICAN *Miles*

From the crossing the Republican the course is due west, crossing five branches of Dog creek at intervals of three to six miles until we reach Station No. 11, 31 miles beyond the Republican, from which point the distances set down hereafter are computed. Station No. 11 is 172 miles west from Atchison and ten miles north. Latitude 39 deg. 42 min., Longitude 98 deg. twelve min.

Creek ten ft. wide, runs south; oak and elm . 32½

Creek ten ft. wide, runs S. oak and elm . . 35½

Creek ten ft. wide, runs scattering burr oak and elm 38½

Creek ten ft. w. runs S.E. oak and elm . . 39½

FROM THE CROSSING OF THE REPUBLICAN	*Miles*
Creek six ft. w. runs S.W. scattering . . .	45½
Creek eight ft. w. runs S. timber, . . .	46½
Creek ten ft. w. runs S. timber, ...	48½
Creek ten ft. w. runs S. timber outcrop of white limestone, ...	49½
Creek eight ft. w. runs south-east; scattering timber and limestone.	50
Creek ten ft. w. runs south-east; scattering timber; chalk cliffs.	53
Creek 10 ft. w. runs S. scattering timber . .	59
Station No. 12 – creek 20 ft. w. runs S. elm, &c; forks into three parts above.	63½
Creek 10 ft. w. runs south; scattering elm and cottonwood	71
Creek 10 ft. w. runs south-east; abundance of timber, principally elm.	74½
Creek 10 ft. w. runs south-east; elm, high, steep bank on east side.	76½
Small creek runs south; no timber. . . .	79
Creek 8 ft. w. runs south; scattering cottonwood and elm.	81½
Delaware creek, 10 ft. w. runs southeast; cottonwood and elm.	84
Station No. 13 – creek 10 ft. w. runs southeast; scattering cottonwood.	86
Creek 10 ft. w. runs south; scattering cottonwood, &c.	90
Creek 10 ft. w. runs south; cottonwood. . .	93½
Creek 10 ft. w. runs south; cottonwood and willow.	94½
Creek 10 ft. w. runs south; cottonwood and elm.	86[96]¼

FROM THE CROSSING OF THE REPUBLICAN	*Miles*
Creek 10 ft. w. runs south-east for many miles; cottonwood	98
Creek, pools of standing water; runs N. into last creek; white, yellow and slate color chalk cliffs; yellow ochre.	100
Lat. 39 deg. 42 min. Long. 99 deg. 25 min. .	103½
A dry creek runs north into creek at 98 miles. A table mountain with monument, a conspicuous land mark, half a mile N.	104½
Creek, pools of standing water; scattering cottonwood and willow.	112½
Creek 8 ft. w. runs south; cottonwood and elm.	113½
Station 14 – Last 15 miles rough and rolling, road crooked. No water for 13 miles. The soil is porous and does not retain it. Timber at intervals, a mile either side.	
Limestone, ...	119
Timber and water one mile north, ...	122
Divide between Solomon and Republ'n, . .	125½
Creek runs north-east into Prairie Dog creek; cottonwood and elm; water 1/3 of a mile above road. No water or wood for the last 17 miles .	127½
Prairie Dog creek, 10 ft. w. runs north-east; cottonwood, elm and ash; very large prairie dog town west of creek.	128½
Station 15 on north bank of Prairie Dog creek, runs east then south-east.	139
Creek 10 ft. w. runs south-east; Prairie Dog creek close to road, separating at this point. .	140
Spring near road.	144
Lat. 39 deg. 52 min. long. 100 deg. 07 min. .	149
Creek 10 ft. w. runs north into Sappa creek; elm and ash.	159

FROM THE CROSSING OF THE REPUBLICAN	*Miles*
Creek 10 ft. w. runs east; elm and ash, . .	161
Station 16 – Timber 1½ mile to north, on Sappa creek.	170
Timber one mile to north on Sappa creek .	174
Timber and limestone ½ mile to north on branch.	176
Sappa creek 20 ft. w. runs north-east then east; cottonwood.	179½
Creek 5 ft. w. runs south into Sappa creek which is close to road	181½
Station 17 – on N. bank of Sappa creek . .	187½
Creek 6 ft. w. runs south-east into Sappa creek which is close to road; ash.	191½
Dry branch; high and very steep banks, . .	193
Leave Sappa creek. Road parallel with it for the last 15 miles.	195
Dry creek runs south-east; scattering timber. Water ½ mile below.	197½
Republican about 4 miles north.	201
Timber on Republican 1 mile to north. . . .	217
Cottonwood and water south of road. . . .	220½
South bank of Republican fork runs east; 200 yards w. and very shoal, sandy bottom; banks 3 to 6 ft. high. No timber at this point; no water or timber on road for the last 26 miles; Lat. 40 deg. 08 min. Long. 101 deg. 27 min.	221
Station 18 on south bank of Republican; scattering cottonwood.	222
Branch runs north; timber and water, . .	224
Soda over surface of ground, ...	228
Latitude 40 deg. 05½ min. Long. 101 deg. 27 min.	230
Scattering cottonwood on bank of Republi-	

FROM THE CROSSING OF THE REPUBLICAN *Miles*

can north of road; soda. Republican 150 yards wide. 237½

Good water in slough. 244

Station 19 on south bank of Republican; no timber; Lat. 40 deg. 00 min. Long. 101 deg. 43 min. . . . . 218 [248]

Water slightly alkaline in slough, ... 249

Lat. 39 deg. 46½ min. Long. 101 deg. 52 min. 265

Dry branch runs north-west, ... 269

Dry branch runs north-west, ... 270

Station 20 on bank of Republican; no timber . 271

White sandy limestone. 274

Branch runs north; good water; a few cottonwood. 279½

A little timber to right, ... 281

Lat. 39 deg. 40½ min. Long. 102 deg. 12 min. 285

A few small trees to right, ... 288

Creek 6 ft. w. plenty of very good water, . . 289

Republican 1 mile to north, ... 290

Republican ½ mile to north, ... 293

Republican ½ mile to north, ... 295

Small quantity of timber one mile north on other side of Republican. 296½

At bank of Republican, 50 yds. wide, . . . 298

Station 21 on bank of Republican. No timber; sandy limestone. Lat. 39 deg. 33½ min. Long. 102 deg. 26 min. 300½

NOTE. – (Something has been said about making a cut-off from station 17 to 21. It is thought that water and perhaps timber can be found at no great distance apart. The branches which we cross, though dry at the Republican have water in them above.)

FROM THE CROSSING OF THE REPUBLICAN *Miles*

Creek 6 ft. w. runs north; good water; Republican 3/4 mile north. It is nothing, above here, but a wide, dry, sandy bed. Water springs from the bed at this point and continues below. . . . 306½

Cross dry sandy bed of Republican, 50 yds. w. runs north-east. 309½

North bank of Republican, dry; hole dug in bed six feet deep, but no water. Yellow conglomerate bluff to north; has the appearance of Castle William, Governor's Island, N.Y. . . . 316⅓

Cross Republican. Dry, deep, sandy bed, 100 yards wide; runs east 319½

Lat. 39 deg. 23 min. long. 102 deg. 49 min. Dug 3 feet deep in bed of Republican; no water 324

Station 22 on south bank of Republican; large spring in bed of river which sinks immediately below 329½

Since first striking Republican our course has been parallel with it and our road nearly level. For the last 23 miles there is no wood or water, but the grass is good. In that distance there are some five miles (not more in all) of deep sandy road – Smoky Hill route comes in from S.E. – South fork Republican comes in from southwest.

Conglomerate Bluff to right. N. Fork Republican 3/4 mile north. South Fork Republican 1½ mile south . . . . 233 [333¼]

Leave road to left and take cut-off . . . 342

Cross North Fork of Republican; dry, sandy bed 30 yards wide, with occasionally a spring; runs northeast; good grass. For the last 13 miles high rolling prairie, little grass and no water;

FROM THE CROSSING OF THE REPUBLICAN	*Miles*
good hard road. Lat. 39 deg. 15 min. Long. 103 deg. 06 min.	343
Strike main road; run parallel with Fork from 343 miles	346
Station 23 on N. bank of N. Fork of Republican; springs in bed; limestone and conglomerate crop out of bluff on south side of Fork for the last 15 miles.	
Pike's Peak in view, bears south about 70 deg. w. distance about 120 miles	350½
Spring in North fork of Republican; a mere ravine at this place	352½
Water in same	353½
Lat. 39 deg. 00 min. long. 103 deg. 20 min. .	358
Head of North fork of Republican . . .	359½
Top of divide; fine view of Pike's Peak; bears south; 70 deg. west; specimens of selenite . .	360
Dry ravine runs south; spring	367
" " " " pools of water . . .	368½
Station 24 on north bank of South fork of Republican; runs south-east for some distance; dry sandy bed 80 yds. wide with pools of water at this point; no timber	373½
Cross same fork, runs south then south-east; dry sandy bed 100 yards wide; water by digging two feet; willow bushes	377
Cross same fork; runs north-east then east; dry sandy bed 100 yards wide; large branch comes in from north-west with large pools of water; shrub willow	380
Small cottonwood and water at fork to left .	383
Lat. 39 deg. 18 min. long. 103 deg. 49 min. .	389
Leave south Fork of Republican which runs from south-west towards south-east . . .	391

FROM THE CROSSING OF THE REPUBLICAN	*Miles*
Top of Divide Ferruginous sand stone . .	396
Creek, dry sandy bed 60 yds. wide; runs north into South Fork of Platte, water by digging two feet; a few willows and cottonwood—Station 25 on west bank	401
Top of hill, sand stone; fine view of Long's Peak as well as Pike's Peak; former bears N. 80 W., latter S. 60 W.	403
Dry branch runs N. pools of good water . .	404
Beaver creek, sandy bottom 12 yds. wide runs north; very good water; a few scattering, small cottonwood and willows	407
Small grove of Norway (long leaved or yellow) pine to left with spring	409
Scattering groves of Norway pine; lat. 39 deg. 24 min. Long. 104 deg. 10 min.	
Creek 5 ft. W. runs N. good water, pine . .	411½
Top of hill, magnificent view of the whole range of mountains from Long's Peak to Pike's Peak; deep broad valley immediately to west .	414
Descend 300 feet	418½
Bijou creek, 30 yds. w. bluff banks 6 to 10 ft. high, bottom sandy, very shoal, runs east of north; scattering willow and cottonwood; pine one mile east and west.	
Top of hill; Ferruginous sand stone, yellow ochre, bright red trap etc., on eastern slope; pine and cedar. No more pine for several miles . .	422
Creek, dry sandy bed 100 yds. w.; water by digging one foot; runs north; bushes; a few cottonwoods one mile north.	423½
Dry ravine runs N. pools of water, . . .	425

FROM THE CROSSING OF THE REPUBLICAN *Miles*

Creek, sandy bed 15 yards wide; good water runs north. 426

Top of ridge bears north and south, ... 427½

Station 26 on Kioway creek, 10 ft. wide sandy bed, very shoal, good water, runs north; willow bushes; lat. 39 deg. 29 min. long. 104 deg. 29 min. 429

Creek 10 ft. wide; very shoal; sandy bottom, runs northeast; good water; willow bushes. . 430½

Take cut off, leaving road to left, ... 433

Dry branch bears N.W. Pools of water; willow bushes. 433½

Dry branch, sandy bed, runs N. two or three trees and some bushes; pools of water. . . . 434½

Creek 20 yds. wide, sandy bottom; very shoal, runs north; a few bushes. 436½

Dry branch runs N. pools of water; a few bushes. 439

Dry branch runs N.E.; bushes. 439½

Creek, dry sandy bed, 10 yds. w; runs N.E.; pools of fine water; scattering cottonwood and pine. 441

Scattering pine. 443½

Groves of pine, ... 444

Creek, bluff banks 3 to 8 ft. high; sand bed 12 yds. W. runs N.W.; good water; scattering pine above; leave pine. Lat. 39 deg. 36 min. Long. 104 deg. 48 min. 446½

Top of hill, Pike's Peak bears S. 10 deg. W.; splendid view of the mountains; a wide valley in the foreground; the lower (black) mountains in the middle, and the high mountains covered with snow in the background. 449

FROM THE CROSSING OF THE REPUBLICAN *Miles*

Pine ½ mile to north.

Strike old road at Cherry creek, on road from Santa Fe; creek 10 yds. w.; runs N.W.; sandy banks and bottom; scattering cottonwood; thence parallel with Cherry creek into Denver city. . 454

Latitude 39 deg. 49 min.; Longitude 105 deg. 07 min. 469

APPENDIX B

[*Log of R. F. Burton's Stagecoach Trip, 1860*] [272]

No. of Mail		*Miles*	*Start*	*Arrive*	*1860*
1.	Leave St. Joseph, Missouri, in N. lat. 39° 40′, and W. long. 94° 50′. Cross Missouri river by steam ferry. Five miles of bottom land, bend in river and settlements. Over rolling prairie 2000 feet above sea level. After 6 miles, Troy, capital of Doniphan co., Kansas Territory, about a dozen shanties. Dine and change mules at Cold Spring – good water and grass	20-24	a.m. 9 30	p.m. 3	Aug. 7
	Road from Fort Leavenworth (N. lat. 39° 21′ 14″, and W. long. 94° 44′) falls in at Cold Spring, distance 15 miles.				
	From St. Jo to Cold Spring there are two routes, one lying north of the other, the former 20, the latter 24 miles in length.				
2.	After 10 miles, Valley Home, a white-washed shanty. At Small Branch on Wolf river, 12 miles from Cold Spring, is a fiumara on the north of the road, with water, wood, and grass. Here the road from Fort Atchison falls in. Kennekuk Station, 44 miles from St. Joseph Sup and change mules . . .	22-23	p.m. 4	p.m. 8	Aug. 7

[272] Taken from R. F. Burton, *The City of the Saints, and Across the Mountains to California* (1862), 505-507.

No. of Mail		Miles	Start	Arrive	1860
3.	Two miles beyond Kennekuk is the first of the three Grasshopper creeks, flowing after rain to the Kansas river. Road rough and stony; water, wood, and grass. Four miles beyond the First Grasshopper is Whitehead, a young settlement on Big Grasshopper; water in pools, wood, and grass. Five and a half miles beyond is Walnut creek, in Kickapoo co.: pass over corduroy bridge; roadside dotted with shanties. Thence to Locknan's or Big Muddy Station	25	p.m. 9	a.m. 1	Aug. 7, 8
4.	Seventeen miles beyond Walnut creek, the Third Grasshopper, also falling into the Kansas river. Good camping-ground. Ten miles beyond lies Richland, deserted site. Thence to Seneca, capital of Nemehaw co. A few shanties on the N. bank of Big Nemehaw creek, a tributary of the Missouri river, which affords water, wood, and grass . . .	18	a.m. 3	a.m. 6	Aug. 8
5.	Cross Wildcat creek and other nullahs. Seven miles beyond Seneca lies Ash Point, a few wooden huts, thence to "Uncle John's Grocery," where liquor and stores are procurable. Eleven miles from Big Nemehaw, water, wood, and grass are found at certain seasons near the head of a ravine. Thence to Vermilion creek, which heads to the northeast, and enters the Big Blue 20 miles above its mouth. The ford is miry after rain, and the banks are				

No. of Mail		*Miles*	*Start*	*Arrive*	*1860*
	thickly wooded. Water is found in wells 40-43 feet deep. Guittard's Station	20	a.m. 8	m. 12	Aug. 8
6.	Fourteen miles from Guittard's Marysville, capital of Washington co., affords supplies and a blacksmith. Then ford the Big Blue tributary to Kansas river, clear and swift stream. Twelve miles west of Marysville is the frontier line between Kansas and Nebraska. Thence to Cottonwood creek, fields in hollow near the stream	25	p.m. 1	p.m. 6	Aug. 8
7.	Store at the crossing very dirty and disorderly. Good water in spring 400 yards north of the road; wood and grass abundant. Seventeen and a half miles from the Big Blue is Walnut creek, where emigrants encamp. Thence to West Turkey or Rock creek in Nebraska Territory, a branch of the Big Blue: its approximate altitude is 1485 feet . .	26	p.m. 6	p.m. 11	Aug. 8
8.	After 19 miles of rough road and musquetoes, cross Little Sandy, 5 miles east of Big Sandy; water and trees plentiful. There Big Sandy deep and heavy bed. Big Sandy Station	23	p.m. 12	a.m. 4	Aug. 9
9.	Cross hills forming divide of Little Blue river, ascending valley 60 miles long. Little Blue fine stream of clear water falling into Kansas river; every where good supplies and good camping-ground. Along the left bank to Kiowa	19	a.m. 6	a.m. 10	Aug. 9
10.	Rough road of spurs and gullies				

No. of Mail		*Miles*	*Start*	*Arrive*	*1860*
	runs up a valley 2 miles wide. Well wooded chiefly with cottonwood, and grass abundant. Ranch at Liberty Farm, on the Little Blue . .	25	a.m. 11	p.m. 3	Aug. 9
11.	Cross divide between Little Blue and Platte river; rough road, musquetoes troublesome. Approximate altitude of dividing ridge 2025 feet. Station at Thirty-two-Mile creek, a small wooded and winding stream flowing into the Little Blue . .	24	p.m. 4	p.m. 9	Aug. 9
12.	After 27 miles strike the Valley of the Platte, along the southern bank of the river, over level ground, good for camping, fodder abundant. After 7 miles Fort Kearny in north lat. 40°38′45″, and west long. 98° 58′11″: approximate altitude 2500 feet above sea level. Groceries, clothes, provisions, and supplies of all kinds are to be procured from the sutler's store. Beyond Kearny a rough and bad road leads to "Seventeen-Mile Station"	34	p.m. 10 30	a.m. 8	Aug. 10
13.	Along the south bank of the Platte. Buffalo chips used for fuel. Sign of buffalo appears. Plum-Creek Station on a stream where there is a bad crossing in wet weather . .	21	a.m. 9 30	p.m. 1 15	Aug. 10
14.	Beyond Plum creek, Willow-Island ranch, where supplies are procurable. Road along the Platte, wood scarce, grass plentiful, buffalo abounds; after 20 miles "Cold-Water Ranch." Halt and change at Midway Station	25	p.m. 2 30	p.m. 8	Aug. 10
15.	Along the Valley of the Platte,				

No. of Mail		*Miles*	*Start*	*Arrive*	*1860*
	road muddy after rain, fuel scarce, grass abundant, camp traces every where. Ranch at Cotton-wood Station, at this season the western limit of buffalo	27	p.m. 9	a.m. 1 45	Aug. 11
16.	Up the Valley of the Platte. No wood; buffalo chips for fuel. Good camping-ground; grass on small branch of the Platte. To Junction-House ranch, and thence to station at Fremont Springs	30	a.m. 6 15	a.m. 11	Aug. 11
17.	Road passes O'Fallon's Bluffs. "Half-way House," a store and ranch, distant 120 miles from Fort Kearny, 400 from St. Joseph, 40 from the Lower Crossing, and 68 from the Upper Crossing of the South fork (Platte river). The station is called Alkali Lake . . .	25	m. 12	p.m. 5	Aug. 11
18.	Road along river; no timber; grass, buffalo chips and musquetoes. Station at Diamond Springs near Lower Crossing	25	p.m. 6	p.m. 10 15	Aug. 11
19.	Road along river. Last 4 miles very heavy sand, avoided by Lower crossing. Poor accommodation at Upper ford or crossing on the eastern bank, where the mail passes the stream en route to Great Salt Lake City, and the road branches to Denver city and Pike's Peak	25	p.m. 11	a.m. 3 15	Aug. 12

APPENDIX C

Pike's Peak and Back

Notes of a Returned Pikes Peaker[273]

JOHN H. EDWARDS

Nebraska City, May 30th, 1859.

FRIEND REYNOLDS: Having just returned from what I term a buffalo hunt, some hundred and odd miles west of Fort Kearny, and supposing that you may have heard of such a place as Cherry creek and Pike's Peak, I propose, having some leisure moments at hand, to give you an account of my trip and the country I have passed through, between Omaha and the fort, and your city and the same, if anything in it will prove interesting, you are at liberty to use the same in any manner you may judge best.

I left Omaha on the twenty-ninth day of march last in company with twenty other unfortunate individuals, who were bound to see the elephant. We intended to have driven as far as Elk Horn city the first day but our horses and cattle got sloughed about fourteen miles out and suddenly introduced us to camp life. There had been no preparation made for camping thus early, consequently we had rather a hard time and passed an uncomfortable night; we however managed to get started early the next morning and reached Elk Horn about noon. This is called a city, but I could find but little to

[273] Published in the *Nebraska City News,* june 4, 1859.

give it the name of even a respectable settlement; we were here kept in camp nearly two weeks, snow bound, and on the eleventh day of april we pulled up stakes and made ready for a start, the snow having kindly consented to leave. Now, in earnest began our hardships. We had no sooner crossed the Elk Horn, than we found ourselves on the Raw Hide Bottom some four miles long and the Lord only knows how deep, however at it we went now knee deep, now hub deep, straining and pulling, pushing and shouting, and finally succeeded in crossing all our teams and then pitched our tents, all hungry, tired, wet and muddy. It was somewhat laughable to see the long faces and sober looks all anxiously awaiting the summons to supper. In a short time that meal was announced and a general rush was the consequence, when instead of nice warm biscuits, strong coffee and beef steaks, we had fried salt meat, weak coffee, and heavy salaratus bread. We however soon disposed of our allotted portions and then all sought such rest as the first night on the road could furnish.

It unfortunately came my turn to stand guard, and I accordingly armed myself with a rifle, revolver, bowie knife and, half scared, began my lonesome task. I imagined every bush or bunch of grass to be a rascally Pawnee, and stood ready to defend the camp by returning into the tent, but there was no opportunity to test my bravery for the Pawnees were undoubtedly as badly scared as I was. It rained hard during the night and we got more or less wet.

The next morning we were all astir betimes and as soon as breakfast was over got under way, intending to reach Fremont and there camp. The roads were bad and our teams had some heavy work to do. When we arrived within two miles of that town we found one continuous mud hole or slough, had to double up teams and take our wagons across singly. Here we went into camp and tried to get some rest. This like all inland towns must have been started on speculation, and a mighty poor speculation at that. The land is somewhat sandy and I do not think will ever be of much importance for agricultural purposes, but answer very well for town lots. Everybody here talked of going to the mines.

Pawnee village is situated on the south side of the Platte, nearly opposite this place, and presents quite a picturesque appearance at this distance. Quite a number of their braves visited our camp and held a talk with us. They are all a miserable set of beggars. We had to lay over here one day in consequence of snow, but got started on the morning of the fourteenth and made some twenty miles to Emerson's. We passed through some good country and quite a number of settlements. We camped at Emerson's, which was a pretty place. The next day we reached Davis' station, only seven miles from Emerson's; the road however was bad enough to call it twenty, so we concluded to stop.

Two days farther brought us to Columbus, which undoubtedly would make quite a city providing there were inhabitants enough. I believe there is only one white woman in town. The country we passed through was rather hard and to save what good land there was they ran the road through every slough they could find. At this point we met Major West, of Omaha, who showed us a great deal of courtesy.

We crossed the Loup Fork here and passed through a

high rolling country, possessing a good soil but little timber. We camped on Prairie creek, a most beautiful stream but little timber. From this on to the Lone Tree the country was sterile and showed much signs of Alkali, and a good many sloughs; at one of these we had to unload all of our teams and take the wagons over with but few pounds of freight. It took us from eleven a.m., till five p.m., to cross, and taking it all together it was rather a hard time. Horses and cattle worn out, men tired and wet, and women frightened. We drove some four miles farther and camped on the Platte; good wood and water handy. There is a sameness in the country from this to Wood river. After crossing this the appearance of the land changes from a low to a high rolling prairie, with a rich loamy soil, and must undoubtedly ere long be all taken up; there are several claims on it now; at one place we noticed a bend in the river of such an extent that some two hundred acres or more could have been securely fenced by building some forty rods of fence. We arrived at Doctor Henry's ranch, twelve miles from Ft. Kearny on friday, the twenty-second of april, and concluded to rest our teams and have a grand buffalo hunt.

On the next morning all hands were up and dressed by four, and guns and pistols overhauled, horses saddled, and men mounted for the start. The party was divided in two parts, one called the north and the other the south party. The party to which I was attached crossed the creek and we wended our way to the bluffs, some five miles distant, and had some exciting sport chasing antelope. We succeeded in killing one and being rather tired turned our faces homeward. These bluffs are different from anything of the kind I ever saw; they not only present a rough, ragged appearance, as you approach, but you continue to climb and slide at a great distance, I do not know how far this unevenness extends, but what part of them I have seen are certainly not fit for any purpose whatever, except to shelter the buffalo and antelope. On reaching camp we were delighted at finding a nice supper of fried fish. The river here abounds with fish and the gentleman in charge of the ranch assured me that what with buffalo, antelope, wild fowl, and fish that they had seldom any occasion to use any salt meat.

About dark one of our southern party made his appearance, and surprised us still more by informing us that they had killed a buffalo and though tired and foot sore, we soon had horses harnessed and hitched to a wagon to bring the animal in. We found that these fellows had been poaching on our side; having hunted all day on their own without killing anything, they crossed the creek and thus saved their credit. We had to take the wagon to pieces and swim the horses, then drive eight miles, cut up the buffalo and back to camp, at which we arrived at twelve o'clock. The majority of our party had not before seen a buffalo and very few indeed had ever tasted the flesh; the consequence was, as soon as breakfast was ready they all pitched in rather heartily with exclamations of "shaw this is no better than beef. I believe the fellow has made a mistake and killed somebody's old cow." I warned the boys not to indulge too freely, but they paid no attention to it and naturally suffered the consequences, for some time afterwards buffalo was at a discount.

Doc. Henry has certainly a most beautiful place and will in the end realize something handsome from it;

the only drawback on him is that the government have extended their wood reservation some three miles further up and down the Platte, making now fifteen miles each way from the fort, instead of as formerly, only twelve. This reservation, as I understand it, includes all the timber on the shores and islands for a distance of thirty miles along the Platte, which is in my humble opinion, much more timber than they can use for the next two centuries. It must make the Doctor feel rather sore, as I understand there is but little timber on Wood river and he was in the habit of getting his from the Platte.

Having rested and refreshed ourselves we bade adieu to the gentlemanly agent of the Doctor and started for the fort. I forgot to state that our party attracted a good deal of notice all along the road, having a party of ladies and children with us. My little girl created some excitement among the Pawnees; they examined her eyes, her hair, hands, feet and every particle of dress she had on. We arrived at the ford at about eleven a.m., and at six p.m., had safely crossed the Platte. It seems to me rather a dangerous undertaking, especially if the water was much higher than when we crossed. There were some three to five hundred immigrants encamped at this point. They had apparently heard some bad news and were very much discouraged. The officers of the fort upon learning our destination tried to dissuade us from going further, stating that they had received reliable assurance that there was no gold out there. We however concluded to see for ourselves and started westward. Flour was selling at ten dollars per hundred and other provisions in proportion, and whiskey at six dollars per gallon, rather cheap that for the kind.

The land west of the fort for some forty-five or fifty miles is rather low, soil in some places crusted over with alkali, in others sandy, and but little that seemed fit for cultivation; timber can be found all along the road by turning towards the river and wading to the islands.

The moment as it were that we left the fort we began to hear discouraging reports; meeting quite a number of footmen and hand carts during the first day, who gave as their experience that they had seen hard times, that the whole thing was a humbug, etc. The second day out we met still more and thought certainly that something must be wrong. They all agreed in their stories, that is, that gold was there but not yet discovered in paying quantities. They were all particularly hard on the authors of certain letters who had positively stated that men had made from three to five dollars per diem; and during the then excited state of mind under which a great many seemed to be laboring I think it would have fared hard with such men as Curtis, Steinberger, Richards and others had they fallen in with some of the returning parties.

We kept on, notwithstanding these rumors, without a wish to return being expressed until the afternoon of the fourth day, when we met Mr. Graham, from Keokuk, Iowa, who had started a large train early. Mr. G. was an old Californian and had several experienced miners with him. When he arrived within some seventy-five miles of the mines he went into camp and then selected a party of twelve with whom he pushed on and made a thorough prospect; he stayed long enough to convince himself that the thing would not pay and then returned. He assured us that provisions were scarce, and that there was a great deal of suffering and want on the road. He gave us some fearful pictures of the destitution that existed among the people and at last succeeded in raising a doubt in our minds as to the propriety of proceeding further. He also informed me that on the next day I would meet Van Ness and Burdine from Coldwater and supposed that I would believe them in preference to him. We had met at least four or five hundred teams on their return, and I cannot tell how many foot passengers.

Among those on foot we saw many who had not more with them than the rags on their back, out of provisions and dependent on the charity of the emigrants. Poor fellows, they did not need words to express their condition as it was legibly printed in their gaunt cheeks, hollow eyes, and haggard appearance. On friday the twenty-ninth of april we reached Cottonwood Springs. Here (if any doubts remained as to the correctness of the reports brought us), they were all dispelled. Van Ness, Burdine, and Jay Crippen passed on the lower road, and hearing that I was still pushing forward, sent me word to turn back. They said they had prospected to some extent and found gold in small particles but not in paying quantities; they also sent me a sad and gloomy report as to the condition of the masses farther west. All was excitement and men who had never known fear were now fearful of starvation; the accounts that reached us from the Smoky Hill route were truly heart rending. It appears that nothing but suffering was experienced on that route. I saw one man, or rather a remnant of a man who had been with a party of four to leave the city of Leavenworth and he was the only survivor. He was worn to a skeleton but possessed of an indomitable courage; all he asked was bread and then would stagger forward on his way home. God grant that he may have reached it in safety. We went into camp some three or four miles above the Springs and held a caucus, the result of which was to retrace our steps.

Near our camp was a large village of Cheyennes who, a day or two previous, had a battle with the Pawnees and killed some fifteen of them. They crowded in and around our camp, handling everything and begging for everything they saw. I was invited by several to smoke, and seated in a circle on the ground, with much ceremony, the kinakanic pouch was drawn forth, the pipe loaded, and the owner drew four long whiffs from it, discharging the smoke to the four points of the compass, then passed the pipe to me. I hated to place the stem between my lips without wiping it but was afraid of giving offence, so I followed suit, looked very serious and passed the pipe to my next neighbor; and thus kept it circling around for sometime, when out, we all arose and then commenced the language of signs. They seemed much in want of flour, tea, coffee and sugar.

The squaws were much attracted by the dress of our ladies and had to examine them pretty thoroughly; they wanted to trade, offering their dirty blankets in exchange for a dress. But what attracted their attention more than anything else was the hooped skirts worn by some of the ladies. Carrie, my little girl, came in for her share of admiration; her hair being very light was handled over and over again. One brave had the effrontery to fall in love with my wife and proposed to buy her. He made her a present of one of his brass bracelets and in return received a string of gold beads; the next day we visited their lodges and a more slovenly, lazy set of beings I never saw. The thought struck me that had Cooper had such examples of Indian life before him the world would never have been delighted with his "Leather Stocking Tales." On tuesday, the third of may, we began our backward march and reached the fort on the following sunday. Having one of our party sick we laid in camp here until the following thursday.

Here we met Doc. Henry, who gave us rather a discouraging account of our proposed route on the south side of the Platte and tried hard to persuade us to return by the northern route. But the river was so high that it was impossible to cross. We consulted our guide book and found that we would likely have to carry water and wood for some distance. We, however, started without either and drove some fifteen miles, found plenty of hazel brush, good water and grass, and camped. The road was over a wet bottom land and good for nothing but grazing. We made about twenty miles the next day, and camped near the Platte, plenty of water and hazel brush. It rained all night, and we remained in camp all day saturday and sunday on account of occasional showers. We moved from this camp on monday morning. The soil grew better all the way until we reached Elm creek, which we did on saturday the twenty-first ult.; we found wood and water convenient to the road up to this point and here we were surprised to see men busy breaking and preparing the ground for seed. A great many have concluded to remain in the territory and make claims. We drove some four miles from the creek and crossed the only hard place we met on the road; this could however at an expense of some four or five dollars be made quite passable. We got across without much difficulty and wended our way towards the bluffs. . . . JNO. H. EDWARDS

APPENDIX D
Letters from Travelers on Arkansas River Trail

LETTER FROM CAPTAIN WICKERSHAM [274]

Half-way to Pike's Peak, April 28, 1859.
In camp one and a half miles from Arkansas river

DEAR MOTHER AND FATHER: We have just stopped to repair a broken axletree. Our team, so far, has done very well, except the yoke of oxen I bought of the negro. They have nearly given out, but they may go through yet. Every day we meet from one to three Santa Fe trains. They have from one hundred to five hundred head of stock, which keep the grass eat off close to the ground, but when we leave the Santa Fe road (sixty miles from here) we shall have better grass. We think we shall get to the mines in about sixteen days. I intend to push ahead unless the teams fag too much; when we have traveled thus far we have averaged twenty miles per day.

I am heartily sick of my office. It is "Captain this," and "Captain that," all day long and sometimes at night. We have an old mule in the train that don't like Indians, and the guard frequently call me when she snorts, to know if I think the mule smells an Indian.

Night before last we rather unexpectedly drove into

---

274 *Missouri Democrat,* may 31, 1859.

a camp of eight hundred Cheyennes and Arapahoes. The chiefs met us on the road and demanded sugar, coffee and tobacco. We had just been informed that this band had robbed a Mexican train of all their provisions. I told them we had none to spare to give them. At this they appeared very angry, and one of them shot at an ox but missed him. I told them that I was Captain, and would whip the whole tribe of them if they again molested one of our cattle. I ordered the men to get their guns, etc., in readiness immediately, and form a line. When all was ready we presented a fine appearancc (198 men); we were capable of accommodating them with 432 shots, as we had quite a number of Colts with us. This manoeuvre somewhat alarmed the natives, and they proposed a compromise, which was that they would show us a good camping ground for the night. They did show us one, in a low place near a stream of water, and near a thick underbrush. I very readily discovered the trick, and consequently ordered the teams out on the prairie about a quarter of a mile. The chiefs laughed at us, and called us cowards; we pocketed the insult, and proceeded to our camp duties. After we had arranged our camp affairs, a lot of them came in and professed great friendship. We gave them something to eat, and then drove them out, put on double guards and went to bed. During the night the sentinels observed them several times, but they did not attack us.

I find human nature has not changed much since my trip to California. Men going to Pike's Peak now quarrel just as much as men did going to California then. We came very near having bloodshed in camp a day or two since. I came up to where two men were quarreling just in time to knock the gun up as one of them fired at the other. The contents of the gun went through a wagon top. Thus you see, with our fighting with Indians and among ourselves, together with other exciting matter, we have quite an interesting time of it.

Next saturday we shall probably divide our train, as grass will be easier procured for a less number, for we have a large quantity of cattle in our train; hence we have to make everything count in order to get feed enough.

There is a horse train of ten or fifteen wagons, two day's travel ahead of us, that burn off the grass everytime they leave camp. The old grass was not burned last year, and the new coming up under the old makes fine feed, if they did not burn it off. I think if we overtake them we shall have a difficulty. A man who is mean enough to be guilty of such an act should be in the penitentiary.

It is now raining hard, and I am writing in the tent, on my tin box. Lowden and Sweeney are cooking; the balance of our mess are reading an old California paper.

News from the mines is very good, but I place no reliance in any of the reports. They may be true or otherwise. I want to see for myself. Nearly every man we meet tells a different story. It seems a man can't travel on this road two hundred yards without forgetting how to tell the truth.

Buffalo, deer and fish are plenty in this section. We have seen two black tail rabbits – some of the boys thought they were young antelope. I will try to get the hide of one to bring home with me. Their ears are about eight inches long. One of the boys to-day shot a buffalo, at a distance of two hundred yards, with my Sharp's rifle. He put the ball through his brain. Some of the boys are now out after more buffalo. Supper is ready. You must excuse me for about three quarters of an hour, as I eat so much now, it takes me about that length of time to get through. You will probably not get another letter from me for some time, as we are past all the mail stations on the Santa Fe Road. I am told it will cost twenty-five cents a piece to get our letters from Fort Laramie to Pike's Peak. Tell brother James I will write him when I get to the mines. My respects to Dod Harris and lady, and all enquiring friends. Your affectionate son,

HENRY F. WICKERSHAM

EMIGRANTS AND INDIANS [275]

Santa Fe Crossing of the Arkansas River, May 10, 1859

MR. EDITOR: As much may be said in regard to some difficulty we had with the Kiowa Indians, I take this opportunity of stating the facts as they occurred. We left Council Grove on the 18th of april with 43 wagons and about 150 men, all Missourians – principally from the counties of Davis, Franklin and Monroe; we have for Captain one Robert W. Gibson, of Rock Hill, Mo., a young man of ability and capacity. We arrived at the Arkansas river on the 1st of may, and next day went ten miles up – five miles above Allison's ranche, and encamped. During the evening numbers of Kiowa Indians come into camp – some begging, some would accept of nothing, even throwing away things that were given them. Finally, at 4 o'clock, one who seemed to be leader of the rest, mounted his pony and struck off through our cattle, yelling, and when about 200 yards from camp, he shot one of the cattle through with an

[275] Kansas City *Journal of Commerce,* may 31, 1859.

arrow. The other Indians made similar noise, but did not shoot. Capt. Gibson and some men pursued them some distance but they escaped.

Next morning the Captain and fifty well-armed men, went to their town near Pawnee Rock, and were kindly received by the chief, who seemed very sorry for the act of his men – he returned to our camp with our Captain, eat, smoked, and finally agreed to replace the ox, which belonged to one Harris, of Brunswick, and he did so. We think the Indians acted without the knowledge of the tribe – which is friendly. Since this, we have seen no Indians, but companies behind have said that we were badly used by them. It is not so. We are all well, and in fine spirits, and all enjoy themselves as much as possible. A number of ladies are with us – both married and single, some from St. Louis county, some from Monroe, some from Brunswick. We intend getting to the mines in three weeks, if nothing happens. We are the only company of Missourians on this road that we know of. The road is the best I ever saw, and grass abundant now, and if I went again I would go this way. Yours,

C. C. BARNES

TOPEKA TRAIN FOR THE GOLD MINES [276]

Camp at Council Grove, May 10, 1859.

J. F. CUMMINGS, ESQ. – Although I did not agree to write for the *Tribune* while out on this trip, yet as we think we have some friends in Topeka who would be pleased to hear from us occasionally, I embrace the present moment of leisure to say a few words about our trip so far. We left Topeka as you know, on monday,

[276] *Topeka Tribune,* june 2, 1859.

the second of may, and came out to Lykin's Run, where we camped. Quite a few of the boys came out to see us, and we spent a few hours with them very pleasantly indeed; so much so, that I for one shall always remember that night with great pleasure. The second night we came to Mission creek, where the team from Chase House broke a wheel, which detained us all the next day.

Thursday morning we were ready to start, but it commenced raining and rained until noon. In the afternoon we made Fremont – (or rather a ravine a few hundred yards west of that flourishing town) – which consists of one concrete house, and any number of choice corner lots, which speculators can have for a consideration. I should like to say a word about the road from Topeka to Council Grove via Mission creek. I did think of devoting a sheet of foolscap to that especial subject, but I have changed my mind.

Suffice it to say, that we have been eight days on this new route, while we could have got here by way of Brownville and Wilmington in four. In short, there was no road or track to be seen except the Kaw Trail, which we followed the whole way – the wheels of our wagons cutting into the prairie sod from six to twelve inches, up hill and down. Finally, if you wish to do humanity and ox-flesh a kindness, advise everybody to come here by way of Wilmington. With the exception of bad roads, we have had a fine time. We have a good set of fellows – have all the game and fish we want to eat. You would be astonished to see the travel there is on this road. I am satisfied that there are six wagons here to one on the Leavenworth road. We are constantly in sight of trains – some of them Mexican traders, but most of them like unto ourselves bound for the land of gold.

Remember us to the boys and the girls too. We never lay our heads down at night but we think of them, and we always remember them in our prayers.

HONAS

Cow Creek, May 18th [277]

J. F. TRIBUNE, ESQ. – How??? – Here we are at Cow creek – 170 miles west of Topeka, all in good shape and fine spirits. The Santa Fe road as far as we have traveled it is the best natural thoroughfare I have ever seen. We have had lots of fun to-day. We have been in the midst of thousands of buffalo for the last three days, and the boys have all had as much sport as they wanted. I mounted a pony today and took after a herd. Singled out two old chaps and gave chase. You ought to have seen them git, – with their large bushy heads down, and their small "narratives" up to the breeze. They go upon a kind of rolling canter, and travel over the ground about as fast as a horse can gallop. We put ten balls into one of them before we brought him down. We have killed seven and the wagons are strung with buffalo meat, drying it in the sun. We stretch a rope on each side of the cover, and string the meat along the rope which gives the wagons the appearance of a meat market.

We have to carry wood in our wagons sometimes for fifty miles, owing to the scarcity of that commodity. Our train numbers at present twenty-six men and two ladies – a team from Burlington, K. T., of two men and one lady, having joined us to-day. Allow me to explain this by saying that the team, proper, is an ox

[277] *Ibid.*

team – not the lady and gentlemen. The face of the country is very level, and one of the best in the world to build a railroad, "barrin the timber." As I have nothing more to say, I'll dry up. Remember me to everybody. The boys all send their regards. Adios,

JOHON

A full analytical index to the set
will be supplied in Vol. XII

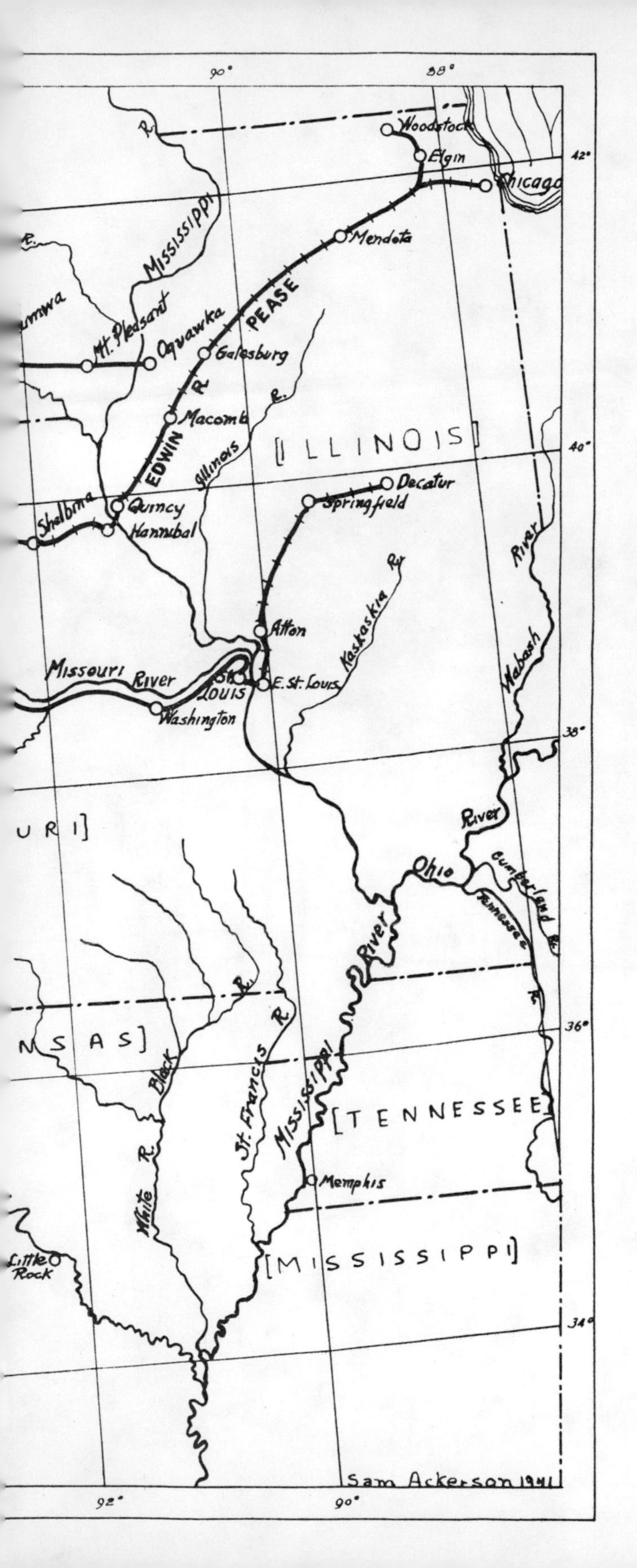

90°
88°
Woodstock
Elgin
Chicago
42°
MISSISSIPPI
Mendota
Mt. Pleasant
Oquawka
Galesburg
PEASE
R.
Macomb
EDWIN
[ILLINOIS]
40°
Illinois
R.
Decatur
Springfield
Quincy
Shelbina
Hannibal
Alton
Kaskaskia R.
Wabash
River
Missouri River
St. Louis
E. St. Louis
Washington
38°
Ohio
River
Cumberland R.
Tennessee R.
36°
Black R.
St. Francis R.
MISSISSIPPI
River
[TENNESSEE]
White R.
Memphis
[MISSISSIPPI]
Little Rock
34°
Sam Ackerson 1941
92°
90°

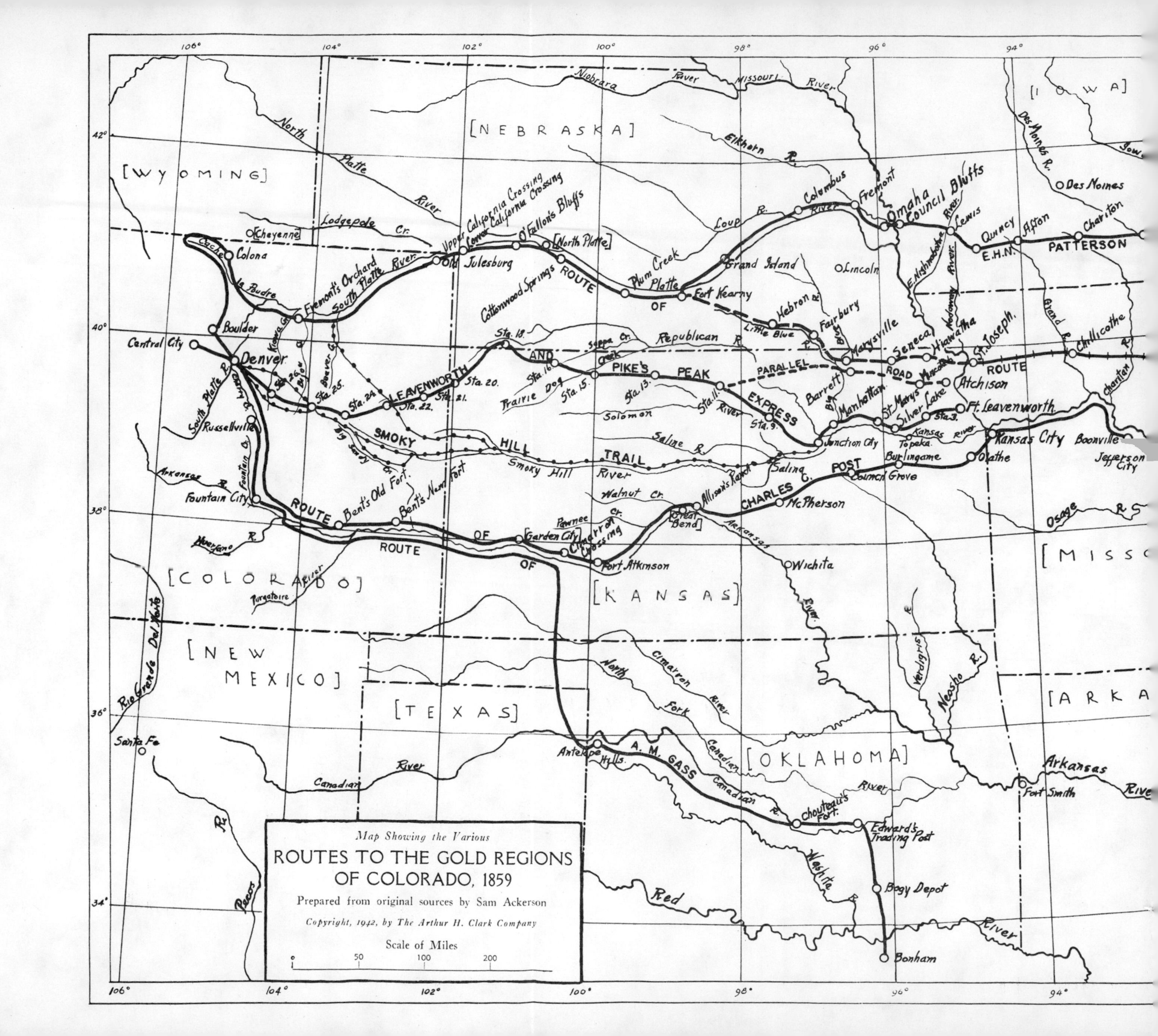
Map Showing the Various
ROUTES TO THE GOLD REGIONS OF COLORADO, 1859
Prepared from original sources by Sam Ackerson
Copyright, 1942, by The Arthur H. Clark Company
Scale of Miles
0
50
100
200
[NEBRASKA]
[WYOMING]
[IOWA]
[COLORADO]
[KANSAS]
[NEW MEXICO]
[TEXAS]
[OKLAHOMA]
[MISSO
[ARKA
Denver
Central City
Boulder
Colona
Cheyenne
Old Julesburg
O'Fallon's Bluffs
North Platte
Fort Kearny
Grand Island
Columbus
Fremont
Omaha
Council Bluffs
Lincoln
Des Moines
Chillicothe
St. Joseph
Atchison
Ft. Leavenworth
Kansas City
Boonville
Jefferson City
Junction City
Council Grove
Wichita
Fort Atkinson
Bent's Old Fort
Bent's New Fort
Fountain City
Russellville
Santa Fe
Fort Smith
Chouteau's Fort
Edward's Trading Post
Bogy Depot
Bonham
ROUTE OF PLATTE
LEAVENWORTH AND PIKE'S PEAK EXPRESS
SMOKY HILL TRAIL
PARALLEL ROAD ROUTE
CHARLES C. POST
ROUTE OF
A. M. GASS
PATTERSON
E.H.N.